Higher
Education
a/ a
Crossroads

Questions about the Purpose(s) of Colleges & Universities

Norm Denzin, Joe L. Kincheloe, Shirley R. Steinberg
General Editors

Vol. 16

PETER LANG
New York • Washington, D.C./Baltimore • Bern
Frankfurt am Main • Berlin • Brussels • Vienna • Oxford

Paul R. Geisler

Higher
Education
Crossroads

PETER LANG
New York • Washington, D.C./Baltimore • Bern
Frankfurt am Main • Berlin • Brussels • Vienna • Oxford

Library of Congress Cataloging-in-Publication Data

Geisler, Paul R.
Higher education at a crossroads / Paul R. Geisler.
p. cm. — (Higher ed; v. 16)
Includes bibliographical references and index.
1. Universities and colleges—Curricula—United States.
2. Education, Higher—United States.
3. Postmodernism and education—United States. I. Title. II. Series.
LB2361.5.G45   378.73—dc22   2005010675
ISBN 0-8204-7914-4
ISSN 1523-9551

Bibliographic information published by **Die Deutsche Bibliothek**.
Die Deutsche Bibliothek lists this publication in the "Deutsche
Nationalbibliografie"; detailed bibliographic data is available
on the Internet at http://dnb.ddb.de/.

Cover photograph by Anton Shevchenko

The paper in this book meets the guidelines for permanence and durability
of the Committee on Production Guidelines for Book Longevity
of the Council of Library Resources.

© 2006 Peter Lang Publishing, Inc., New York
29 Broadway, New York, NY 10006
www.peterlang.com

Printed in the United States of America

• CONTENTS •

• A CKNOWLEDGMENTS •

To Charlie, John, Bill, Marla, and all my teachers for your inspiration, mentorship and guidance during my journey towards erudition; I tender my sincere appreciation & respect.

To Marc, for your friendship, love and steadfast encouragement during my quest for enlightenment; I utter my deepest affection and gratitude.

To Susan, Nicholas & Benjamin, for your patience, unwavering love & resolute understanding; I extend profound admiration and reverence.

Et A Joyce, ma mère et premiers merci d'enseignant pour enseigner me "m'enseigner," et pour permettre de que m'errer dans ouvre des espaces.

prg

Having Arrived at a Crossroads

The productive man is born old and dies young. The productive man turns time around. You will recognize a thinker by the way he goes from truth to possibilities. As life goes from repetition to negentropy.

—Michel Serres (1995, 17)

Like many complex phenomena requiring significant structural analysis in order to be better understood, a myriad of interconnected and complex historical, social, personal, and cultural factors have dynamically contributed to the evolution of the modern, corporatized, and increasingly externally controlled American university. In considering the impact, effects and affects that today's corporate university has had, and continues to have upon its subjects and society at large, a complex and fundamental paradox presents itself for deconstructive analysis and discourse. To be precise, it has recently become apparent that the current "state of things" in America's Ivy Towers has arrived at a Crossroads. More specifically, the character, identity and functional utility of many of today's colleges and universities has evolved, or morphed into an institution in flux, an institution in disarray, and perhaps most importantly, into an agency of concern for those deeply involved with the mission of "higher education." As primary players and investors of a larger demographic concerned with the collective sociocultural, political, environmental and democratic future, today's higher education machine problematically engenders a profound level of disquietude for the myriad and deeply interconnected sociocultural roles that legitimate academicians' value and respect. More specifically, a palpable "hidden curriculum" that

Henry Giroux has described as a "creeping vocationalization and subordination of learning to the dictates of the market" (1999, 16), can now be seen not only as the defining principle of primary & secondary schooling, but also at all levels of education, including many of our revered universities and colleges. Just as the legendary bluesman and iconic father of rock and roll, Robert Johnson, confronted his Crossroads in rural Mississippi, today's university is now situated at a crossroads of similar levity. The 21st-century American university can be visualized as tenuously floating in the middle of a crossroads, and thus must soon decide which road to take—the relatively modern road paved by curricula geared towards hyper-vocationalization and technocratic disciplinization, or take the older, more traveled road leading towards the academic ideals and mission of the historical university. The older, more traveled road is metaphorically positioned to imbibe the original and philosophical foundations of education intended to enhance and progress individual enlightenment, and contribute towards social progress and the betterment of *all* living entities. Legend renders an account that Robert Johnson sold his soul to the devil in return for his considerable musical talent, and thus indirectly, his historical legacy in the annals of Western cultural history. Metaphorically speaking, those deeply concerned with the fate of the Ivy Towers wonder just what our institutions of higher learning will be forced to surrender in exchange for its "talent," and cultural legacy.

The paradoxical challenge (between vocational disciplinization and genuine characteristics of liberal education) presented by today's hidden curriculum sparks a certain passion, purpose and constructive promise for those concerned with the invention of new, counter-discourses capable of challenging the status quo that is the contemporary, corporate university. Although written in the context of K-12 teacher education, William Reynolds' candid comments concerning his role as a public intellectual are indeed applicable to the current discourse.

> So as a teacher and an academic I need to be concerned with "wide-awakeness." To be wide awake to our part and our choices in the concerns of the historical moment is to move toward a passionate engagement with social criticism. The movement toward wide-awakeness is to be tempered with the thoughts of the problems that will be encountered. (2003, 66)

To be wide awake in today's academic world requires all members of the Academy to not only be competent in their chosen disciplinary fields, but they must also be actively attuned to the myriad political, sociocultural, philosophical and transformative issues now facing the American higher education machine. Using healthcare as a metaphor for this challenge, academicians and policy makers concerned with the present and future state of things in the Ivy Towers should be aware of, and become actively involved in helping to diagnose, manage and rehabilitate the various maladies now affecting and infecting many American institutions of higher learning. In medical terms, "dys" means abnormal or irregular, a prefix I intend to make judicial use of in order to establish and co-opt an array of medical metaphors to color my discursive palette. Collectively, the various (dys) conditions that will be introduced make up what I am calling, Dysacademia—a pathological condition replete with signs, symptoms, and complications.

Thus situated, there are two increasingly parasitic and interconnected agents (dys) effecting the utility, existence and identity of the American Academy today. Each can be directly linked either to Foucault's discursive analysis on the operation of power, or to the deconstruction of surveillance put forth by Deleuze and Guattari. Together, the subaltern dynamics and operative action(s) that *control* and *censorship* now have upon on most, if not all aspects of contemporary society are wreaking havoc in many of our hallowed institutions of higher learning. Having gestated and mutated over the years due to myriad passive and aggressive forces, control and surveillance have morphed into a potent plague that is slowly (dys)rupting the metabolism and vitality of today's Ivy Towers. Subtle, yet strong evidence for Dysacademia can be clearly found operating in several initiatives designed to further control and degrade higher education in America.

First, there is a proposed "Academic Bill of Rights" initiative being promulgated by hyper-conservative activist and President of the Center for the Study of Popular Culture, David Horowitz. Led by Horowitz's substantial monetary war chest, and supported by a growing political and corporate constituency, the ABR is self-reportedly "about what is appropriate to a higher education, and in particular what is an appropriate discourse in the classrooms of an institution of higher learning" (Horowitz, 2005, 1). In Horowitz's phobic mind, too many professors today "behave as political advocates in the classroom, express opinions in a partisan manner on controversial issues irrelevant to the academic subject," and thus, indoctrinate immature students before they have the "sufficient knowledge and ripeness of judgment to be entitled to form any definitive opinion of his own" (p. 1). Knowing who provides the financial sustenance for Horowitz's Center for the Study of Popular Culture, and that he routinely uses openly conservative and biased think tanks and their incestual media outlets to voice his concerns and promote his purportedly "neutral" initiatives, it's not difficult to dissect what really lies at the heart of the ABR: the conservative driven silencing and censoring of perhaps the last openly democratic (as in literal translation, not political party) bastion of free thought and discourse in this country.

The second subterranean initiative at work brings us back to the work of such influential scholars as Ralph Tyler, Ivan Pavlov, and the numerous other curriculum planners and behavioral psychologists who effectively set the table for the majority of our educational agendas over the last century. Empowered by a new commission appointed in the fall, 2005, by U.S. Secretary of Education, Margaret Spellings to study the effectiveness of higher education in the United States, The Commission on the Future of Higher Education is "examining whether standardized testing should be expanded into universities and colleges to prove that students are learning and to allow easier comparisons on quality." Headed by G. W. Bush crony Charles Miller, this committee is working off the self-stated consensus that "a nationwide system for comparative performance purposes, using standard formats," is clearly lacking in higher education (Arenson, 2006, 1).

According to Spellings, Miller and the remaining committee members, this enterprise is substantively grounded upon recent studies citing the inability of current college graduates to analyze and deconstruct literature samples and to perform basic math skills as measured in small-scale standardized tests applied to relatively heterogeneous and small samples (United States Department of Education, 2005). In Miller's eyes, public reporting of collegiate learning via standardized tests "would be greatly beneficial to the students, parents, taxpayers and employers," and thus he envisions a "national database that includes measures of learning" that would be imposed upon the Academy on multiple levels. In other words, our current administration is aggressively approaching the adoption and implementation of fundamental "No Child Left Behind" mandates for all institutions of higher education receiving any amount of federal funding—private and public, big and small, research and teaching, general and liberal arts. In typical modernistic rhetoric, the extreme and neoconservative pundits of our current epoch are now trying to further boil down an historically complex and chaotic institution shaped by numerous political, social and cultural tributaries in order to predict, control and interpret "higher education" outcomes and effectiveness in simple, monolithic and predictable terms measurable by standardized tests. Together, the potential power of the Academic Bill of Rights combined with widespread standardized testing to gauge institutional effectiveness will add to the already powerful dynamics currently at work in many of our institutions of higher learning.

The third activity increasing at a rapid, almost epidemic pace concerns the increasing effects that formal private and government constituencies are having upon the utility and character of the university—external accreditation. All schools of higher learning are required to be accredited by regional, or national accrediting bodies in order to receive federal funding, state recognition, and of course, to be considered "legitimate" to many consumers looking for "quality" education. This fact is of little surprise to anyone working in the educational fields, as regional accrediting bodies have been in existence for several years. But many academics may not be aware that the accreditation craze is now becoming increasingly more finite with what they are demanding from the institutions and the disciplinary programs they now accredit in order to substantiate their legitimacy. In a nutshell, the utilitarian foci of accrediting agencies are becoming increasingly geared to the documentation of outcomes and learning objectives; an emphasis placing even more external control and power over the various constituencies of the Academy.

If that wasn't enough to agitate the academic spirit, the last few decades have seen a proliferation of "professional" accrediting bodies that have become very specific and hyper-structured with regards to evaluating and accrediting various academic major programs of study. In addition to the institution itself requiring regional accreditation in order to operate and sustain itself, and thus requiring that a multitude of standards and guidelines be met in order to be recognized as a *quality* institution of higher learning, many of the non liberal arts based professional programs are now being accredited with even more restrictions on what they teach, how they teach, and how they evaluate student learning outcomes. From administrative and institutional marketing perspectives, the mantra has now largely become "if there is an accreditation out there for a specific program, get it!" For parents and prospective students, accreditation status represents a stamp of quality, an assurance of sorts for the significant investment made in higher education, and a "competitive advantage" over rival institutions of learning.

Effectively, this layered and controlling bureaucracy has resulted in an even further marginalization and de-emphasis of liberal arts based courses and programs of study at many institutions of higher learning. For those intricately involved in managing and teaching in accredited academic majors, this powerful external control mechanism provokes a diminution of faculty autonomy and suffocates the freedom to construct and modify curricula, or to employ critical pedagogies that possess the potential to actually liberate the mind and spirit. Michel Foucault's operational "definition" of this process is known as *biopower*, an extremely ardent mechanism that describes how prolonged immersion in a controlling environment erodes the necessity and utility of the original external control mechanism. Rather, the external mechanism that initiated the humbling and convoluted transformation is no longer required to be present or in play, in order to have the same controlling effects upon the subjects. The end result of this ontologically and epistemologically stifling dynamic is that subjects of such power eventually self-control and self-surveil without the need for an external source; thus transforming into objects of power, and passive, unknowing participants of Foucaultian biopower.

In the chapters that follow, I have co-opted certain elements of postmodern and poststructural theory in an attempt to describe how the three (dys) pressures have helped fabricate two architectonic phenomena that have been progressively spawned by the control and censorship dynamics witnessed in today's Academy. Both of these spectacles have deeply affected my perception of the world, and my existence in it, as a multidisciplinary thinker and academician. Both phenomena possess their own sub-constructs and influences that prohibit simplification or empirical isolation, yet both occupy and identify the culture and effective utility of today's University, can be seen as "sequelae" (unintended consequences) of the 3 aforementioned elements of Foucaultian biopower.

The first trend centers explicitly on the organic subjects of the educational machine that give life and vibrancy to the institutions—the professorate and the student body. It is my observation that various social, cultural, educational and economic initiatives now overtly influence the objectives and motivations of far too many contemporary students. Resultantly, too many students outside the upper echelon of critical, motivated and capable students now resemble docile bodies functioning under the pretext that the purpose of attaining a university degree is primarily, or resolutely even, for professional and economic success and stature. If this is indeed true, one can only imagine what widespread standardized testing will do to the living bodies of future University students and educators.

The second pronounced development focuses on the more inorganic dynamics at play—the increasing effects and affects that various external forces are having on the function, utility and culture of the University. As a program director of an accredited allied health educational program, I am increasingly concerned with the escalating influence(s) exerted upon the University by various external forces demanding to control what is taught, how things are taught, how learning is measured, and how the University "documents" their respective educational outcomes. Institutional and academic program accreditation standards and guidelines that are typically evaluated in complex and overburdening "self-studies" are now having an increasing influence not only over the various institutions themselves, but also over various and myriad programs of study. These effects are not strictly inorganic however; the organic subjects involved in teaching and learning in these programs are effected deeply by these external forces as they increasingly dictate and control how academicians educate and exist in the Academy.

Thus by indirect extension of this phenomenon, university and college students are equally (dys) affected. As one can surmise, the interaction between previously existing docile subjects and increasing external control create a deeply profound and disturbing cycle of re-production; each time becoming exponentially more significant. Now, the U. S. government's Department of Education want to become more involved in higher education by threatening to pull federal funding for any institution that fails to comply with proposed stan-dardized tests and guidelines, and to silence "radical" professors who speak against and pedagogically challenge the meta narratives that dominate our current cultural discourses. As one can readily see at this point, proposed initiatives like the Academic Bill of Rights, higher education standardized testing, and an increased reliance upon accreditation programs to ensure "quality" outcomes promise to deepen and further complicate the effects these various dynamics are having upon our higher education institutions, and the educated elite they produce. Something is indeed askew with certain elements of postsecondary education today in the United States. If the univer-sity takes the newer road allowing the accreditation movement to gain additional momentum, and if formal implementation of the Academic Bill of Rights and standardized testing becomes "real," the contemporary American university will only deteriorate further, and perhaps even find it impossible to change paths. In effect, the Univer-sity risks following in the legendary footsteps of Mr. Robert John-son—it may inevitably sell its soul to the devil in exchange for its performative future. This text intends to examine the myriad factors that define, characterize and represent just "what" the university is "for," what it should "do," and "whom" it should benefit if we are to concern ourselves with higher education in the United States.

In reflecting upon Jacque Derrida's primary thesis in Eyes of the University, one can't help but wonder, "What does university respon-sibility represent?" (2004, 83). Does the University (represented collec-tively heretofore, as "University" with a capital "U") functionally exist for performative and neoliberal motives intended to contribute to the gross domestic product and neocolonial aspirations of our na-tion's citizenry and political machine? Looked at differently, is the modern day American University analogous to society, in that it ex-ists to produce disciplined, performatively valuable subjects capable of contributing to the economic well-being of society at the expense of other noteworthy constructions? If so, just how will this "well-being" be measured and quantified for those interested in such outcomes? Is the University's modern day utility simply to contribute to our grossly inflated notion of free enterprise, hyper-consumerism and postcolonial agendas—otherwise known as global capitalism, but disguised as democracy? The spirit of the Academic Bill of Rights cer-tainly calls for such an egregious censorship and myopic agenda, while standardized testing and accreditation initiatives collectively promise to boil higher education down to measurable outcomes and hollow indications of effectiveness in most disciplinary fields. Or rather, does the University still exist to promote and promulgate other, more critical, personal and philosophically based higher ideals that are, in essence largely uncontrollable, immeasurable and much more chaotic in nature and scope? Does higher education still liberate the constrained self and/or advance the subjective intellect? In effect, one has to ponder if "higher education" is indeed still "high" in today's postmodern times. If education wishes to remain high, it must resist the temptation to sell it's soul by remaining respectful of, and creatively reconciling the older, more historical road first laid out with the evolution of university education in Europe, with the more contemporary technocratic one so prevalent today.

In an attempt to situate my theoretical position, and thus my analysis and criticisms, it is necessary to expose the autobiographical underpinnings associated with my particular educational state(s). More specifically, my first reading of E. O. Wilson's 1998 modernist and deeply homogenous manifesto, Consilience (that all knowledge can be connected via "consilient," or Unitarian or universalistic thinking), forced me to take a pronounced and introspective look at my personal educational experiences, my intellectual state of mind, and eventually the epistemological dimensions of the various university students I have interacted with as and educator in higher education. Although I eventually came to realize the Cartesian and polemical nature of Wilson's central thesis, this text nonetheless sparked a deep catharsis, forcing me to reexamine my educated state, and my role as an academic in a highly specialized field. Thus positioned, I don't intend to construct a modernist meta narrative categorizing all institutions of higher learning as dysfunctional; only that the phenomena I describe do exist on a disturbingly widespread level. Thankfully, there are indeed many colleges and universities that fall under some other category. They are genuinely and stubbornly operating as counter-examples of the subsequent discourse(s) to follow; they have not yet sold their soul in order to take the new, performative road. If my criticism is productive, perhaps it will resonate in the consciousness of others who have inhabited similar spaces and times. My modest objective is merely to provide a deconstruction capable of initiating and supporting a discourse surrounding restorative thinking and rehabilitative actions for the University.

Chapter 1 will thus serve as the platform from which I intend to portray my experiences, observations and analysis of the current state of higher education in the United States. I will subsequently introduce the term "Dysacademia" into the discourse surrounding higher education ("dys" having been introduced earlier, and the opposite of "eu," meaning good, or well in medical parlance). With these lived experiences in tow, I have gradually come to realize that up until my entry in the academy (which came comparatively late in life for me), I was in many ways like most of my undergraduate students. For most of my life I can earnestly admit that I was effectively suffering from certain medically derived metaphorical (dys) conditions such as dysbulia, dysgnosia, dyserethesia, and dyslogia (conditions expounded upon in Chapter 2) that gestated as a complication of the Dysacademia I myself had been deeply immersed; of the inherent and profound connections between this "fragmentation of the disciplines" and the corporate professionalization and performative nature of the academy that treats students like consumers, and produces ready made degrees for highly specific industrial means. These lived experiences and ruminations have led me to further investigate the archaeological underpinnings that shape the contemporary University's character, collective utility and identity.

Together, the various manifestations of "dys" can be seen as interconnected and interdependent maladies capable of portraying the discourse of Dysacademia. Just what do these various pathologies of the University add up to when all is said and done? The professor as Dysacademic; the curriculum as Dyscurriculum; higher education as Dyseducation; or, just a general and widespread "dys" that merely mimics the society it was intended to directly influence? One may already be pondering the next question regarding just "whom" is actually getting dys'd in the end--the individual objects, or the collective citizenry and society at large? It is my deepest hope that together, the various dysconditions presented herein are capable of serving as effective metaphors capable of effectively vaporizing the "University as simulacra" prophecy Bill Readings laments in elaborating upon what's really going on in our modern institutions of postsecondary training (1996). Interestingly, the metaphorical approach I am using to articulate the many tentacles and subsequent discourse of Dysacademia in Chapter 2 typifies one of Michel Serres' favorite "methodologies" for articulating complex ideas. Because Serres detests "ultratechnical language" and its inherent power to exclude and inevitably "kill," he has become known for his artistic and deft implementation of various poetic and graceful metaphors, and use of otherwise simple terms and language to express his complex ideas and propositions of thought (Serres & Latour, 1995, 24). In borrowing liberally from Serres' inclination that "Hiroshima is in everything that he does" (Serres & Latour, 1995, 15), I consider Serres' inventive, experiential and chaotic philosophy of education to be part of everything that I do as a subject in the University machine.

In Chapter 2, I extend Foucault's notion of discipline in order to describe the hyper disciplinization of the disciplines that has rapidly occurred in our cultural history. That is, I intend to situate the gradual hyperfragmentation of the disciplines that started with the University of Berlin in 1910 (Ford, 2002, 39), and augmented by events, circumstances and outcomes associated primarily with the industrial revolution, World War II, the Cold War, the information technology boom, and now the desire to make the globe one big, open market as the nascent source and force that now defines the inorganic operations and character of the typical contemporary American University. In *Chaos of Disciplines* (2001), sociologist Andrew Abbott analyzed the specific history, development and current condition of the social sciences, and then applies this discourse to the relative state of other academic disciplines. Essentially, it is Abbott's contention that any discipline can actually be represented by self-similar fractal patterns and chaos; and that there is actually much less to disagree about amongst and between the different disciplines. Presented from the ground up (the individual disciplines), Abbott calls for a curriculum with less boundaries, and one that illuminates the fractal connections between different types of knowing.

Abbott clearly points out that academic disciplines do a much better job of staying connected than do the professions; but steers clear of intonating that academia does in fact, do an admirable and effective job of teaching an eclectic, interstitial, or interdisciplinary approach to its students. In fact, he actually identifies several of the now established traditions of the American academe as being responsible for much of our current state of intellectual disrepair. Chiefly, he lays blame on the specialized PhD—academic major reproductive cycle, and the standard reliance and emphasis on academic majors and all of their financial and administrative underpinnings as being the primary disciplinary structures responsible for preventing a true, interstitial curriculum and pedagogy. This of course begs the question(s) regarding the various political, economic and sociocultural forces, both internal and external, that have contributed to the preponderance of hyperspecialized academic programs and their impact on the educational processes found in the University. Further, I aim to illustrate how this comminution of learning and enlightenment into the disciplines has intertwined with various other social, political and cultural factors previously described and further articulated by Foucault, Deleuze, Lyotard, Derrida and other scholars to help spawn what may now be seen as a pronounced disciplinary, control based and neoliberal/performative culture (Dysacademia) thriving in many of our colleges and universities.

Chapters 3 and 4 focus on the various neoliberal influenced and censoring forces that are increasingly morphing and controlling our academic institutions of higher learning, with a particular emphasis on the effect(s) that external agencies and processes like accreditation and a potential Academic Bill of Rights have/will have upon our academic practice, utility and eventual outcomes. As a program director of a nationally accredited allied health education program, my experiences and subsequent frustrations with the increasing amount of control exercised over "what" and "how" I teach provides much of the nutritive substance for these two chapters. In short, my interdisciplinary education and practical experiences have become marginalized by the controlling power of the accreditation machine. My hope is that other educators constrained by similar controlling forces can draw parallel analyses and insights from my application of Deleuze's discourse on control and censorship in the University.

The latter chapters change dispositions 180° from a cynical, attacking perspective into a more optimistic or inventive voice; from a deconstruction, to a (re)construction. My attempt to posit an intellectual pharmacopoeia capable of addressing the concerns expressed comprises the foci of Chapters 5 through 7. Chapter 5 takes a meticulous look at the postmodern nature of knowledge, closed versus open systems, chaos, and their intertwining effects on the nature of knowledge, and its subsequent construction of subjective epistemologies. If, as noted and self-professed amodern philosopher Michel Serres says, "the goal of instruction is invention" (Serres & Latour, 1995, 133), and the "goal of teaching is to have teaching to cease," is accepted as a feasible and appealing premise, then pedagogy today may be exposed as being more "necrotic" (dead, as in lacking nutrition and energy) than alive; or at least because of its relatively closed and static nature, "quasi-necrotic." Simply put, in these current times of classroom discipline, rabid standardization, measurable outcomes, censorship, surveillance and teacher accountability that so typify our 21st-century educational paradigm, the typical American student now has very little opportunity or initiative to invent his/her own knowledge; and thus, very little ability to teach the self. As the "founder" of cybernetics Norbert Wiener expressed 50 plus years ago, this is hardly a novel argument.

> Our elementary and secondary schools are more interested in formal classroom discipline than in the intellectual discipline of learning something thoroughly, and a great deal of the serious preparation for a scientific or a literary course is relegated to some sort of graduate school or other. (1954, 132)

From this perspective, Chapter 6 will advance a "curriculum reconceptualized" by integrating what I see as complementary concepts from various scientific frames of thought to the larger framework of pedagogy, curriculum and the student in a postmodern manner that allows and encourages students to act, to draw, and to invent. Specifically, many if not all of the central constructs that characterize open systems theory (OST), cybernetics and information theory, and chaos and complexity theories can be applied to a postmodern University curriculum, and in so doing, connect the central theoretical tenets of these analogous theories to the central problem put forth by Wilson's Consilience. Appreciated as such, Chapter 6 intends to create a postmodern educational paradigm that maximizes mobility, growth, wandering and eventually negentropy (or, complex order) in an attempt to connect and interrelate specific and pertinent elements of OST, chaos and cybernetics. Hopefully this plastic paradigm will be capable of providing a platform for "Undisciplining the Disciplined" by intertwining the philosophical creations of Michel Serres, Gilles Deleuze and Felix Guattari; a platform capable of supporting and nourishing a theoretical conception I am calling *POST*, or postmodern open systems theory. It is intended that a *POST* framework will effectively extrapolate and coagulate specific conceptual elements from open systems, chaos, information, multiplicities, and rhizomes, and subsequently connect and interrelate these complimentary concepts as constituent structures of an alternative postmodern curricular discourse that provides openings, possibilities, multiple lines of flight, and rhizomatic recursions that prove capable of developing critical epistemologies; and thus too, subjective and contextual ontologies. In an attempt to adhere to the poststructural notion that "theory is not prescriptive," it's merely "idiosyncratic," the current discourse will be offered "up front" with the full awareness that its effectiveness, if any, can only be embodied by a discourse structured by invention, hope, prospects and multiplicity (Pinar et al., 1995, 56).

From there, I wish to add a poststructural intellect to these concepts by elaborating more upon the pedagogical and cultural thoughts of Michel Serres, Gilles Deleuze, Felix Guattari in an attempt to articulate what a *POST* education might "feel" like in the final chapter. As students progress through a curriculum reconceptualized as such, they won't likely proceed in a linear and scientific fashion of objectivity and controlled order; rather, they will have the opportunity to transform from entropy (disorder) towards negentropic (order) and complex forms, and in a more fractal, rhizomatic and postmodern manner that is not predicted, controlled, or manipulated by objective ideals, essential knowledge, or modern absolutes—much like an artist, a dancer or a writer. In looking at education in this light, Bill Readings' hypothetical wondering of "How long does it take to become 'educated'?" takes on even more weight and significance for those concerned with the intellectual development of personal, critical and local subjectivities (1996, 25). Chapter 7 is a (re) constructive effort to articulate a cohesive and inventive paradigm for a postmodern and poststructural curriculum embodied by subjective potential, wandering and empowerment.

As the sections of this text gradually unfold, and as I labor to articulate the various points of my analysis, I intend to continue interpolating, juxtaposing and taking full advantage of the many extraordinary and profound metaphors, ideas and perspectives on philosophy, education, knowledge, learning, and life that Michel Serres has given us in his many creative and Hermetic works. Thus said, a Serresian expression of thought will be amalgamated throughout my analysis, culminating in an articulation of possibility and hope that I believe provides multiple and exciting potentialities for the invention of new, more promising dialectical discourse(s). A new discourse that possesses the potential to displace and disposition the current meta narratives currently occupying the center of the discourse that is the contemporary University; a discourse that has the healing powers to dismiss the various dysconditions that shape and define the current discourse; a discourse that possesses the power to dismantle and disavow Dysacademia. In the introduction to their forthcoming book dealing with the potential for expanding curriculum theory research and practice, Reynolds and Webber elaborate on the notion of "dis/positioning" the conversations, on creating multiple Deleuzian "lines of flight," and on discovering the new; the focus of which will be the centerpiece of my concluding chapter.

> We wish to distinguish this volume from current models of research and offer the possibility of refusing them, questioning them and directing practitioners towards this idea of adopting lines of flight" or multiplicities...It advocates multiplicity...It is a question of discovering the conditions under which something new might be produced. This discovery of, or working toward the new is at the heart of multiplicities and lines of flight. (2004, 2)

Higher Education at a Crossroads' ultimate ambition is simply to deconstruct one account of today's higher education machine, and to subsequently create original, multiple, and discursive "line(s) of flight" for curriculum, inquiry, and travel. The closing chapter will attempt to do just this; to invent a new discourse, a discourse of open possibility and empowerment, and a discourse that centers the self at/in/between the heart of the University by dis/positioning Dysacademia. By offering a 3rd option, a 3rd curriculum, a 3rd pedagogy, and a 3rd space—a postmodern, postdisciplinary approach to cultural, social and subjective learning, it may prove capable of critical ontological and epistemological transformation of multiple individual subjects. In light of this recognition and its profound effects on the development of the intellect and self, I propose embracing an educational conception that is more "postdisciplinary," in that it reflects and requires Michel Serres' "multiple multiples" thoughts concerning the infinite possibilities associated with ways of seeing, hearing, speaking and knowing (1995). This counter-narrative for myriad free and open spaces and possibilities occupy the spaces of the closing, constructive chapter. A curriculum conceived as such has the potential to dismantle power, disciplinary boundaries, and homogenous meta narratives and modes of thought that have recently worked to inhibit invention and wandering of the subjective self; and instead opens up various and multiple spaces for thought, knowledge production and deconstruction, transformation and wandering of the self. A postmodern, postdisciplinary curriculum that works to connect various modes of thought, all the while respecting the differences and similarities that exist to give shape and form to the respective disciplines, thus creating a fragile synthesis of thought, or what Serres calls a "syrrhese" (Serres & Latour, 1995, 122), that is interlaced with a postmodern sensibility reflective of Lyotard's observations on postmodern knowledge from over 20 years ago.

The potential utility of such a curriculum will be presented as a potentiality of thought and discourse that holds promise for deconstructing old and existing discourses, while also allowing for the generation of new and multiple discourses of difference that can better enable "higher educated" students to understand how power and knowledge are inextricably linked in all, if not most of our social endeavors. It is hoped that students enmeshed within a Serresian 3rd Curriculum will prove capable of recognizing how power, authority and meta narratives operate, define and constrain most, if not all aspects of their lives, their being and their ethics. Perhaps it will enlighten the 3rd educated as to their responsibility as one of the higher educated, an awareness that goes beyond performative and neoliberal measures and markers of identity and position. Thus recognized, students educated in the postmodern 3rd University may be truly capable of inventing their own knowledge, of traveling in and amongst the middle and dystopic spaces, and of inventing their own authentic and democratic self(s) in profound, untold and myriad ways. For me, as is for Serres, this is the ultimate and empowering purpose of education and the only true sign of "intelligence"—that being the ability "to invent" (Serres, 1997). In the end, the relative value and utility of my finished theoretical inquiry will be based upon its ability (or inability) to enable curricular thought and practice to discern new from old, inventive from stifling and reified; or to produce a language system or conceptual scheme that is capable of producing a meaningful and enumerative discourse (Short, 1991, 211).

In other words, if my research does not cause its consumers to think, reflect, reiterate, and eventually to invent something else; something personal, and something ontologically new, it is just that--"re-search." I'm in a search that I hope provides the spark for others who are looking to search, not to re-search. Humbly, I'm not searching for the essential answer or solution for all of higher education, nor am I denying the very real utility of professional expertise, disciplinary competence, and economic vitality. "Re-search" for Serres is old, copied, redundant, and most importantly structurally iterative; whereas invention is generative, fresh, noisy, chaotic, synthetic, entropic and risky; it is here that my mode of inquiry and scholarly intentions steadfastly harmonize with Serres' thoughts on productivity and invention.

Inventive thinking is unstable, it is undetermined, it is undifferentiated...it bleaches the body. (1995, 35)

Culture in America is quite an enigma—we are reported to be the wealthiest, the best educated, and the most advanced society in the world, yet we also have some the highest rates of social disharmony amongst so-called "developed nations." If we are such a highly educated society and people, why can't the majority of our college graduates "read" difficult texts, or critically analyze literature? Why do we have such high divorce and suicide rates? Why are so many of our citizens on mood enhancing and sleep enhancement medications? Why do we have the highest obesity rate in the developed world? Why do we have such pronounced "mid-life crisis" phenomena in our country? Why has elective plastic surgery to enhance and modify aesthetic features proliferated into the latest cultural, "must have" craze for an increasing percentage of our populace (including teenagers)? Why does the average American professional change careers numerous times in his/her lifetime? Why are so many highly educated people so "well off", yet so unhappy and ill prepared to handle life's many complexities and uncertainties? This begs the question, "just what does most of our populace actually become "educated" in?

To me, this disturbing sociocultural paradox is at heart educational, philosophical, social and political. We teach too many of our students "how to", and "how not to" dance, to read, or to draw; yet we rarely "let" them invent their own dances, interpretations, or drawings. We allow, no, we subject our students into singular, myopic, closed and typically performative ways of seeing and being in the world. The (dys)educated become accustomed to singularity, political correctness, and Cartesian thinking and Newtonian ideals of perfection; while becoming uncomfortable with philosophical uncertainty, sociocultural controversy, or critical discourse(s). We treat the (dys)educated as nimble consumers, and as such, we happily sell them what they seek in the name of customer service—a performative education void of critical or philosophical mass, and the cultural capital to take advantage of capitalism (just what is "student centeredness" these days?). And, like a caged animal, the (dys)educated get fidgety, anxious and confused when confined in restricted ontological and epistemological spaces for too long. Eventually, the (dys)educated lose the instinct or ability to return into the invigorating turbulence of open spaces; they become fearful of complexity and change, and eventually face the reality that they have little reference from which to act, to think, or to feel. Some eventually realize that their higher education only prepared them for a fraction of the challenges life in a complex world presents. Higher education should rightfully "be" about critically exploring an developing multiple, chaotic, and unknown open spaces, as much as it is about professional preparation and economic viability.

If our personal journeys continue to be unstable and turbulent, productive and noisy; if we are successful in treating our various [dys] ailments, in finding our spaceships, in leaving the womb of comfort and familiarity; we too will turn time around, we will die young. We can only hope we become younger as we become more erudite. Further still, if our personal pedagogies prove to be turbulent and negentropic; if we can find the energy and the means to overcome Academic dyskinesia; if we are allowed to lead our students into open, 3rd spaces; if we can lead our selves and our students to the outside, into the rain, away from the shadows of their youth; if we can let University students dance and draw without boundaries and preconceived outcomes, they too will grow young, they will prove capable of treating and preventing their own dysacademia. Imagine the possibilities…both old and young becoming young together; dysacademia can be eradicated and unfettered learning and growth can flourish amongst the higher educated. The University can become the university again, but only by recognizing what lies at the vortex of the crossroads and subsequently being cognizant of what each road promises for its travelers; then and only then can a path be chosen, and well traveled towards erudition.

The Lived Curriculum
& Dysacademia

In the relations of the university to society, in the production, structure, ar-
chiving, and transmission of knowledges and technologies (of forms of
knowledge as technologies), in the political stakes of knowledge, in the very
idea of knowledge and truth, lies the advent of something entirely other. To
answer, what to answer for, and to whom?: the question is perhaps more
alive and legitimate than ever.

—Jacques Derrida (2004, 89)

In noticing that many University students today don't seem to be in
possession of the more historical and intellectual notions of what
higher education can do for liberating the intellect and the spirit, and
for transforming individual ontologies with open and creative energy,
a despairing realization can be appreciated. Directly stated, an overwhelming percentage of contemporary University students seem to
be contently operating as the central mechanistic devices that drive
the economically laden "human capital theory." As such, they have
innocently and passively been complicit in the conversion from subjects, to objects; they are part of a mechanistic production and can
thus be viewed as capable, but docile consumer objects of production
(Apple, 1995, 39). Or to borrow Paolo Freire's now infamous term, today's higher education subjects have become the objects of the "banking phenomenon" of pedagogy; whereby concrete knowledge and
facts are merely deposited into their sub-consciousness, idly sitting
there, collecting dust and eventually, growing mold. Sadly, these performative objects are diligently working under the impression that
these deposits will gain significant interest following graduation in
the form of lifelong economic prosperity, and perhaps even personal

fulfillment. But this concern is not unique to any one academic's situatedness, nor is it a novel observation. Jean-Francois Lyotard put forth a notion of "performativity" and applied it specifically to this type of education; whereby the "other" facet of knowledge (that being, its transmission) is now just a "subset of the social system," and where higher education is now perceived as being operationally based on the best possible input/output equation (1984, 46).

In Lyotard's performative education, the "desired goal becomes the optimal contribution of higher education to the best performativity of the social system," with two kinds of indispensable skills created in the process. First, performative students in the University acquire the specialized skills necessary to "tackle world competition" as they are locally relevant to the global market; and secondly, higher learning has to supply the social system with the skills needed to maintain its own internal cohesion. It is largely within Lyotard's contentions that "in the context of delegitimation, universities and the institutions of higher learning are called upon to create skills, and no longer ideals," and "the transmission of knowledge is no longer designed to train an elite capable of guiding the nation towards its emancipation, but to supply the system with players capable of acceptably fulfilling their roles at the pragmatic posts required by its institutions," that will center my critique of higher education and the production of performative subjectivity. Most assuredly, Lyotard could not have foreseen the potential connection between this type of critical discourse and the daunting, but foreseeable possibility that college and university professors may soon be forced to give standardized tests in order to prove their effectiveness and educational value to our nation's citizenry (or more appropriately, the government).

With such economical and technical motivation towards learning, often by both parties (student and professor), it is also apparent that today's University products are largely incapable of their own epistemological creations, of meaningful knowledge synthesis, or of de- and reconstruction of complex phenomena or critical issues. In fact, a recent book entitled *Our Underachieving Colleges* penned by former Harvard President Derek Bok on the failure of many academics to study, incorporate or even much care about new and creative forms of pedagogy supports this fear (2005). Citing numerous, large-scale studies, Bok summarizes by notifying us that an alarmingly high percentage of today's college and university graduates "who start college with average critical thinking skills only tend to progress over the next four years from the 50th percentile of their class to approximately the 69th percentile." There's more alarming news according to Bok, this time with direct implications for the teaching body(s) in the University.

Most undergraduates leave college still inclined to approach unstructured "real life" problems with a form of primitive relativism, believing that there are no firm grounds for preferring one conclusion over another. Further studies indicate that problem-based discussion, group study, and other forms of active learning produce greater gains in critical thinking than lectures, yet the lecture format is still the standard in most college classes, especially in large universities. Other research has documented the widespread use of other practices that impede effective learning, such as the lack of prompt and adequate feedback on student work, the prevalence of tests that call for memory rather than critical thinking, and the reliance on teaching methods that allow students to do well in science courses by banking on memory rather than truly understanding the basic underlying concepts. (2003, 1)

Situated as such, is knowledge then treated like an industry, or as a valuable commodity in the American University? Or looked at from a Kantian-Derridean perspective, does the University have a more metaphysical and ontological intention centered on a more substantive and liberating discourse of responsibility that appeals to "a pure ethico-juridical instance, to pure practical reason, to a pure thinking of right, and correlatively to the decision of a pure egological subject"? (Derrida, 2004, 90). This is not a simple question to address, nor are the various factors that have contributed to the construction of the contemporary University and its propensity for producing docile objects; but the implications for failing to attempt such an undertaking are dire and disturbing.

In their landmark text *Understanding Curriculum*, Pinar, Reynolds, Slattery & Taubman (1995, 14) take considerable effort to present a scholarly, yet admittedly cautious synopsis of the historical and cultural events, processes, and phenomena that have defined and shaped curriculum in the United States. In walking a constant tight rope with their literary mapping of the topography that *was* and *is* curriculum, Pinar et al., explicitly state their intent to avoid supplanting yet another meta narrative as to "what" curriculum should specifically *be* for their readers, while attempting to describe and elucidate the complex field that "is" curriculum. Inspired by Joseph Schwab's 1969 characterization of the American curriculum field as "moribund," Pinar and colleagues assert that our pre-1970s curriculum was "balkanized," and thus ineffective at critically or genuinely educating most of our populace. As a result of myriad sociocultural developments that emerged and flourished in the post-WWII epoch (most notably, the increasing overemphasis/blind reliance on behaviorist psychology as the pedagogical method of choice, and the escalating post-Sputnik eminence of math and science as "valuable" and desirable knowledge), the 20th-century American curriculum can be historically distinguished by the hasty and profound technologization of our society, culture, and even our body(s).

As various branches within the social sciences progressively embraced a modern, empirical and objective method of inquiry for all
things social such as education, the classrooms and brick pathways of
many of our educational institutions became virtual Petri dishes for
myriad scientific and industrial modes of operation, application and
identity. Specifically, models of industrial efficiency and various
sources of "objective" data from cognitive and educational psychology collectively intermingled their central tenets and presumptions
with Ralph Tyler's (1949) curricular ideas to effectively fabricate a
very mechanical, linear and industrial based method of pedagogy
that often belied sound theory, or even rational educational thought.
The result of this pedagogical mess is that it took almost 70 years for
curriculum thinking, writing and discourse to occur differently; for it
to be "reconceptualized"; for the "other" (approach, self, place, etc.) to
be considered and articulated in both theory or praxis; for the existing
paradigms to be deconstructed and dialectically challenged; and subsequently, for new discourses regarding our curricular phenomena to
be generated, invented and substantiated.

As Pinar et al. state, the contemporary curriculum field of the
early 1970s no longer saw curricular problems as "technical problems," but rather as "why" problems (1995, 8). The evolving paradigm shift for curriculum studies that began in the early 1970s and
1980s with the generative and promising scholarship of Pinar, Joseph
Schwab, Elliot Eisner, Herbert Kliebard, Philip Jackson, and others,
produced new curricular sub-discourses that critically challenged the
concepts, research methods, status and function of curriculum within
the larger field known as education (Pinar et al., 1995, 12). Admittedly, the foci of much of this early curriculum theory and criticism
by Pinar and his contemporaries concerned K-12 education problems
and shortfalls in the United States; but perhaps they can now be seen
as prophetic, as it concerns higher education in the United States, as
well. Sadly, much of American higher education can now be considered in need of solemn and extensive attention from curricular theorists and vested academicians alike, as it can effectively be argued
that it too, has naively followed American primary and secondary institutions of learning on the path to functional obsolescence.

In effect, *Understanding Curriculum* has helped to initiate the process of reflecting upon what was "not" in *my* lived curriculum; my
high school curriculum, my undergraduate curriculum, my master's
curriculum, and my life's curriculum. At that moment I can explicitly
recall taking another look at Pinar et al's table of contents, reflecting
upon all levels of my formal educational experiences, and then performing a simple contrast-and-compare analysis between "what was"
and "what was not" in my curricular memories, with what was presented in Pinar's landmark 1995 text. I actually found myself "check-
ing off" those things that I had experienced, as well as those that I did

not, and needless to say my "had not" list was much longer than my "had" list. This "retro" analytical process of substantiating my lived curriculum was extremely revealing, deeply frustrating, and yet also terribly exciting and potentially liberating for me in myriad ways. Despite the many negative and anxious emotions that I encountered in analyzing my "lived curriculum" and its many nulls, the experience also provided a sort of cathartic spark for me in both my professional and educational worlds. In particular, these reflexive and candid moments allowed me to better understand what my collective educational, professional and personal experiences provided me in the form of redemptive and transcendent curricular experiences.

Personal Situatedness & Curriculum Inquiry

Finally, it goes without saying that after a certain age, questions of upbringing lose more and more of their pertinence, as a person becomes the father (sic) of himself—as he takes responsibility for his decisive and definitive education. Only the lazy and the infirm remain dependant on their initial upbringing—an ailment that should be treated. (Serres & Latour, 1995, 20)

As the third son in my family to attend a private liberal arts institution in search of "higher education," I can now realize that I was largely unaware of the larger purposes and missions of higher education, and its intended and potential transformative powers both before I entered, and while I was in college. And although I thought at that time that I knew the fundamental differences between a liberal arts college and larger, public university, I know now that I was naïve in that regard as well. Somehow I knew, or at least thought I knew that liberal arts colleges were more demanding, more intensive, and thus more rewarding than their larger, broader in scope, public counterparts. But in looking back, I don't suppose I knew precisely why, or how. I somehow thought that all liberal arts colleges would be fairly comparable in terms of curriculum, pedagogy and their transformative abilities—after all, college is college right? Although I knew I was going to my chosen baccalaureate institution primarily because of their reputable program in my chosen disciplinary field, I suppose that I also took some comfort in knowing that it was also a "reputable" liberal arts college. Theoretically then, it would offer me the same form of emancipative education that I saw my older siblings experiencing at their respective & highly touted New England liberal arts campuses. After all, I too wanted to be liberated by "the college experience"—but liberated from "what," to "where," or in what "ways" I wasn't quite sure.

Despite my subsequent academic successes in my chosen specialized and technical field of study and my liberal arts core classes, I became increasingly disenfranchised with the overall quality, depth and breadth of my own undergraduate education as time progressed. Where were the conversations on Plato, Marx, Toni Morrison, and W. B. Dubois in *my* curriculum? Where were the critical and profound debates and dialogues about the various epochal sociopolitical issues at my undergraduate college? When was I going to get the opportunity to discuss politics, postmodern theory, multiculturalism, critical theory and religion? When was I going to find myself embroiled in an intense intellectual debate with one of my professors over truth, justice, multiculturalism, or democracy? When was I going to figure out if I should join the Young Republicans or the Young Democrats club? Truth must be known that I graduated from a 4-year liberal arts college without ever having heard of any of these people, nor the trendy "isms" that color the intellectual landscape.

Although something seemed amiss to me during my early undergraduate years, my relative level of intellectual immaturity and ignorance didn't allow me the opportunity to explicitly articulate the nature of my "angst." In short, I felt that I knew "something" was missing from my higher educational experiences, but I really had no idea what that thing might be. Even though I felt a discernable level of what I now can recognize as epistemological and ontological anxiety, I wasn't able to pinpoint exactly what that void represented, nor what was needed to fill it, and thus to satiate my epistemological and ontological angst. To borrow from Pinar's expression of what curriculum was, is, and/or ought to be, I didn't quite know what was missing from my experiences simply because "I didn't know what I was missing." I didn't quite understand the shape, form, or the subsequent professional and personal consequences that my missing curriculum would eventually reveal as my life experiences came into being. At the current stage of my life, I feel that I can now ask myself why it was that I had never even heard of the term "postmodernism," despite the fact that I was at the time enrolled in a liberal arts college during very active and pronounced postmodern times.

I was a good student; I graduated on time, passed the grueling national certification exam in my field on the first attempt, and had been accepted to the graduate schools of my choice, including the two premier programs for graduate study in my field. Yet despite this "obvious" academic "excellence" at my chosen reputable liberal arts college, I'm quite sure that I had never even heard of the Western Canon, modernism, postmodernism, postcolonialism, cultural studies, multiculturalism, or poststructuralism during my tenure. Worse yet, despite leaving with a bachelor's of science degree I had not yet been required to didactically or socially engage in any meaningful study about the environment, politics, power, education, ethics, or morality, and their inherent and critical connections to the institution(s) of "big" science, and our democratic way of life. In fact, I don't even think that I knew the difference between the "left" and the "right" and all the associated trappings that accompany one's political leanings. For me, identity, truth, and language were simple, linear and fixed concepts that could be thought out rationally and critically; they were essential and sovereign entities that I had bought, ingested and reproduced like other, "good" students. Upon matriculation, I was a certified allied health care provider; a consumer, producer and provider of medical and health science, yet I knew not of the potential and real challenges, pitfalls, and limits of scientific epistemology and the method(s) used to generate such knowledge. I knew not of the inherent power relations between knowledge, authority and scientific discourse, the meta narrative it generated and possessed, or the subsequent hierarchical position that science held over other forms of knowing. From professional and civic standpoints alike, I knew not of the various cultural and social factors that can, and do complicate our medico-scientific institutions, and their subsequent delivery of services to our diverse and heterogeneous populations. Something was *different*…something was omitted from my "higher" education, and also from my highly specialized and scientific master's curriculum; and thus also from the potential intellectual and liberal enlightenment that awaited me upon my matriculations.

Disturbingly (and perhaps a very real reflection on the times, as well as a strong supporting argument for my central thesis), the completion of a doctoral degree in curriculum theory was the illuminating force required for me to begin to understand at least a part of my lived and disciplined curriculum. Exposure to and immersion in curriculum theory helped me to see that in effect, I had become "disciplined" by my chosen "discipline"–a powerful concept and self-realization that now underlines and shapes of the primary theoretical framework of this book. Because of the strong autobiographical and theoretical connections this impression has to my overarching analysis, I will elaborate further upon the meaning and impact in forthcoming sections of this text, but suffice it to say that I can now more readily realize both the impact and significance of Messer-Davidow, Shumway, and Sylvan's situational comment regarding disciplinarity and its multiple discourses, "socially and conceptually, we are disciplined by our disciplines" (1993, vii.).

That is, I have gradually come to the self-awareness that despite the purported breadth and depth of the required liberal arts core classes that I had endured and passed with flying colors, things felt disconnected, incomplete, less liberating, and *less* than challenging. Reflecting a *void* more so than it does some positive entity or variety of *other*, I was different. In the words of John Michael, I had at least partially succeeded in becoming a "technocratic intellectual," but was far off from being considered, or considering myself what he calls a "critical intellectual" (2000, 2). But as chance would have it, the gradual passage of time, continuous internal reflections and deconstruction of my own subjectivity, and the advent of new and varied learning experiences would eventually coalesce to help me reformulate a more clarified insight regarding the complex ontological and epistemological nausea that I had been experiencing.

After eleven subsequent years of myriad clinical and professional practice in the field of sports medicine, including working for a Fortune 500 healthcare company for five years, I opted for a lifestyle change in order to take a university teaching position at a midsized, general state university in the Southeast. Although excited by the pending change in professional scenery, I must admit I was very anxious about entering *the academy* and the potential reception I would receive from my new colleagues; they themselves highly educated and disciplined professionals in their chosen fields.

Although I was resolutely confident in the knowledge and skills needed to teach my discipline at the university level, I was dreadfully fearful of not being able to hold my own in an intellectual debate with my colleagues who after all, were in custody of something I didn't possess—impressive academic vitas. Even worse, I was twice as fearful of "getting caught with my pants down" in any type of critical discourse with an external colleague from another department or college from within the university. This being said, I decided to take a proactive approach to enhancing my intellectual agility, and as Serres alludes, to "treat my ailment" (1995, 20) by hitting the books in an effort to avoid being categorized as "that guy who teaches athletic training" (my field and profession, by training). In short, I wanted to become the "father of myself" so as to be rightfully respected and recognized as an academic; as someone with a certain degree of intellectual fiber, and as someone who, quite frankly "belonged" in the academy. I suppose that I must also confess that I wanted to "right" what I perceived as my educational shortfalls, and to make others take notice of my pending intellectual transformation. I wanted to belong; I wanted people to taken notice of me as an academic first, to consider my actual disciplinary home only as an afterthought. To do this, to become the father of myself and subsequently set a new path for growth, I had to continue to deconstruct both my lived and living curricula in ways that revealed the subjective nature of my consciousness and the voids that I felt existed in my epistemology, ontology and axiology.

To "re-invent" myself, I had to find spaces and methods capable of opening up new passageways and possibilities that would allow a reformation and altered evolution of my subjectivity. For Jacques Derrida, such a "critique of consciousness, of the subject, of self-identity and of self-proximity or self-possession" represents his intentional notion of decentering structure and the humanistic construction of the sovereign subject (1988, 280). For Serres, who chooses to represent complex poststructural notions such as Derrida's deconstruction of the subject in a more poetic manner because he detests ultratechnical vocabulary, and its propensity to exclude and discourage, this means that I had to leave "the shadow cast by my father's house" and the "landscapes of my childhood" in order to re-invent my own pedagogy and to launch my own wandering (Serres, 1997, 8).

As chance would have it, while browsing through the university bookstore one day without any particular agenda in mind, I happened across a book that inspired my ontological and epistemological consciousness—*Consilience: The Unity of Knowledge,* by Harvard biologist and Pulitzer Prize winning author, E. O. Wilson (1998). Promoted as an "intense intellectual journey" for its readers on the jacket, *Consilience* was just what I desired for my intellectually myopic mind. Meta narrative aside, my first reading of *Consilience* opened my mind's eye to other forms of knowing, to various philosophical debates in the diverse fields of knowledge, and most importantly, to how much I *did not know*. In short, my "non knowledge" was critically and enthusiastically exposed by my experiences with *Consilience*, and although I have now largely moved away from much of Wilson's modernist ideology for unifying knowledge around one meta narrative (biology) that some critics have called "fascist pseudo-science" (Rosenthal, 1998, 3), the current intellectual journey that I now find myself in the midst of was effectively fertilized for future augmentation by other texts, other authors, and other erudite experiences. Despite the inherent limits and subsequent critiques of Wilson's construction (upon which I will pontificate upon further in Chapter 3), the depth, intensity and breadth of discourse contained within *Consilience* afforded me the primary intellectual nutrition and confidence to converse about "something" outside my professional field on a variety of topics, issues, and debates. Because it gave me new ideas, new knowledge, and new curiosities, it effectively provided me the self-assurance to discuss something "other" than athletic training with those outside my professional identity; it filled some of my voids. *Consilience* gave me the stimulus to look for other things, to read other texts, to wander into other spaces, to ask other questions, and most importantly, to feel comfortable leaving behind the landscapes of my childhood, to cure my ailment.

Becoming Rewired: Undisciplining the Disciplined Self

Cultural anthropology from Marvin Harris, the theory of the mind from Howard Gardner and Steven Pinker, and the philosophy of science from Bertrand Russell, Albert Einstein, Bruno Latour and Paul Feyerabend soon began to take up spaces on my nightstand, in my book bag, and most importantly in my consciousness. The language(s), questions and opinions contained within these diverse "extra disciplinary" texts gradually worked their way into my own now mushrooming vernacular, and thus, a funny, unanticipated occurrence "happened on the way to the ball" that was/is my self-deconstruction. The more I read, the more I wandered; the more I saw and heard, the more I realized what I couldn't see and hear; and as time passed, the younger I began to feel. Although I obviously wasn't aware of the language of poststructural discourse at the time of these events, the deconstruction and subsequent reemergence of the self I was in the midst of can be seen, not as the liquidation of the subject (mine), but rather as Michael Peters argues, the rehabilitation, decentering and repositioning of the subject; a *tour de force* that represents the actual intention and practice of Derrida's poststructural thinking (Peters, 1997, 71). For Michel Serres, such chaotic and turbulent experiences represent what he sees as the essential and authentic meaning of learning, knowledge and living, a domain of thought in which he spends considerable time and energy addressing in his work, particularly his treatise on education, *The Troubadour of Knowledge*.

> Learning launches wandering. (1997, 8)

> The creator is born old and dies young, the opposite of those who are realistic and, as they say, have their feet on the ground, know how to be born infants and die senile like everyone else. (1997, 104)

Serres & Latour discuss the meaning of meaning making as well.

> Authentic epistemology is the art of inventing, the springboard for passing from the old to the new. (1995, 14)

As my deconstruction crept along on my own volition and direction (or more appropriately, a lack of?), I suddenly began to take greater notice in the arts, in nature, in ethics; and in the larger, more global sociocultural conditions that define and challenge our current epoch. I began to pay more attention to cultural events, politics, social commentary, and other more meaningful and dialectical discourses; and as such, my life began to take on a different meaning, a different quality, a more pronounced turbulence, and thus, a different purpose. I began to be even more critical of my past educational experiences and the structural influences of my "father's house," and how they worked to shape my consciousness and subjective self. Thus experienced, I arrived at a more genuine ability to reflect on and analyze my lived curricula, on what was "there," and on what was missing. I was ravenous with curiosity. Gradually, I found myself better able to "put my finger" on some of the issues affecting my subjective and rather nascent "state," and soon I realized that Serres was on to something— it was time to become the father of myself, to take responsibility for my own learning and exploration, to construct my own reality, and thus to reformulate and adapt my own subjectivity.

I was becoming increasingly interested in, and somewhat conversant in myriad "other" things—other ways of knowing, other ways of seeing, hearing, and feeling; other "others." On a different but obviously interconnected level, I also began to look more critically at the educational experiences in which my current students and my own two sons were currently enmeshed in, a process that revealed a stronger sense of urgency to discover more about their respective living curricula. I began to notice and to feel the effects and affects of the humanist pedagogy that I had experienced almost exclusively as a student at multiple levels. I began the disciplinary process of critically challenging my own epistemology, of "de-essentializing" and "de-privileging" my disciplined notions of knowledge described by Messer-Davidow et al. in their critical analysis of the discourses that shape and define the various disciplines (1993, 3). I became more readily cognizant of the fact that I too was reproducing many, if not most of the homogenous and modern principles and truths embedded in our historically grounded essentialist paradigms of thought and pedagogy. In making his point regarding the calculation of the subject, Peters explicitly connects Derrida's deconstruction to pedagogy in a manner reflective of my ongoing autobiographical deconstruction and theoretical exposition.

> Derridean philosophy offers an active interpretation, resistance, and re-evaluation of humanist pedagogy, of forms of pedagogy based on the sovereign subject—which is to say, the predominant forms of pedagogy existing today that structure our pedagogical institutions, theories, and practices...the question of pedagogy is never far from Derrida's concerns; that when he poses the question of style, of new styles of writing and thinking, he is engaged in rethinking traditional humanist pedagogical practices and the founding principles of our educational institutions. (2003, 64)

Induced by the deconstructive catharsis that was now consuming my consciousness, my various theoretical perspectives, ways of doing, and ways of being began to shift drastically towards a being that reflected a more postmodern sensibility. This new way of "being" in the world, although not yet, nor will it ever be complete brought about subsequent and pronounced adjustments in both my parental and professional manners of praxis. I began to avoid, dislike even, structure and disorder; I increasingly began to seek out and embrace chaos and chance, to look for things that I was trained not to look for; I began to feel comfortable in the gray areas, and to shun the black and white poles of dichotomy. I was in effect and finally in my mind at least, just starting the life long and time reversal process of becoming "higher educated." Interestingly and perhaps somewhat paradoxically to *structure philiacs*, this subjective transformation was occurring at the same time that I was becoming more deeply involved in a more postmodern and critical approach to higher education.

Because of myriad circumstances, I soon found myself enrolled in a curriculum theory and cultural studies doctoral program. Over time, the various and sundry intellectual, cultural and phenomenological experiences that I have been fortunate to experience as a result of my collective life events have progressively dilated various and multiple channels of social and academic opportunity for me; and it was/is my doctoral studies that provided the *coup d'etat* for me to put it all together and to make sense of *my lived curricula*. Collectively, the authentically liberal and emancipative experiences that I have been fortunate to be in the middle of have vigorously opened multiple passageways for a deeper ontological exploration of my self, my future, and my soul. For Gilles Deleuze, "lines of flight" such as these are required to resist fascist power regimes that cage the individual self, and thus are necessary for revealing avenues for escape, and for fostering the exploration and execution of desire.

> We set against this fascism of power active, positive lines of flight, because these lines open up desire, desire's machines and the organization of a social field of desire; it's not a matter of escaping "personally from oneself," but allowing something to escape, like bursting a pipe or a boil. (1995, 19)

For Serres, the soul is constructed through experience, joy, sadness and magnitude, and represents "the kind of space and time that can be expanded from its natal position toward all exposures" (1997, 31). Serres' conception of the soul can only be exposed by learning things, things in an invented, turbulent and experiential 3ʳᵈ place, and is thus best represented by a "vacant intensity, potential world and thought right in the middle of the body which is like a rose window, or a small sun" (34). In this sense then, my doctoral studies can be seen metaphorically as an offensive lineman that functions to open holes in the defense for me, the running back with the ball, so that I can run through and advance to new, as of yet undetermined spaces. My subsequent experiences with curriculum studies has effectively coalesced with my other lived curricular events to open and maintain multiple lines of flight, to expose and nourish my desire, and to give accent, expression, and spirit to my soul.

In effect, the dilation of these inquiring passageways has allowed me, as Serres proposes, to be the "father of myself...to take responsibility for my own decisive and definitive education" (Serres & Latour, 1995, 20). And indirectly, my recent intellectual enlightenment and autobiographical reflections provided a different lens with which to view my role as an academic, and to better crystallize my personal philosophy of higher education on the larger scale. The curriculum that I had struggled to find since my entrance into college in the early

1980s, the journey that I had been seeking for so long had finally materialized, and thus, the deep intellectual transformation that I felt I was missing had finally come about for me in very powerful, transcendent and liberating ways. In reference to my particular voyage of lived curriculum, Lyotard answers his own question regarding the state of being educated by using a spaceship metaphor, "When we know more or less which is the far off planet that we desire, and when we do all that we can to set off for it" (cited in Peters, 1997, xx).

For Lyotard, as for me then, education can be seen as the examination of, and subsequent following of the inner desire that lies deep within all of us, and consequently charting a course that allows for the invention of the self. In Lyotard's parlance then, it wasn't until after my entry into the academy and my subsequent immersion in doctoral studies that I was able to locate my "planets," to leave behind the shadows of my father's house and the landscapes of my childhood; and thus find the appropriate vehicles needed to travel to, from and within the opened and far off spaces. Alternately, my *currere,* or what Pinar refers to more specifically as the "running of the course," had finally heard its starting gun, and I was now beginning to enjoy this new form of action research on myself that was consuming much of my time and energy (Pinar, Reynolds, Slattery & Taubman, 1995). But why had I wasted so much time? Why was I getting older, and not younger prior to this?

My soul then, is what I yearn to nourish and cultivate through unstructured experience and wandering; through an endless and perpetually plastic expansion of my epistemological and ontological self. Perhaps most excitedly for me then is the new found realization that the metastatic, contextual and infinite nature of this experiential soul searching process ensures that multiple and unforeseen corridors of inquiry will forever remain open and available to me, and my desires - thus allowing my mind and my self to cross over multiple, untold static thresholds towards an unknown and perpetual intellectual transformation that evades sovereign truth and essential constructions. In effect then, "I will never again know what I am, where I am, from where I'm from, where I'm going, through where to pass" (Serres, 1997, 8), because I now know that "nothing gives greater direction than to change direction" (4). I am not yet satiated...my hunger and my thirst persist...I want to be exposed to others and to foreign things...I want to run through the holes. Again, Serres poetically elaborates upon contextual and virtual growth and learning of the self (1997).

> Now nothing can make an exception of this experience. Doubtless, everyone, one day at least, experiences this formidable dilation of his being—in explosive volume, strength, and potential—this free break, this unemployed

greatness, that remains virginal no matter what one does, the infinite regret
of remaining to one side: the infinite possibility of learning. (1997, 34)

Subsequently, one recurring and perhaps rhetorical question began to dominate my consciousness as I continued to garner experience and insight as a university educator, a parent, and as an infantile
scholar of curriculum theory—"Shouldn't *all education* be equally
transformative, emancipatory, and eventually self-generating in some
similar manner for all of its subjects?"

A Personal Crossroads

Although in retrospect, I am not exactly sure what I was thinking
when I decided to reinvent my professional self as a university educator, I can now safely say that I certainly wasn't thinking realistically,
but rather more ideologically. True, I had been far removed from the
university for over ten years and deeply enmeshed in a world of corporate culture and anti-intellectualism for a long time by the moment
I entered the academic ranks, but I suppose I also maintained a quixotic sense that the academy remained the "last" bastion of higher
thought, exploration and transformation for all those contained
therein. My quasi-midlife crisis had met its elixir. Much to my naivety, I thought that the university was immune, or at least too far
removed from the capital culture that had by then, infested much of
our society and ways of being in our hyper-capitalistic culture. Although ignorant at that time as to what had *really* happened to the
university culture in the last several decades, most of my excitement
in taking my initial academic position was based upon a desire to
dive into learning and teaching with students as equally malnourished as I had been. I couldn't wait to engage in real learning and
meaningful dialogue with my students by applying the "real world"
knowledge that I had acquired...to watch them get knocked down
and stand back up, only to be "enlightened" further...to be challenged by students interested in technical knowledge *and* other
worldly pursuits of truth, knowledge and experience.

It wasn't long, less than three months in fact before I became radically aware that higher education had "changed," that it was "different" from what my perception of what it "should" be, or at least,
radically different than what mine had been. Not only were most of
my students not interested in deep and complex insights, knowledge
and inquiry into areas of thought "not related" to their chosen major,
but most were also pathetically disinterested in genuinely learning
major, disciplinary domains of knowledge, its intricacies, its complexities, and its applications beyond rudimentary, cookbook levels.
Rather, far too many of my students were (are) more interested in
"what they need to know" to move on...to pass this class, or that

one…to graduate…to pass the national exam…to gain admission to graduate or professional schools…to get a job. In effect, they were after the "codified data" or knowledge necessary to "perform," and subsequently secure gainful employment in the field. They had already been sufficiently "disciplined" to study "a discipline," to see learning strictly from within a behaviorist's perspective, and to excessively value and compete for grades and outcomes. They were/are for the most part subversively enrolled in what amounts to the "UPD," or what can metaphorically be considered as the *University of Professional Development*. Viewed in this vein, it made me wonder just what my "role" actually was as a professor and educator, why I was working as hard as I was to learn the art and science of teaching, and why I was so concerned with being "scholarly" beyond my specific discipline. Where were all those dynamic, interesting and challenging students? Just what does it mean to be an "effective teacher"? Where were those interdisciplinary dialogues and spontaneous moments of intellectual debate that I envisioned occurring on most, if not all campuses of higher education? What kind of "product" was I helping to manufacture? What impact would my students have upon society once they "finished" their higher education? How many of them would realize one day that they were shortchanged, as I had been?

In my early semesters prior to my personal intellectual catharsis, I suppose that I could somewhat tolerate, almost expect even a certain level of student apathy towards non-major courses and the inherent and critical connections to democracy, sociology, and ontology that other modes of thought possess. After all, I have always prided myself on being more of a pragmatist than an idealist. But what I was not prepared for was for the majority of my students to be so fundamentally disinterested in meaningful and challenging learning experiences respective to their chosen major…to be so disinterested in learning just for learning's sake…to dismiss my energy and passion for learning and engagement as just another eccentric teacher. I couldn't help repeatedly and exasperatingly wonder just what had happened to college students today…to high schools…to education in general, as I worked my way through my initial semesters as a university teacher, program director, and non-doctored member of the academy. Now I know…they had become disciplined at a young age before they even got to the university, and the process was now continuing unabated for a bulk of their university experience.

Over the course of time, the deconstruction of my lived curriculum that I have put forth here has profoundly impacted both my theory and praxis as a university educator, program director, mentor, advisor and role model for the undergraduates under my guidance each academic year. Perhaps most evident, and thus of most significance and relevance to the larger analysis that I am undertaking, is the passionate impact these still evolving changes have had on my pedagogical world view regarding curriculum as *lived and embodied text*. Thus expressed, the lived/unlived curriculum that I am now experiencing as someone on the other side of the podium, as a member of the professorate provides the central precept for my structural analysis and discourse surrounding our contemporary institutions of postsecondary education, its affective powers on the self, desire, and the educated soul.

In noticing that very few of my students possess much of the more historical and quixotic notions of what higher education can do for the intellect, the spirit, and the individual ontological development (subjectivity), I have come to believe that far too many students, parents and educators are content with being cogs in the central mechanistic devices that drive "human capital theory," and its production of capable but docile consumer objects of production (Apple, 1995, 39). Lyotard went so far as to apply his notion of "performativity" to education, whereby the "other" facet of knowledge (that being its transmission) is now just a "subset of the social system," whereby higher education can be perceived as based on the best possible input/output equation (1984, 46). Lyotard believes that with regards to education, the "desired goal becomes the optimal contribution of higher education to the best performativity of the social system," with two kinds of indispensable skills created in the process. First, students acquire the specialized skills necessary to "tackle world competition" as it is locally relevant to the global market, and secondly, higher learning will have to supply the social system with the skills needed to maintain its own internal cohesion.

Michael Peters extends Lyotard's critique further by arguing that any analysis of the commodification of education is not completely clear unless an analysis of what the "student is buying" is conducted (1995, xxii). Specifically, Peters wonders aloud just "what the student is buying?" Do students and their families think they are purchasing "the skills of the teacher," "the program or course," or the "certificate or qualification" awarded upon graduation? Pointing out that education might be the only market endeavor in which the student-consumer actually gets to participate in the production of the service they are buying, Peters charges that active participation is an essential and inherent part of the "product" that is being purchased, and without it (active participation), there actually is no "product" produced, or delivered to the consumer (xxii). Theoretically, Peters is more correct than not, the student "does" get to participate in the production of the product they are consuming, but realistically, how many actually do just this?

It is my contention that the compounding effects of our currently fragmented, disciplinary-control based, and neoliberal influenced agendas are the primary prophylactic forces working to prevent and deny students from engaging in the production and construction of their personal, democratic and subjective educations. Instead, most students enter the academy with specific goals of gaining an education in order to improve or maintain their social, cultural and class positions, and to ensure life long rewards as members of the cultural elite. In referring back to Lyotard's "Spaceship" metaphor for a contrasting approach to learning and education, those subjects who allow themselves to become objects deeply embedded in our market based society without investigating their true inner desires, may instead find themselves occupying what Lyotard refers to as a "rusting spaceship."

> If adults are often tough and sad, it is because they are disappointed. They do not listen well enough to the invitation to grace which is in them. They let the spaceship rust. (1995, xx)

With such economical motivation and technical foci towards learning as a consumerist based activity, it has also became apparent to me that these same students are largely incapable of then producing their own epistemological creations, of meaningful knowledge synthesis, or of de- and re-constructing complex phenomena, or critical issues pertaining to our ecological and social sustainability. And in all honesty, I saw in them what I was now able to see in myself following my undergraduate and master's experiences 10 years earlier— highly and technically trained, but certainly not what one might call critically educated. Stanley Aronowitz comments further on this observation in *The Knowledge Factory*, by acutely distinguishing between true "higher education," whereby students are enlightened, transformed, and critically educated, and "postsecondary education," whereby technocratic and industrial modes of production predominate the pedagogy and the curricula (2000). As it regards the other primary factor of higher education equation, John Michael's coining of the "technocratic intellectual" is an apropos descriptor that effectively identifies the professorate as a fait accompli in this mess I am calling Dysacademia (2000, 2). Obviously, this implies that higher educators must embrace Michael's and Giroux's similar call for teachers to be critical intellectuals capable of resisting the corporate university and maintaining the academic values linked to culture, ethics, open thought, and transformation of the self; reminiscent of pre-modern universities.

Thus, here I now sit at a crossroads of sorts, at a place and time wherein I find myself reconceptualizing both my lived curriculum, *and* the current curriculum in which I am wholeheartedly engaged in as a college educator empowered to teach in, and direct an accredited allied health education program. Firmly affixed in the vortex of these crossroads sit the various challenges, issues, and discourses surrounding my personal, educational and institutional responsibilities and ideals. Am I here to help produce students according to a fixed recipe that guarantees economic and professional success? Do I just take the easy road, and *discipline* my students with my *disciplinary* knowledge, thinking and being, while ignoring the existence of other modes of thought and ways to see and be in the world? Have the internal and external administrators that control and discipline me figured out all that I need to know, and how to transmit authoritative knowledge in order to ensure academic excellence and produce exemplary disciplinary professionals? If so, what kind of research and teaching initiatives should I undertake, and, what will I be missing if I ignore "other" issues that pertain to higher education and the higher educated? Or, does my academic utility call for something much deeper and more critical than merely contributing to the technocratization of our society? If that's the case, how should my various service, scholarship and teaching expectations be shaped so as to constructively address this fundamentally paradoxical set of academic challenges? William Reynolds reflects on this sort of "tugging of the professional heartstrings" in his essay entitled "Curriculum Theory in the Age of Dole & Clinton" by pondering the effective utility and value of his own academic work and how it subsequently contributes (or doesn't) to the much needed social criticism of our national educational condition.

> I begin to think that maybe I should be more concerned about what type of articles and books I am writing than how many I write. Whose interest do those articles and books serve? Who, besides other curriculum scholars is reading what I am writing. (2003, 64)

For Reynolds, as for other members of the academic professorate dedicated to an impassioned critique of our social and cultural milieu, the modern university can readily be seen to exert pronounced and multiple effects on "how" professors think, work, and teach. In a nutshell, there now exists a very profound and dubious affective disorder wallowing in higher education that challenges our historical and practical notions of academic productivity, utility and responsibility. Today's critical educator in the academy is now, perhaps more than ever, confronted with an array of disconcerting and complex questions pertaining to the validity and value of their scholarly work, what "counts" as effective teaching and learning, and in the end, what is expected of them in order to fulfill their role as public intellectuals, and to receive promotion and tenure. In accordance with the various critical analyses of postsecondary education already put forth (Readings, 1996; Aronowitz, 2000; Katz, 2002; Giroux, 2003; Reynolds, 2003), I am contesting that this "affective disorder of the academic self" can be justly coupled to the increasingly corporate and performative identity and utility of many, if not most of our colleges and universities today. Simply said, the corporate university has power, shapes power and exerts power in a subversive fashion over all of its constituencies, right down to each and every last teacher and student. Stanley Aronowitz elaborates on the far-reaching impact this new world university directly has upon its professorate, and thus indirectly too upon the production and transmission of knowledge for, and to the student body.

> Symptomatically, we now speak of a corporate "culture," which in the academy signifies a displacement of the old intellectual culture of the sciences, humanities, and the arts. Research and writing goes on, but it becomes increasingly instrumental to the overarching goal of individual survival, let alone advancement, in the academic hierarchy. But in their official roles, faculty are more than ever urged, cajoled, and even threatened to direct their scholarship and research to the ever-decreasing pots of grant gold on penalty of losing resources such as computer time, assistants, equipment, promotions, and tenure. (2000, 67)

Perhaps this testament is just an overt and tedious example of "preaching to the choir," but what may not be so obvious is the insight that the corporate university doesn't "give power" to its subjects, it doesn't empower the self; but rather that its subjects are the direct and unequivocal *objects* of its power. That is, today's university doesn't empower the self as it once did when the pedagogy of *Bildung* emphasized the development of character and culture by teaching "the rules of thought" (Readings, 1996, 67), but rather it controls and normalizes individual subjects within the confines of disciplinary knowledge and specialization, a priori established standards and guidelines, and sovereign yet opaque notions of academic excellence and quality. Giroux's definition of corporate culture and its particular relevance to the pedagogy of higher education are reflective of my innermost concern for the contemporary university, and for my professional future within.

> Corporate culture is an ensemble of ideological and institutional forces that functions politically and pedagogically to both govern organizational life through senior managerial control and to produce compliant workers, spectorial consumers, and passive citizens. (1999, 9)

Dysacademia Contaminates the Ivy Towers

Framing the fundamental structure of my argument is a critical analysis of today's higher educational machine, or what Bill Readings communally calls "the University" to represent the status quo institutions, and not the exceptional (1996). For Michel Foucault, this means that I will attempt to elucidate a "discourse" that outlines and shapes current University's operative dynamics, particularly as it pertains to larger, more research focused institutions of higher learning. Discourse then, as defined by Foucault, is a discursive practice that becomes part of itself by framing and giving meaning to the objects and phenomena it describes without reference or insinuation to essential forms, objective realities or sovereign truths (1980, 122). Discourses are found everywhere one looks, schools, religion, disciplines, social clubs, professional practices, each replete with its own language, codes, norms, and boundaries of thought. Discourses, and the discursive practices they live off of and promote, produce and work on the assumption of normativity, of ideals, and absolutes; and they all contain subversive and usually unseen connections between power and knowledge that must be exposed and brought to light.

> It is in discourse that power and knowledge are joined together...Discourse can be both an instrument and an effect of power, but also a hindrance, a stumbling block, a point of resistance and a starting point for opposing strategies. (1980, 100)

Implicit in this particular situatedness is an understanding that the arguments contained in forthcoming sections are not meant to essentialize or generalize all institutions of higher education in the United States into one myopic characterization. In this particular and local instance, I will be articulating the discourse of the University as I have come to see, feel and experience it, not as it "really," essentially, and globally exists. My analysis and subsequent argumentation is intended to present a particular discourse that represents a unique structural analysis of present-day higher education and its "hidden curriculum"; how it manages to constrain and limit subjective and epistemological freedom, how it effectively ignores its larger roles that society requires of it, how it has operatively "flip-flopped" to mirror and submissively respond to culture, rather than to produce, acquire and resist culture (Readings, 1996, 119), how power functions and reproduces itself through the formation of passive subjectivities, and the inherent connections it has to neoliberal and corporate values promoting excellence and cost-efficient quality. Likewise, I also intend to take full advantage of Foucault's study of a discourse's recursive power by utilizing my analysis of the discourse surrounding today's university as a "starting point for opposing strategies" that may one day prove capable of generating new, socially conscious, and ontologically open discourses.

As noted in my introduction, and in following the lead of both Derrida (2004) and Readings, I will use "University" with a capital "U" to represent the collective institution of higher education as it pertains to my analysis and commentary of the corporate university. Most notably, it is my contention that far too many factions of today's University can be characterized as highly "dysfunctional," in that it (the University) now operates largely in a "state of being" far removed from its original social mission, liberal roots, and democratic utility. In short, the University writ large can now be seen to "only serve itself" (Readings, 1996, 40). In coining what he calls "The University of Excellence" because of the inextricably neoliberal and professional agendas that influence most, if not all initiatives, policies, and allocations, Readings goes so far as to state that the University has no referent, but instead, that it's merely a "simulacrum of the idea of a University" (54). Indeed, to those not ordained to engage in serious and meaningful social criticism, the image and conception of the University as an archetype of higher intellectual thought, debate, and self-transcendence is unknowingly just that—a simulacrum.

In complementing the grave and serious concerns put forth by Readings, Stanley Aronowitz's thematic declaration that there now exists a specific and tangible difference between true "higher education" and vocationally oriented "postsecondary training" has strong and credible merit, as well (2000). Specifically, because of myriad reasons and factors separate unto themselves, yet somehow all genealogically and archaeologically connected to economics, power or science (or a combination thereof), higher education institutions in the Western world today can be seen as highly fragmented, corporatized, and ontologically disoriented with regards to their "other" social, humanistic, and ethical responsibilities. Building upon Kant's analysis of the role and purpose of the European University in "The Conflict of the Faculties," Derrida takes great pains to similarly address the state of the University in more recent times by categorizing the University as "being –ill" (mal-etre), and in so doing, iterating a "discourse of responsibility" intended to place true philosophy at the center of university education once more (2004, 87). As such, the inherent connections that readily exist today in Academia pertaining to impressions of excellence, corporatization, specialization, technocratization, performativity, and control requires a perfunctory structural analysis that is capable of revealing the affective and effective nature of the contemporary university. A deconstruction of the discourse which is the Ivy Towers is indeed warranted .

CHAPTER TWO

(De)Constructing Dysacademia

No learning can avoid the voyage. Under the supervision of a guide, education pushes one to the outside. Depart: go forth. Leave the womb of your mother, the crib, the shadow cast by your father's house and the landscapes of your childhood. In the wind, in the rain: the outside has no shelters. Your initial ideas only repeat old phrases. Young: old parrot. The voyage of children, that is the naked meaning of the Greek word pedagogy. Learning launches wandering.

—Michel Serres (1997, 8)

In previously presenting the autobiographical exposition of my lived curriculum as the operative foundation for this text, I would like to expand upon Readings' critique of the University and Aronowitz's eloquent and well-articulated analysis of postsecondary education, put forth in *The Knowledge Factory* (2000), in order to articulate a (decon) structural analysis of higher education which reveals and postulates an institution in Byzantine disarray. And, in keeping with the various elements of my autobiographical position that can be directly attributed to my formal training and background in the allied health sciences, I aim to color my discourse surrounding the contemporary university by borrowing select terms and conditions from the medical sciences in order to pontificate various metaphors that represent the current physical and mental wellness of the Ivy Towers. I would like to introduce and assert *Dysacademia* as an umbrella term to describe the discourse of the contemporary university, its operations, its identity, and its effective (dys) servitude, as I see and experience it. "Dys," in Greek means "bad; difficult; disordered" (Miller & Keane, 1983, 346), and thus I chose the prefix "Dys" because of its medical inferences, as well as because of its association to various and multiple pathological and disconcerting conditions of the living self; to life in general. Thus situated, I wish to take advantage of the metaphorical power and discursive relevance of this particular prefix by juxtaposing various medical states and conditions of the body associated with "dys" into my structural analysis of the University. It is my specific argument that Dysacademia, and the many affiliated dysconditions I will subsequently employ to help shape and articulate the analysis of the discourse, have profound and subsequent effects and affects on both the University's inorganic (the University as institution) and organic sub constituencies (the living elements, namely the educators and students).

Dysacademia & the Inorganic

Inorganically, the discourse of Dysacademia can be conceptually embodied on three separate, yet deeply interconnected and interdependent levels that operationally and qualitatively influence the contemporary University's effective identity. First and foremost is the reiteration of Lyotard's "performative university" (1984), or as Readings calls it, "the University of Excellence" (1996, 32) in an attempt to show how corporate America and contemporary politicians have transformed the educational landscape in our society. More specifically, the "new world" corporate University described by Bok (2003), Giroux (2003; 1999), Aronowitz (2000), and others has worked "hand in hand" with our increasingly consumerist and materialistic society to drastically alter the ideological mission, educational landscape, and effective utility of higher education in the West today. Perhaps Giroux states it most succinctly and effectively in his brief but theoretically dense critique of the contemporary university, *Corporate Culture & The Attack on Higher Education and Public Schooling*.

> The cost-accounting principles of efficiency, calculability, predictability, and control of the corporate order have restructured the meaning and purpose of education. (2003, 23)

In short, it is my central concern that far too many students enter, exist and depart college and university today specifically and resolutely to a) increase their lifetime earning potential, b) improve their respective families' class and social position, c) to get specific job training that promises significant material compensation, or d) any logical and interspersed combination thereof. Indeed, it is the third reason (job training = more money) that has had the greatest effect on the modern University and the modern student, as private and public monies are allocated en masse in order to develop and promote academic majors that promise significant and speedy bounties for local, regional and national economies; or as Giroux bluntly puts it, "if it's not profitable, it's not funded" (1999, 20). Because of the far-reaching influence and outcomes associated with corporate culture's role in the University, the discourse pertaining to the neoliberal disposition of today's University, as articulated by Giroux, Readings and Aronowitz will be interwoven into the analyses presented in later chapters, with an attempt to coalesce the argument that "corporate culture" rules.

Neoliberal Influences in Higher Education

Widespread budget shortfalls, the renewed pleas from conservatives to squelch academic freedom and to eliminate tenure, and the increasing neoliberal fragmentation and technocratization of the curriculum; these are just a few of the many current challenges that threaten to destabilize the historical, intellectual, socio-cultural missions of the American university system. In *University in Ruins* (1996), Bill Readings goes so far as to say that because of the decline in our national cultural mission, the wider social role of the University as an institution is "now up for grabs"; and that both the place and nature of the contemporary university are now nebulous and problematic for intellectuals vested in our academic and social futures (2). In short, it is Readings' critical contention that the University has succumbed to the capitalistic demands associated with the Western neocolonial globalization project, and thus, it no longer participates in the historical project for humanity that once served as the original legacy of medieval Enlightenment; that being "the historical project of culture" (5).

Ever the more cynical, Lyotard believes that the "desired goal becomes the optimal contribution of higher education to the best performativity of the social system," with two kinds of indispensable skills created in the process (1984, 48). First, students acquire the specialized skills necessary to "tackle world competition" as it's locally relevant to the global market, and secondly, higher learning will have to supply the social system with the skills needed to maintain its own internal cohesion. It is within Lyotard's contentions that "in the context of delegitimation, universities and the institutions of higher learning are called upon to create skills, and no longer ideals," and "the transmission of knowledge is no longer designed to train an elite capable of guiding the nation towards its emancipation, but to supply the system with players capable of acceptably fulfilling their roles at the pragmatic posts required by its institutions" (48), that I center the current critique of higher education and the production of *performative subjectivity*. Added to this sad and counterproductive industrial based development is Norbert Wiener's observation that the pursuit of higher education is no longer driven by a "deep impulse" to transform and grow intellectually, but rather by the desire to attain a certain "social prestige" (1954, 133).

In his efforts to "map out" the framework of his discourse on education, markets, standards, God and inequality, Michael Apple identifies four different "groups" of players from the political and religious "right" who have/are drastically affecting the educational topography in the United States (2001, 11). Of these four principal groups, only the first one—*neoliberals*—is relevant to the current discourse. Neoliberal activists and ideologists from the right, as Apple terms them, are "deeply committed to markets and to freedom as 'individual choice'"(11). In other words, neoliberal theory is based strictly upon the idea that a "free market economy" is the democratic and just pillar upon which to base educational reform, budgetary decisions, and other curriculum policies upon because it is "available to everyone." As a definition, Apple imports the work of Robert McChesney to better articulate the multifarious aspects of neoliberalism.

> Neoliberal initiatives are characterized as free market policies that encourage private enterprise and consumer choice, reward personal responsibility and entrepreneurial initiative, and undermine the dead hand of the incompetent, bureaucratic and parasitic government, that can never do good even if well intended, which it rarely is. (2001, 17)

As he builds his critique of the "Right" education, Apple goes on to elaborate how neoliberal influences have changed the scenery in education by "aiming to provide the educational conditions believed necessary both for increasing international competitiveness, profit, and discipline" (65), by "setting the market loose on schools so as to ensure that only 'good' ones survive" (68). Central to this corporatized process of schooling is the centralization of practices that promote fiscal and pedagogical accountability and efficiency, and industrial based models of management, with a concurrent marginalization of "other" forms of learning not deemed vital to economic sustainability and vitality (humanities, liberal arts, social sciences), along with the inherent and varied interests of the students. In dire contrast to *classical liberalism*, where state power is disdained and the individual is a free entity with an autonomous human nature, Apple qualifies *neoliberalism* as an ideology that favors the state's "neutral" role in the creation of appropriate markets and individuals as market players which signifies a subtle shift in the school's emphasis, "from student needs to student performance and from what the school does for the student to what the student does for the school" (71). Although much of Apple's criticism focuses on primary and secondary education in the United States, there is no doubt that his points regarding the encroachment of neoliberal policies, and the resultant missionary shifts it induces can aptly and justly be applied to higher education, as well.

In his chapter entitled "Higher Education, Inc.," critical theorist Henry Giroux does just that—he critically illustrates contemporary society's neoliberalist impact on higher education by bringing to light the "hidden curriculum" of higher education, and by drawing numerous uncanny congruencies between Wall Street and the Ivy Towers (2003). Perhaps most indicative of the subtle, but perceptible transformation, that Giroux is attempting to articulate can be found in the changing role of the University president.

> The new breed of university presidents is characterized less by their ability to take risks, think critically, engaging important progressive social issues, and provoke national debates than they are for raising money, producing media-grabbing public relations, and looking good for photo shoots. (2003, 170)

But perhaps the most disturbing and penultimate example of the impending neoliberal conservative threat on academic freedom that both Apple and Giroux highlight can be witnessed in the administrative desires of James Carlin, a multimillionaire ex-business executive, who as chairmen of the Massachusetts State Board of Education in 1998 launched a fourfold attack on the academic professorate (as cited in Giroux, 2003, 175). Specifically, Carlin attempted to convince other policy makers and the public that 1) higher education should model itself after successful corporations, 2) that professorial tenure should be eliminated, 3) that faculty members had too much democratic power to shape university decisions, and 4) that all "non essential research" not central and relevant to the market economy of the state of Massachusetts was to be condemned.

This "university as corporation" discourse operates as a major component of the neoliberal machinery that characterizes our postmodern economic, social, cultural and political conditions. Giroux's comments regarding the neoliberal era and its technocratic effects on higher education, the student-consumers, and thus society at large subsequently, clearly reflect the concerns put forth by Lyotard, Wiener, and others as they pertain to our social coherence, and so are also current with the sub-discourse I am attempting to articulate.

> In the neoliberal era of deregulation and the triumph of the market, many students and their families no longer believe that higher education is about higher learning, but about gaining a better foothold in the job market. Colleges and universities are perceived—and perceive themselves—as training grounds for corporate berths. (2003, 167)

Secondly, the overly performative and neoliberal function of the new world, corporate university can be seen to work in concert with the fragmentation and specialization of the academic disciplines to severely limit the potential levels of subjective, personal and contextual learning and self-transformation that might occur for most students. In essence, the pronounced proliferation of Foucault's disciplinary society discourse has worked in concert with neoliberalism and performativity to have now taken full hold of the academy, and as such has multiple contributing factors, associations, and consequences that require deconstruction. The specific dynamics of our essentially economically driven, and academically supported disciplinary society can be seen then as inextricably operating with various financial, economic and material factors to produce an even more complex system. This neoliberal disciplinary system can be seen then, as both a by-product and as the perpetuator of our overly technocratic and capitalist education system—a system that, sad to say has dominated Western culture since the advent of the industrial revolution, and one that has arguably grown even more pronounced during our current "techno-cybernetic revolution."

Thus stated, the various historical, social and cultural factors that contribute to this (de)evolution necessitate a deconstructive analysis that is capable of rendering the corporate University that Readings (1996), Aronowitz (2000), Giroux (1999; 2003), Gould (2003), and countless others have described. With this task firmly in mind, a genealogical analysis of the development of our disciplinary society will thus be undertaken in an attempt to connect the disciplinary dynamics described by Foucault with the proliferation of economically laden neoliberalist agendas in the modern University. Using Foucault to set the table for their discussion on disciplinarity, Messer-Davidow et al. describe genealogy as a "means of de-essentializing phenomena," and capable of helping us "to understand just how these elements became the disciplines they are, rather than something else" (1993, 4). Further, genealogy "insists that knowledge not only is a product of power but also is itself a nonneutral form of power" (5), and so it is my explicit intent to genealogically analyze the academic learning of disciplines in a critical and problematized manner by further examining the specific socialization of individuals into disciplines, disciplinary professionals, and thus active constituents of our disciplinary society.

Lastly, Deleuze has written that we have gradually re-evolved from Foucault's notion of a disciplinary society to a control society, a contention well supported and expertly connected to pedagogy by William Reynolds (2003), and Rebecca Martusewicz (2001). As Deleuze points out, we have been gradually entering a society of control, one characterized by "new weapons," technology, communication, and varying other forms of social control (1995, 177). Chiefly stated, disciplinary societies are confined by *molds*, while control societies are *modulated* by different ways of doing business, school reform, technological advancements, and other social transmutations that in Deleuze's words, "never allow us to finish anything." Similar to, sometimes difficult to discern the difference between, and all together linked to a point whereby one must be considered whenever the other is discussed, control and disciplinary based societies operate symbiotically and interdependently in the modern University in many complex and discursive manners. And as one may logically surmise, both control and disciplinary societies also work collectively with neoliberal and performative functions to reinforce, reproduce, and perpetuate the existing power structures that exist in Dysacademia today. Deleuze is explicit with his educational critique and the subsequent conversion of our schools to institutions governed and characterized by disciplinary control and surveillance, a.k.a. training.

> One can envisage education becoming less and less a closed site differentiated from the workplace as another closed site, but both disappearing and giving way to frightful continual training, to continual monitoring or worker-school kids or bureaucrat-students. (1995, 175)

Operating as a discursive element of power and authority, and deeply connected to the economic realities of our current social epoch then, the control society that is the modern University can be seen to have weighty effects on the teachers and students filling the classrooms and offices, the production and dissemination of knowledge, and the resultant pedagogy and curricula employed within. In addition to various and more subtle examples of "corporatized" control that now occur on a daily basis in the modern University, the increasing love affair that policy makers, administrators and the general public now have with accreditation arrangements can be seen as outward manifestations of control and power in concerted operation with monolingual disciplinary modes of thought, and neoliberal centered agendas to both stimulate and propagate Dysacademia. Chapter 3 will further analyze the various manners and materializations in which control and surveillance operate in the contemporary University, and how they are inextricably connected to the disciplinary and neoliberal tendencies that now define my articulation of Dysacademia.

Dysacademia & the Organic

Organically, Dysacademia and its offspring, *Dyscurriculum* and *Dyspedagogy*, must be analyzed according to how it effects its living constituencies on at least two separate, yet interconnected levels, 1) the consequences that it has fashioned for the deliverers and providers of higher education, the professorate, and 2) in terms of its subsequent and unquestionable role as an accomplice in the public manufacturing of far too many socially and intellectually apathetic objects molded mostly for economic, technical and professional needs. As it regards the first organic element, the professorate, Dysacademia's organic effects can be conceptualized by making use of Lyotard's "death of the professor" (1984, 50) in relation to the various control and accreditation mandates, and Dysacademia's residing corporate culture. Together, these inorganic attributes can be thought to effectively produce the *dysacademic*. As Giroux would most undoubtedly confer, the *dysacademic* can be seen as a mutation of the professorate that can be directly traced to the "deskilling and anti-intellectualizing" that accompanies the corporate model of teaching (1999, 36). For the Dysacademic working from within *Dysacademia* then, the inevitable condition that results over time as a complication of the constant control, surveillance, and performativity expectations can be seen metaphorically as a form of "*dysbulia*" (weakness or perversion of the will, Miller & Keane, 1983, 348). Dysbulia wears down the professorate, it makes them submit, it makes them play by the rules, and in time, it kills them. Thus, the pivotal and urgent question for critical pedagogues now regards the effective role of the contemporary professor in the postmodern university. Is it to teach the self, or to train the body? Or, as Giroux points out, to "emphasize the translation of educational exchange into financial exchange"? (1999, 35). Is it to resist the corporate culture, or to submit to the standards of excellence and profit? Chapter Three's emphasis on control, standards and excellence, and their operative effects on the University will incorporate an analysis of the current state of the professor as part of a larger discourse concerning our transition to a Deleuzian control society, and its subsequent contributions to Dysacademia.

Dyserethesia ("impairment of sensibility"), *dysgnosia* ("any abnormality of the intellect"), and *dyslogia* ("impairment of the power of reasoning") (Miller & Keane, 1983, 347–348) can be seen to exemplify the constraining and dysfunctional effects that Dysacademia has upon its organic constituencies; especially the student body. The development and shaping of individual consciousnesses, epistemologies, ontologies and subjectivities in the spirit typical of the University ideals of Kant or Humboldt, seem to sadly be a thing of the past (Readings, 1996). In simple terms, the state of dyscrasia that now exists in the University as a result of the disciplinary influences and fragmentation, control based policies, and neoliberal dynamics have had a profound and complicating affect upon both the professorate and student body in terms of knowledge production and construction, ontological freedom, and the subsequent creation of critical subjectivities (or lack thereof). Specifically, the inherent connections between power, authority, and knowledge and their subsequent predication upon disciplinary knowledge and meta narratives leads to the formation of largely monolingual and fixed subjectivities in the modern University; a university without Reason (Kant), or Culture

(Humboldt), or moral development (Readings, 55). Because multiple and open modes of thought, freely disassociated from economic and authoritative motives and/or habits, are not regularly promoted or pursued in the modern University, students can successfully pass through the various technocratic and specialized curricula without ever embracing a more postmodern sensibility of heterogeneity and multilingualism; without ever developing their own culture, without ever constructing their own knowledge, and without ever learning the power of thinking, of speculative utterances. Furthermore, the pronounced neoliberal and corporate influences that now dominate most public universities, as well as our general societal mindset, can be seen as accomplices in the development and promotion of impaired sensibilities, reasoning and intellect as materialism, consumerism and egocentrism become the dominant modes of consciousness in our younger generations. Stated as such, this sentiment has led Readings to require that "we accept that the modern University is a ruined institution" (129). As a ruined institution then, David Kirp poses the "ultimate question" for all publicly supported institutions of higher learning, and for those empowered to make policy and fiscal decisions that impact the Academy.

> The ultimate question is this: Can the public be persuaded that universities represent something as ineffable as the common good—more specifically, that higher education contributes to the development of knowledgeable and responsible citizens, encourages social cohesion, promotes and spreads knowledge, increases social mobility, and stimulates the economy? Can the argument convincingly be made that the university offers something of such great value that it is worth subsidizing despite bottom-line pressures? (2003, 2)

From the student perspective, the role of the University and its affective disciplinary powers over its legions of subscribers must be analyzed from an epistemological, ontological and even axiological perspective. In short, a Dysacademic in charge of carrying out and implementing a Dyscurriculum more than likely contributes to the production of multiple states of *dysgnosia* (any abnormality of the intellect) and *dysbulia* (the will) either willingly or not. In this pathological state of "dys," the intellect is sadly characterized by homogeneity, linearity, myopia, and homonormativity; all sublimely laced with neoliberal ideals and initiatives tied to the various markets that now control most, if not all of our social policies and values. To be blunt, the modern University works from within, and towards a paradigm largely defined by narrow-mindedness and vocational specialization. To be more clear, the central purpose and long-term action potentials that higher education promises and provides (used to?, supposed to?) for the nation's students must be critically assessed and weighed against the social and cultural costs of doing business in its current manifestation. Again, Kirp's insight here is valuable as it pertains to the "purpose" of the University.

> Embedded in the idea of the university—not the romanticized idea, but the university as its truest and best—are values that the market does not honor: a community of scholars and not a confederacy of self-seekers; an openness and not ownership of ideas; the professor as a pursuer of truth, not simply an entrepreneur; and the student as an acolyte whose preferences are to be formed, not a consumer whose preferences are to be satisfied. (3)

In the end, *Dyskinesia* ("impairment of the power of voluntary movement"), and *dysbulia* (weakness or perversion of the will) (Miller & Keane, 1983, 347) may prove to be the most powerful and apropos metaphors to embody the hyperfragmentation of knowledge and its contributions to Dysacademia, and its resultant power to (de) limit and control subjective movement, evolution and transformation of the individual self to spaces and times beyond those embodied by professional and neoliberal initiatives. By going to college in order to study for a job, rather than to study for learning as learning, for self-transcendence and transformation, or for the open and chaotic formation of subjective ontologies and epistemologies, young students unknowingly, yet actively contribute to their own dyskinesia and dysbulia. Students enrolling in institutions of higher education in order to attain postsecondary training effectively limit their own ability to move beyond, amongst and between the various spaces of knowledge and being that exist for anyone interested in such voluntary movement. In time, this perversion of freedom and movement can be seen to work on the will, as dyskinetic individuals become comfortable and learn to avoid the exhilarating and empowering turbulences associated with active movement and perpetual, untold change. And, because colleges and universities are all too happy to "offer what the customer wants" and what the economy needs, the process becomes deeply and problematically symbiotic for all parties involved. David Kirp, author of the recent critique on the marketing of higher education entitled *Shakespeare, Einstein, and the Bottom Line* (2003), reflects upon this tendency in an excerpted article criticizing Governor Mitt Romney's explicit business plans for corporatizing the entire Massachusetts university system in a current *Boston Globe* commentary.

> Such ideas exemplify an age when priorities in higher education are determined less by academic values than by the interests of multiple constituencies—students, donors, corporations, politicians. In today's university, the student is a "customer" and the professor is an "entrepreneur." Each campus unit is a "profit (or loss) center," and each institution is busily promoting its "brand" and looking for its "niche market," whether in money capital or intellectual capital. (2003, 1)

Young doctoral students and newly minted assistant professors fall into and become part of this same trap, as doctoral degree programs have also become highly specialized and market driven, producing highly competent, yet myopically educated researchers and scholars for multiple specialties and subspecialties (Abbott, 2001). Although the humanities and some of the social sciences seem more immune to this socially induced transformation, it is probably not incidental that the natural, technological, and military science related fields (those deemed more economically viable and useful) are not as lucky. Again, Kirp's analysis is on the mark.

> What's troubling today, however, is the single-minded fixation on marketplace and managerial values. The winners are those with the skills valued by the market. The losers are advocates of the liberal arts, who can't prove their bottom-line value, and students from poor households, who are increasingly priced out of higher education. (1)

This "downsizing of the disciplines" according to their perceived market value can be seen then, as just another example of the profit standard mantra that the corporate University utilizes to calibrate their operations according to standard supply and demand operating procedures (Giroux, 1999, 25).

Specifically it is within the critical contentions put forth by Lyotard, and mirrored in the scholarship of Aronowitz (2000), Giroux (2003), Readings (1996), and others that "in the context of delegitimation, universities and the institutions of higher learning are called upon to create skills, and no longer ideals," and "the transmission of knowledge is no longer designed to train an elite capable of guiding the nation towards its emancipation, but to supply the system with players capable of acceptably fulfilling their roles at the pragmatic posts required by its institutions" (Lyotard, 1984, 48), that I am centering my critique of higher education and the production of performative subjectivities within. Inherent in these (de) transformative processes are myriad factors that have contributed to the educational and social demise of many of today's institutions of higher learning, especially mid- to large-size public institutions. Complex in nature and scope, today's commercialized academia stems from myriad sources, such as rapidly rising university costs since the 1970s (largely due to the tremendous costs associated with biotech and high-tech research projects), and shrinking federal and local funding sources (Kirp, 2003, 1). As such, these developments have forced universities into a survival mode as they have all scrambled to look for viable and sustainable funding sources, and creative ways to boost enrollment and decrease attrition. In other words, higher education today may now be more readily described as one of the central metabolic forces that nourish and sustain the human capital theory of economic reproduction. In *The Knowledge Factory*, Stanley Aronowitz elaborates more fully on the changing nature and function of postsecondary education in our culture.

> Most colleges and universities are part of an academic system in American society whose success is measured by, among other criteria, how much it contributes to the economy. (2000, 11)

The gradual institutional transformation that occurred largely in the 20th century and described as the "university-corporate complex" by Aronowitz (16), is not a "new thing," however. In fact, this complex and progressive transformation actually began as early as 1900, and subsequently evolved as a consequence of myriad social, political, industrial, economic and scientific factors that occurred throughout World Wars, the Cold War, and our current postmodern epoch. In the end, the result is that most, if not many of our current public universities now resemble mid- to large-size corporations more than they do centers of higher thought, or institutions of cultural production and dissemination.

> A new generation of administrators, schooled in business practice, has acquired ever-greater power in the retooled universities. Those officials, veterans of government streamlining and corporate downsizing, have brought all the fashionable management and budgeting nostrums—ideas like TQM (total quality management), revenue-center management, and emphasis on "core competencies"—to higher education. The intention is to make universities run more like businesses…Those borrowed innovations have been problematic because universities aren't like widget-making firms or the post office and organizational strategies can't be created by the logic used to assemble cars. (Kirp, 2003, 1)

Seen then as a bothersome *sequalae* ("a morbid condition following or occurring as a consequence of another condition or event," Miller & Keane, 1983, 1015) to the inorganic operations of the University, the role that Dysacademia plays (whether implicitly, or explicitly) in preventing the free and open development of critical and individual subjectivities, in denying the necessary space(s) needed for the development of social and cultural agency, and in drastically altering the history, identity, and undertakings of the intellectual professorate requires an inclusive and interconnected analysis.

The Academic Paradox:
Postmodern Knowledge & Modern Students

If, as noted and self-professed *amodern* philosopher Michel Serres says, "the goal of instruction is invention" (Serres & Latour, 1995,

133), and the "goal of teaching is to have teaching to cease" (22) is accepted as a feasible premise, then pedagogy today may be exposed as being more "necrotic" (dead, as in lacking nutrition and energy) than alive; or at least because of its relatively closed and static nature, "quasi-necrotic." Simply put, in these current times of classroom discipline, rabid standardization, measurable outcomes, surveillance and teacher accountability that so typify our 21st-century educational paradigm, the typical American student has very little opportunity or initiative to invent his/her own knowledge, and thus, very little ability to teach the self. As the "founder" of cybernetics Norbert Wiener expressed nearly 50 years ago, this is not a novel argument.

> Our elementary and secondary schools are more interested in formal classroom discipline than in the intellectual discipline of learning something thoroughly, and a great deal of the serious preparation for a scientific or a literary course is relegated to some sort of graduate school or other. (1954, 132)

For Wiener, education in the 1950s was already being viewed as a closed and myopic system, one wherein young minds were no longer implored to think, to invent, or to experience knowledge for themselves; young actors were "taught" how to act rather than being allowed to express their art forms from within, and young writers were schooled in "how" to write from expert sources, rather than being allowed to invent their own form of communicative art. In short time, highly specialized and advanced degrees, especially the PhD, were the standard bearers of knowledge and communication needed to impart learning and skill onto the masses, leading inevitably to the multiple meta narratives of authority and truth that now define academia (Abbott, 2001). To Wiener, "forms" of knowledge and occupational skill now superseded critical and intellectual mass as part of a fast moving trend towards an "ever-increasing thinness of educational content"; while the artistic desire to invent was rapidly being structured around particular methods and forms, and thus, subsequently extinguished in all but the most extraordinary of students (1954, 133). In harmony with Serres' and Wiener's critical calls for invention to serve as the primary focus of education, Katherine Hayles suggests that the creative writer is perhaps the best example of a free-floating and chaotic inventor, capable of connecting various epistemic cultures. Working from the "third territory" then, somewhere between order and disorder, is what allows the creative writer to communicate beyond one particular field of study, and thus better capture and articulate the "aura of cultural meanings that surround chaos" (1990, 19).

In noticing that very few of my students possess much of the more historical and romantic notions of what higher education can do for the intellect, the spirit, and the individual ontological development (subjectivity), I have come to believe that far too many students, parents and educators are content with being cogs in the central mechanistic devices that drive "human capital theory," and its production of capable but docile consumer objects of production (Apple, 1995, 39). Lyotard went so far as to apply his notion of "performativity" to education, whereby the "other" facet of knowledge (that being its transmission) is now just a "subset of the social system," whereby higher education can be perceived as based on the best possible input/output equation (1984, 46). Lyotard believes that with regards to education, the "desired goal becomes the optimal contribution of higher education to the best performativity of the social system," with two kinds of indispensable skills created in the process. First, students acquire the specialized skills necessary to "tackle world competition" as it is locally relevant to the global market, and secondly, higher learning will have to supply the social system with the skills needed to maintain its own internal cohesion.

Michael Peters extends Lyotard's critique further by arguing that any analysis of the commodification of education is not completely clear unless an analysis of what the "student is buying" is conducted (1997, xxii). Specifically, Peters wonders aloud just "what the student is buying?" Do students and their families think they are purchasing "the skills of the teacher," "the program or course," or the "certificate or qualification" awarded upon graduation? Pointing out that education might be the only market endeavor in which the student-consumer actually gets to participate in the production of the service they are buying, Peters charges that active participation is an essential and inherent part of the "product" that is being purchased, and without it (active participation), there actually is no "product" produced, or delivered to the consumer (xxii). Theoretically, Peters is more correct than not, the student "does" get to participate in the production of the product they are consuming, but realistically, how many actually do just this?

It is my contention that the compounding effects of our currently fragmented, disciplinary-control based, and neoliberal influenced agendas are the primary prophylactic forces working to prevent and deny students from engaging in the production and construction of their personal, democratic and subjective educations. Instead, most students enter the academy with specific goals of gaining an education in order to improve their social, cultural and class positions, and to ensure lifelong rewards as members of the cultural elite. In referring back to Lyotard's "Spaceship" metaphor for a contrasting approach to learning and education, those subjects who allow themselves to become objects deeply embedded in our market based society without investigating their true inner desires, may instead find themselves occupying what Lyotard refers to as a "rusting space-ship."

> If adults are often tough and sad, it is because they are disappointed. They do not listen well enough to the invitation to grace which is in them. They let the spaceship rust. (in Peters, 1997, xx)

With such economical motivation and technical foci towards learning as a consumerist based activity, it has also become apparent to me that these same students are largely incapable of then producing their own epistemological creations, of meaningful knowledge synthesis, or of de- and re-constructing complex phenomena, or critical issues pertaining to our ecological and social sustainability. And in all honesty, I saw in them what I was now able to see in myself following my undergraduate and master's experiences 10 years earlier—highly and technically trained, but certainly not what one might call critically educated. Stanley Aronowitz comments further on this observation in *The Knowledge Factory*, by acutely distinguishing between true "higher education," whereby students are enlightened, transformed, and critically educated, and "postsecondary education," whereby technocratic and industrial modes of production predominate the pedagogy and the curricula (2000). As it regards the other primary factor of higher education equation, John Michael's coining of the "technocratic intellectual" is an apropos descriptor that effectively identifies the professorate as a fait accompli in this mess I am calling Dysacademia (2000, 2). Obviously, this implies that higher educators must embrace Michael's and Giroux's similar call for teachers to be critical intellectuals capable of resisting the corporate university and maintaining the academic values linked to culture, ethics, open thought, and transformation of the self; values and principles reminiscent of premodern universities where philosophy (the love of knowledge) and reason were the *raison d'etre*.

CHAPTER THREE

Disciplinary Practices
& Neoliberalism Mesh

1discipline n 1: PUNISHMENT 2: a field of study: SUBJECT 3: training that corrects, molds, or perfects 4: control gained by obedience or training: orderly conduct 5: a system of rules governing conduct

2discipline vb 1: PUNISH 2: to train or develop by instruction and exercise ex In self-control 3: to bring under control (~troops); also: to impose order upon

— The Merriam-Webster's Collegiate Dictionary (1997, 221)

Disciplines provide the rationale for the departmental structure of U. S. colleges and universities and strongly influence faculty appointments; hiring, promotion, and tenure practices; teaching assignments; student recruitment and enrollment; and even accounting practices, and moreover, disciplinary frameworks still organize most faculty members' understandings and interpretations of information and experience.

— Lattuca (2001, 1)

An Imbalance of Component Elements

Recently, a colleague of mine and I were chatting about education, students, scholarship and a myriad other connected topics of critical significance for members of the professorate. This particular colleague was a young, newly indoctrinated assistant professor with an impressive track record and affinity for high-level scientific scholarship. Nonetheless, he also expressed a genuine interest in other, more holistic pursuits of knowledge and intellectual engagement. As time passed, we gradually became more acquainted courtesy of our informal, but frequent exchanges regarding academic and philosophical discourses pertaining to what we perceived as social and academic maladies. A few days prior to the aforementioned engagement, I had lent him a newly published compilation of Albert Einstein's various speeches, papers and positions on education, science, philosophy, economics, war, and myriad other topics of interest to him. Although at the time I took it to be a fairly innocuous interchange between colleagues and office mates, he expressed to me that he "didn't know Einstein was such a philosopher!" to which I rather sarcastically replied, "What did you think the 'Ph' stood for in 'PhD'?" After reflecting upon this short interchange for a day or so, I later asked him, if during his doctoral program he had "any philosophy or history of science courses"; to which he honestly and rather sheepishly answered, "no." As it turned out, this casual and brief interchange of ideas bestowed additional insight for me regarding the nature of "terminal" education, scholarship and the academic pursuit of knowledge; insight that coalesced with my previously articulated autobiographical experiences in education to formulate much of the impetus for the current discourse. Essentially, and on a more general level, I began to become more interested in how it came to be that someone with the highest academic degree achievable had no formal class work in either the history or philosophy of his parent field(s).

In order to explicate one of the major etiological factors that contributes to my central metaphor Dysacademia, discipline, there exists an additional "dys"-condition that begs introduction to the discourse surrounding the University curriculum, and its subsequent state of effective utility. *Dyscrasia* (a morbid condition usually referring to an imbalance of component elements, Miller & Keane, 1983, 347) is a medical term usually reserved to describe circulatory irregularities in the human patient, but in its current usage can be seen to embody the pathologically fragmented and disciplined condition of a different sort of patient—higher education. Stated as such, dyscrasia is being used currently to describe the typical 21st-century college educational experience that is, for myriad historical, cultural, social and political reasons, fragmented, imbalanced, and disciplined by the disciplines and the surreal borders they construct and perpetuate. As Lisa Lattuca explains in the introductory sections of her text on interdisciplinary, the exponential growth of knowledge in the 20th-century, particularly in the sciences, reveals how disciplinary cultures and perspectives could discourage and prevent inquiries and explanations that crossed the socially constructed disciplinary boundaries.

> Disciplines, it now seems clear, are powerful but constraining ways of knowing. As conceptual frames, they delimit the range of research questions that are asked, the kinds of methods that are used to investigate phenomena, and the types of answers that are considered legitimate. (2001, 2)

And, as disciplines and the knowledge they produce grow, they also become more complex and eventually splinter into multiple and disparate subspecialties that complicate and disunite things even further. In some cases, the sub-specializations resemble, respect and connect to their parent fields, and even sometimes cross borders with other disciplines and sub-disciplines; but as time progresses the larger, more realistic practice that takes place more resembles a comminution of knowledges, languages, and views with strong ancestral loyalties and genealogical ties that ironically, work to restrain the subsequent development of non-disciplinary knowledge. Logically then, disciplined and fragmented education leads to disciplined and *a priori delimited* ways of seeing and being in the world, a sentiment best captured by Lattuca's notion that "the more schooling we have, the more entrenched our sense of disciplinarity can become" (1). Viewed metaphorically on multiple levels then, our modern postsecondary curricula can be characterized as being dyscratic because of its fundamentally and epistemologically *comminuted* disposition (the act of breaking, or condition of being broken, into small fragments, Miller & Keane, 1983, 255), a recognition that's analogous with the central premise put forth by E. O. Wilson in *Consilience* (1998). Because education and the intellectual pursuits of knowledge and self-transcendence have in effect, been broken into multiple sub-disciplines and technical specializations for myriad reasons then, the overall (dys)effect can be seen as "an imbalance of the component elements"—dyscrasia.

Academic Dyscrasia: Utterance & Discipline

Historically, genealogically, and archaeologically, academic dyscrasia has many interrelated factors that require further inquiry and analysis, the most notable of which being 1) the inherent connections that exist between knowledge and power, and their subsequent connection to the evolution of disciplinary societies, as brought to our attention by Michel Foucault (1977), and 2) the strong neoliberal underpinnings that oblige much of our educational missions today as alluded to in the previous chapter, and elaborated upon more fully by Aronowitz (2000), Giroux (1999; 2003), and Readings (1996). Epistemologically speaking, the comminuted and dyscratic dyscurriculum being articulated here can be considered as an inorganic structural phenomenon that actively and perfunctorily contributes to a fundamental change in how knowledge is produced, invented, shared, and dialectically challenged (or not). In using a neighborhood community as a metaphor in which all the neighborhood parents work together to "keep the neighborhood kids in line," Lattuca laments the evolution of our disciplined and specialized society.

> The growth of specializations parallels the decline of the front porch from
> which everyone could survey their territory. Now the more private world of
> the backyard deck excludes all but a select few. (2001, 3)

Exposed as such, the dyscratic state of higher education can thus
be seen as an institutional accomplice in the perpetuation of various
meta narratives of authority, discourses of power, and neoliberal incentives that exist between and amongst the academic disciplines that
constitute higher education. Obviously, the inorganic existence of
dyscratic curricula in the University has the potential for profound
and disturbing affects for its organic constituencies, most notably the
myriad restrictions and constrictions that Dysacademia has had upon
the developing ontologies and epistemologies of both the student
body, and the professorate.

In addressing both the genealogical and archaeological factors
that have contributed to the evolutionary development of disciplinary
societies, one can't help but also consider the rather Derridean
"tinted," and *different* definitions that Webster's dictionary provides
for the word, concept, or phenomenon known as "discipline." Essentially, the "sign" discipline must be signified, conceptualized and understood as having multiple, and very different meanings that *effect*
and *depend upon* the other, relative to the particular time and space in
which the word is used/viewed/understood. In other words, "discipline," like "communication," is a "performative act" in that it is not
exclusively a semantic or conceptual act, nor a semiotic operation, nor
a linguistic exchange, and defining it doesn't involve a phenomenon
of authentic meaning or signification (Derrida, 2000, 87). Simply put,
the use and thus the meaning, of *discipline* is contextually relevant, but
not predetermined...it is a "performative utterance" that is different
every time it is spoken, written, and analyzed (2002, 13). Interestingly,
it is this performative difference between discipline as a specific "field
of study," discipline as "training that corrects, molds, or perfects",
and discipline as "punishment" that begs for a discursive analysis
relative to the conception of Dysacademia being presented.

Centering & Decentering Disciplined Knowledge

In *Consilience: The Unity of Knowledge,* Edward O. Wilson (1998)
claims that the extreme proliferation of overzealous and narrow-
minded inquiry, characteristic of the evolution of the different
branches of learning in modern times, has caused the various disciplines to become far too fragmented and specialized for our social
well-being. In particular, Wilson points out that the production of
knowledge within the arts, humanities, social and natural sciences has
become so divergent and monofocal that experts firmly and myopically entrenched in their fields are not only largely incapable of fully
understanding the complexity and comprehensiveness of their own

discipline specific knowledge, but also the inherent connections and practical relevancies of each discipline to others, as well. In effect, Wilson renews the position put forth by C. Snow in *The Two Cultures* (1964), by contending that the major branches of knowledge (science and the humanities) have become so divergent that they cannot fully understand or appreciate the historical foundations, breadth, depth, or complexity of their own discipline specific knowledge.

In medical parlance, one might say that learning and the construction of knowledge have thus become comminuted, or from a physical science perspective that knowledge has become "atomized." In short, the average college student now goes to college or university, not to "become educated" in a manner that reflects intellectual transcendence and breadth of consciousness, but rather to attain a specialized, technocratic, and highly disciplined degree. With the modern University all too happy to oblige aspiring neophytes, the eventual outcome of this process takes the shape of a disciplined citizenry with a limited cognitive flexibility, and one largely void of the critical mass historically associated with higher education, with the higher educated. And as is the case between the professionals and academics within the various disciplines and pedagogues, the *everyday* educated person is thus likely denied a more meaningful knowledge and understanding of the world, its many complexities, and its many interconnected nodes of significance and interpretation (Wilson).

> With rare exceptions American universities, and colleges have dissolved their curriculum into a slurry of minor disciplines and specialized courses. While the average number of undergraduate courses per institution doubled, the percentage of mandatory courses in general education dropped by more than half… Win or lose, true reform will aim at the Consilience of science with the social sciences and humanities in scholarship and teaching. Every college student should be able to answer the following question: What is the relation between science and the humanities, and how is it important for human welfare? (1998, 13)

As such, techno-fragmented and *non-consilient* intellectuals are also seen to be largely incapable of translating and understanding knowledge from outside their fields, or the various interconnections and transmutations that inherently and chaotically exist within the margins of all fields (Wilson, 1998). For Peter Galison, this means that actual and accessible "trading zones" that may prove capable of highlighting those areas of knowledge that are connected and interdependent can't be realized (1997, 803); an epistemological shortcoming that inevitably, and exasperatingly contributes to a limited scope and depth of knowledge concerning the object under inquiry. To Galison, trading zones focus on "finite traditions with their own dynamics that are linked not by homogenization, but by local coordination," and represent a localized, "social, material, and intellectual mortar bind-

ing together [of] the disunified traditions of experimenting, theorizing, and instrument building" (803). In a dialogical attempt to demonstrate what he sees as an utter and profound lack of appreciation for
the true existence of epistemological boundary crossing, trading
zones, Wilson provides various examples of social, cultural and scientific issues (the human mind, religion, the environment) that he sees
requiring explicit knowledge of the innate and dynamic interconnectedness of the humanities and the arts with the different branches of
science. In considering such vexing human problems, Wilson charges
that the epistemological and ontological states of many of our current
administrative professionals, policy leaders and politicians not only
mirrors the condition of the different branches of learning within the
academy, but that this recognition should also prove difficult for all
those concerned with our social and ecological well-beings.

> Every public intellectual and political leader should be able to answer that
> question as well. Already half the legislation coming before the United States
> Congress contains important scientific and technological components. Most
> of the issues that vex humanity daily—ethnic conflict, arms escalation, over-
> population, abortion, environment, endemic poverty—cannot be solved
> without integrating knowledge from the natural sciences with that of the so-
> cial sciences and humanities. Only fluency across the boundaries will pro-
> vide a clear view of the world as it really is, not as seen through the lens of
> ideologies and religious dogmas or commanded by myopic response to im-
> mediate need. Yet the vast majority of our political leaders are trained exclu-
> sively in the social sciences and humanities, and have little or no knowledge
> of the natural sciences. (1998, 13)

Obviously, one can see Wilson's academic and professional biases
in play here, his ideological proclivity for the natural sciences, and his
relative lack of a postmodern sensibility for seeing "the world as it
really is." Nonetheless, Wilson's motivation for crafting a consilient
worldview is certainly founded upon the apprehension of a pronounced (dys)academic narrow-mindedness in many of our elected,
public and corporate leaders. Admitted as such, this consciousness of
nonConsilience that Wilson laments is pregnant with potential illness
and eventually disaster, if it is not adequately addressed through profound and much need educational, social and cultural changes. Because of the inherent relevance to Dysacademia and our subsequent
dyscratic curricula, Wilson's central concern that our academic disciplines have become "islands unto themselves" calls for an extended
deconstructive analysis that may hold promise for revealing some of
the genealogical and archeological factors that have contributed to the
current (dys)state.

Unfortunately though, all is not well in Wilson's theoretical arguments for a consilient way to see and understand the world by connecting the various ways of knowing. As Wilson makes his arguments

for a more heterogeneous and open discourse of knowledge, which ironically would imply a more postmodern, non-centered and perhaps chaotic approach to knowledge free from a central and domineering hegemonic authority, he makes (at least) two fundamental and deeply disturbing missteps that reveal his affinity for reductionist thinking and modern meta narratives of power. In the final analysis, these two failings dilute both the strength and potential application of his arguments, especially for postmodern thinkers and practitioners. As previously stated, Wilson goes to great depths to provide specific examples of the inherent and "natural" interplay and unity of disciplinary knowledge between various historical, social and human phenomena in an attempt to demonstrate and justify his desire for Consilience. Herein lies Wilson's first and perhaps most worrisome ideological blunder. More specifically, it is not the examples that Wilson uses to make his point that have received sharp criticism, but rather, his subsequent theoretical and structural (or sufficient lack thereof) analysis. Steve Rosenthal's "Marxist Critique" of *Consilience* is quick to point out that Wilson's mistakes actually start with his decision to center human nature as "the unifying concept of Consilience" (1988, 1). Additionally, Wilson's arguments can be seen to fall short of his intended goals because he fails to address the many historical, social, and cultural factors involved in the construction of knowledge, the inherent connection existing between power and authority, and the postmodern skepticism associated with univocal perspectives that portray authenticity, objectivity, and realism. A double derivative of his sociobiological and reductionist heritage, Wilson's analysis of human nature as a strictly hereditary and biological phenomena responsible for driving and determining our behavior, culture and social practices effectively ignores and dismisses the capitalistic and disciplinary aspects of human nature that have shaped, among other things, racism, religious hatred, sexism and war (Rosenthal, 1998, 1). Thus recognized, Wilson's reductionist and materialistic approach to human nature, and thus to the subsequent construction of knowledge, reveals a strategy deeply laced with imperialistic and fascist motivations that weaken and diminish the potential impact of his overarching arguments.

While mistake number one proves to be extremely troublesome for poststructural and postcolonial theorists because of its essentialist claims to human nature and identity, mistake number two further draws the ire of postmodern thinkers because of the foundationalist character of the meta narrative structure he proposes. In drawing up his blueprint for a consilient approach to knowledge, Wilson directly locates the discipline of biology ("the science of life") as *the just* and deserving center of his consilient methodology.

I say the master problem, because the most complex systems known to exist in the universe are biological, and by far the most complex of all biological phenomena is the human mind. If brain and mind are at base biological phenomena, it follows that the biological sciences are essential to achieving coherence among all the branches of learning, from the humanities on down to the physical sciences. (1998, 81)

By centering biology as the focal axis of knowledge, the more heterogeneous and interconnected counter-discourse that Wilson intends to propose is paradoxically transformed into just another modern, hegemonic discourse defined by one "true center." It makes Galison's "trading zones" operate in and out of, and go through one central port in order to trade. For Michel Serres, Wilson's inclination to center the discourse, to take space, and thus to dictate the language and character of that space, represents a type of violence; or a metaphysical death in that any type of *inclusion* automatically produces an ancillary and reactive *exclusion*. Or to put it more straightforwardly, Serres believes that any attempt to permanently occupy space, especially the center space, on the supposition of authoritative knowing represents a parasitic act of violence; for Serres, "to know is to kill" (1995, 20). Considered in this light then, the operative definition put forth by Amariglio, Resnick and Wolf may be helpful for understanding the complexity, nature and power of "a discipline."

A discipline arises in the course of struggles to limit discourses involved in the production of formal knowledge to a determinate set of objects of analysis, questions about that object, methods of investigation, and modes of demonstration of the nature and determinations of (presumably) these same objects. (1993, 151)

In reference to the current critique then, the more homogenous and interconnected counter-discourse that Wilson intends to propose is fundamentally transformed into just another modern, hegemonic discourse defined by a true center that effectively denies the potential energy and voice of other discourses, languages, and spaces. In the end, Wilson's blind faith in the biological center of a consilient discourse effectively supplants one meta narrative in lieu of another— the one he is purportedly attempting to deconstruct ironically. From a postmodern perspective then, Wilson's variety of Consilience can actually be seen as structured by disciplinary barriers that can/will/do prevent true osmotic exchanges of knowledge and ideas across, amongst, and between the various disciplines. Thus revealed, his theoretical proposition for a more heterogeneous and open discourse to connect all branches of knowledge can be seen then as contradictory and antithetical to the postmodern, de-centered and perhaps chaotic approach to knowledge that he tantalizes the reader with in the early passages of *Consilience*. Thus viewed, the postmodern potential of Wilson's ambitious efforts can be critically exposed for what it really represents, a modernistic essentialism merely and sadly dressed in *postmodern drag*.

Saul Cohen's analysis of our disciplinary culture illustrates the inherent contradictions in Wilson's desires for a "center" of knowledge, while simultaneously extending Serres' concern for epistemological death by acknowledging the difficulties inherent in striving for a balance "between those energies that contribute to the healthy, integration evolution of a discipline, and those that lead to its fragmentation" (1988, 1). In addressing this problem Cohen says, the learned society that is the disciplinary body must "guard against becoming so protective of its organizational territory as to become an *end unto itself*, thus abandoning its proper role as the means for achieving the expressed needs and desires of its disciplinary practitioners" (1). What Cohen seems to be saying here is that practitioners who are sensitive and open to a more postmodern, or postdisciplinary approach to knowledge and inquiry are paradoxically faced with a very complex and challenging tendency to "slip back into" modernist ways of thought by drawing boundaries, and protecting their turf. An additional and paradoxical challenge to working outside and in between the disciplines is brought to light by Lattuca, that being the notion that interdisciplinary work is not credible enough because it is "not disciplined enough" (2001, 3). But as Cohen, Abbott (2001), and Messer-Davidow, Shumway, & Sylvan (1993) effectively point out, this territorial and predatory tendency is a learned thing that comes with learning the boundaries and spatial configurations of one's disciplinary territory, not a natural or congenital trait as Wilson might contest (Messer-Davidow et al.).

> To focus on the learning of disciplines is to problematize disciplinarity in an obvious way; the socialization of individuals into disciplines produces them as group experts, thereby supporting the authority of disciplinary knowledges and the correspondingly lower status of nongroup members as disciplinary knowers. If we think of disciplines as (in part) groups with members, it is much harder to regard them as neutral enterprises wherein minds discover pure truths about various phenomena. (1993, 5)

As a result of these two major ideological weaknesses and misappropriations found in Wilson's thesis, numerous scholars have largely dismissed Wilson's end product citing its overly fascist, modern, and sociobiological underpinnings; and its subliminal attempt to replace one authoritative meta narrative with another (Gould, 2003; Rosenthal, 1998). But, if one temporarily displaces Wilson's sociobiological tendencies for an "essential scientific order" and also his modern biocentric meta narrative, perhaps all is not lost from the actual issue under consideration—that being the disciplinary fragmentation of knowledge and inquiry, and its resultant impedimentary effect on the acquisition of critical knowledge. If the various disciplines of knowledge are indeed shattered into a multiple and contingent archipelago of epistemic cultures, each abounding with their own languages, modes of inquiry and areas of interest, as Wilson, Lattuca, Cohen, Ford, and Messer-Davidow, et al. all summarily contest, then it can likely be appreciated that many academics, educated elite, public intellectuals and service professionals are both working from within, and trapped inside of distinct and remote disciplinary worlds. Wilson is on the mark with his critique of the limitations of such disciplinary fragmentation and specialization, "the best of their analyses are careful and responsible, and sometimes correct, but the substantive base of their wisdom is fragmented and lopsided" (1998, 13).

I for one, concede the criticisms levied against Wilson, and in a manner that reflects the *reconstructive* potential of postmodern analysis can displace his ideological and theoretical shortcomings in hopes of developing a different "line of flight "for my subsequent analysis of our disciplined Dysacademia. With this concession firmly in hand, I concur with the observations of William Doll (1993), Stephen Jay Gould (2003), Andrew Abbott (2001), C. Snow (1964), Marcus Peter Ford (2002), and most notably those of Michel Serres (1982, 1995a, 1995b, 1997) in noting that the academic disciplines have indeed disfavorably *hyperfragmented* into multiple modernistic homogenous narratives, all competing for the same space, time and exposure, and eventually authority and disciplinary power over other forms of knowing. And in a performative sense, this hyperfragmented disciplinarity also has profound effects on the *disciplining* of the various selves that constitute the Academy, the professorate and the student body, collectively. Thinking in Derridean terms of performativity then, the discipline that it takes to expertly learn one's chosen discipline works to produce an intensely specialized and proficient disciple of a disciplinary practice that, because of the discipline required to excel in that discipline, largely precludes one from becoming disciplined in other disciplines, and in the meantime also inhibits the undisciplined extrusion into interdisciplinary and nondisciplinary modes of thinking, seeing, and knowing that may prove capable of deconstructing the original disciplinary knowledge, and thus loosening the constraints and effects that disciplinarity has upon the disciple. For Serres, compartmentalizing knowledge in the modern disciplinary way induces a like disciplining of the academic pursuit of knowledge, a practice that is stagnating, (de) inventive, parasitic, and highly suggestive of power and control at work.

> The more classification there is, the less evolution there is, the more classes there are, the less history there is, the more coded sciences there are, the less invention and knowledge there are, the more administrating there is, the less

movement there is…Parasitic growth has brought everything to a standstill. (1995a, 94)

In Carl Boggs' analysis, the elite specialists and bureaucrats that have been spawned from the fragmented education that Wilson and others have described since the 1800s, "comes with advanced levels of industrial development and the rationalization of social life that accompanies it," can be represented collectively as "technocratic intellectuals" (1993, 3). Technological intellectuals are a "new class" of specialized and economically driven experts serving to "legitimate" their disciplines, professions, associations, and ultimately the smooth functioning of bureaucratic state capitalism and other forms of our neoliberalist society through the perpetuation of specialized languages, forms of thought and disciplinary behaviors. Not surprisingly then, techno-intellectuals can primarily be found thriving in state governments, universities, corporations, the military, the media, and even the culture industry itself; incidentally, all institutions of power and legitimacy in the socio-cultural and political arenas. Again, the technical words and subsequent identities that give shape and meaning to technical intellectuals are problematical for Serres, due primarily to their exclusionary power.

Nearly all technical words are harmful in science and philosophy; they serve only to separate the sectarians of the parish from those who are excluded from the conversation so that the masters can hold on to some form of power. (1995b, 7)

In contrast to Boggs' elaboration of the techno-intellectual, Michael Peters has worked to articulate an analysis of what he sees as the antithesis of the technocratic intellectual, the "critical intellectual" (2000, 2). Admittedly difficult to describe, critical intellectuals can be viewed as having lost much of their authority and influence over what Peters calls "popular politics." Quite simply stated, "a critical orientation toward a more general audience on more general topics" represents the popular politics that Michaels feels is missing from the "politics intellectuals as technicians practice." Sympathetically, Wilson argues that scholars and political leaders alike need to embrace more of a "consilient" approach to knowledge, understanding, discourse and inquiry in order to address and manage the many complex problems of our contemporary cultural epoch. For Wilson, "a balanced perspective cannot be acquired by studying disciplines in pieces but through pursuit of the Consilience among them" (1998, 13). This apparent and discursive lack of "critical intelligentsia" in the public spheres that Wilson, Boggs and Michaels all lament can in my view, be genealogically linked to Wilson's central arguments regarding the fragmentation of our academic disciplines; and as such, provide much of the initiative for undertaking the current critical inquiry surrounding the Academy today. Thus, the question now becomes "how did our disciplines come to be so fragmented and specialized?"

Disciplines & Disciplinarity: Our Academic Crutch

> Socially and conceptually, we are disciplined by our disciplines. (Messer-Davidow, Shumway & Sylvan, 1993, vii)

Systems scientist Ervin Laszlo has commented on the awkward social and professional quandaries that can arise as a direct result of this modernistic development of disciplinary specialization, in simple terms that most professionals and academicians might appreciate with candid reflection upon the specific and atomistic epistemic culture that defines and shapes their "chosen discipline."

> The literary historian specializing in early Elizabethan theater may not have much in common with a colleague specializing in Restoration drama, and will find himself reduced to conversation about the weather when encountering an expert on contemporary theater. (1996, 2)

And as Laszlo points out, modern educational paradigms that are built upon and shaped by a fragmented episteme results in a construction of knowledge that has been largely pursued in isolation; a process that effectively presents fragmentary and authoritative pictures of "reality" to the disciplined pursuer of knowledge. Observably, this development hampers the ability of the learned subject to openly pursue and construct knowledge with depth and integrated breadth; a restriction, that inevitably circumvents the subjective formation of a coherent picture of the various contextual and local networks, and organizational hierarchies of knowledge represent a more holistic appreciation for the complexity and interrelatedness of knowledge (1996, 2). In reflecting upon the dire condition of our now, unnatural world and the subsequent and urgent eco-challenges that face our cultural epoch, Serres connects Mother Nature's illness, and our relative inability to treat them, with our technical specialization culture.

> It is we who still have a say: administrators, journalists, and scientists, all men of the short term and of highly focused specialization...we're inept at finding reasonable solutions because we're immersed in the brief time of our powers and imprisoned in our narrow domains (1995b, 30).

But if education is/was designed to liberate and transform the self, and to spawn creative and critical thought for the betterment of society, just how did we become so inhibited and static? How did we become so disciplined, or as Serres more aptly utters, "inept"?

In *Knowledges: Historical and Critical Studies in Disciplinarity,* Ellen Messer-Davidow, David Shumway and David Sylvan have collected a series of essays centered on a critical and multidimensional analysis of "disciplinarity." For the editors, "disciplinarity" is not merely the study of what knowledge is produced, nor of specific disciplines themselves, but rather "what makes for disciplinary knowledge as such," or the concern of "the possibility conditions of a discipline" (1993, 1). In short, the various scholars addressing the study of knowledge and disciplinarity in *Knowledges* are centrally concerned with the discourse that *is* disciplinarity, and as such, are interested in "a radically heterogeneous inquiry" that investigates and ponders "a diverse set of terms and a large methodological repertoire" from various disciplines. As it attempts to critically deconstruct the discourse that is/are the disciplines, to "defamiliarize the disciplines," to de-essentialize the disciplines, and to deprivilege traditional notions about knowledge, disciplinarity can thus be seen to have a profoundly dispersed and Foucaultian nature (Messer-Davidow et al.).

> It is neither a field in itself nor a metafield in which one can study disciplines. It is neither the essence of disciplines nor their foundation. Rather, disciplinarity is about the coherence of a set of otherwise disparate elements: objects of study, methods of analysis, scholars, students, journals, and grants, to name a few. To borrow from Foucault, we could say that disciplinarity is the means by which ensembles of diverse parts are brought into particular types of knowledge relations with each other. (1993, 3)

Disciplinarity viewed through a postmodern lens critically attacks the "socializing practices" that the various disciplines have had upon the construction of the self, and the various knowledges that define our cultural and historical epoch. In describing socializing practices as the discursive utility of disciplinarity that has discursive effects not only on institutions and professions, but also on human bodies, Messer-Davidow et al. suggest that students, scholars, and scientists alike are all trained in the work of their disciplines, right down to the style and form of reading, writing, and thinking. As a form of bio-power then, disciplines must be seen as "institutionalized formations for organizing schemes of perception, appreciation, and action, and for inculcating them as tools of cognition and communication" (7). In a passage that explicitly represents the academic manifestation of Foucault's disciplinary societies, while also supporting Andrew Abbott's accounts of disciplinary structure (2001), the editors of *Knowledges* effectively arrive at the deconstructive heart of their text.

> To focus on the learning of disciplines is to problematize disciplinarity in an obvious way: the socialization of individuals into disciplines produces them as group experts, thereby supporting the authority of disciplinary knowledges and the correspondingly lower status of nongroup member as disci-

plinary knowers. If we think of disciplines as (in part) groups with members, it is much harder to regard them as neutral enterprises wherein minds discover pure truths about various phenomena. (1993, 5)

The Social History of the Modern University

This notion of disciplinarity, the discursive centerpiece of the edited collection by Messer-Davidow and colleagues on knowledge, is obviously a Foucaultian tethered discourse that effectively embodies the performative powers of its root word, "discipline" in myriad ways and forms that impact, and relate to the current analysis of Dysacademia. Thus recognized, a discursive analysis of disciplinarity and its performative connections to Foucault's analysis of discipline and disciplinary societies must be undertaken by those intellectuals and academics interested in the deconstruction of the virtual boundaries that effectively encumber true interdisciplinary thought, and epistemological invention. In order to do this, to look at how our academic disciplines have become immobilized and disciplined, requires us then to perform an historical analysis capable of uncovering and demystifying the archaeological and genealogical factors that have contributed to the condition that I am calling Dysacademia.

In *Beyond the Modern University*, Marcus Peter Ford (2002, 1) laments the future of our societies and the role that modern universities will/will not have in improving the outlook of life in the year 2050. In setting the primary concern for his critique of the modern university that sadly defines our postmodern times, Ford straightforwardly points a finger at American higher education and accuses the modern university culture of doing very little to prevent, circumvent, or correct the environmental devastation that is now seen to be happening before our very eyes. In charging that the modern university is far too involved in economic initiatives and modes of capitalistic reproduction built upon a consumerist ideology, Ford wonders aloud what role higher education in the West should play as we confront an expanding human population, estimated to reach 10 billion by 2050.

> ...what should be the primary objective of higher education?...higher education should help make the world a better place by enabling human beings to live more meaningful and satisfying lives and by helping to promote social justice and environmental sustainability. It begins with the critical assessment that the university is currently failing in this role, having in some ways lost its moral commitments, in other ways having committed itself to false and destructive modes of thought, and yet in other ways having made it difficult to know what to think or do. (2002, 2)

Ford's concerns over our ecological and human futures is incorporated here not to divert the focus towards ecocentric initiatives, ecoliteracy, or any related environmental sub-discourse, although they are important for all of us, but rather to help illuminate the far-reaching impact that disciplinary modes of thinking can have upon our global condition and future. This passage regarding the modern university's "postmodern failings" is also central for better understanding the subsequent historical analysis of the modern university that Ford expertly provides in order to set up the counter-narrative that makes up his book's subtitle, *Towards a Constructive Postmodern University.*

In mirroring my theoretical intentions, Ford first deconstructs the social histories of the "modern university" that now "actively participates in the breakdown of human communities and the destruction of the natural world," and then to avoid being stuck with the postmodern, relativist, nihilist tag, works to reconstruct an image of a more postmodern university that "is devoted to strengthening human communities and mending the natural world, a university that will be a force for good" (2002, 4). Ford is also clear to critique those closest to the university, those that work within it, for failing to recognize higher education's shortcomings. In fact, this observation proves to be extremely ironic, hypocritical even, in that the esteemed and honored "institution of critical reflection and thought" fails to look at itself in the mirror.

> The task of criticizing higher education has been left to those outside the university — to journalists, pundits, politicians, and others. (2002, 3)

Furthermore, Ford's work is extremely relevant to the current exposition because he too places a great deal of conviction in the academic disciplines' culpability regarding the current plight of higher education, and thus too, for our environmental and social futures.

> Academic disciplines are a particular way of structuring thinking that has proved to be very powerful and yet undermines the very possibility of a coherent worldview. As long as the university is committed to the disciplinary form of thinking, the university cannot make sense of the world. Seen through the lens of academic disciplines, the world lacks coherence and meaning. The various assumptions and findings of one discipline are unaffected and unchecked by those of another. (2002, 7)

Because of the synoptic value and relevance of Ford's historical analysis, I will provide a brief but germane summary of his account of the modern university's disciplinary evolution in order to better develop the framework for my analysis of disciplinarity and its contributions to Dysacademia, and to interrelate this historical account to the subsequent and coupled conversations regarding the evolution of our disciplinary societies.

In the interest of pithiness, Ford divides the historical evolution of the Western university in the last 1,000 years into three fundamental categories, 1) the cathedral schools of medieval Europe, that were essentially extensions of the Catholic Church in the years 1150—1648, and best embodied by the University of Paris, 2) the nationalistic universities that saw the initiation of church and state, and thus secular institutions of higher learning like Germany's University of Halle in 1694, and finally, 3) the more modern universities founded upon an economic route to peace and prosperity, such as America's University of Phoenix (2002, 22). At the University of Paris, the seven liberal arts (grammar, logic, rhetoric, geometry, arithmetic, music and astronomy) were recast within the context, and under the ideological umbrella of Christian theology, and most of the curriculum focused upon the learning of Latin (the language of the Church) and logic ("highest truths"). So powerful and dominating was the emphasis on theology at that time, it took longer to become a doctor of theology (16 years) than it did to become a medical doctor (8), or a lawyer (7) (24).

In 1648, the "Treaty of Westphalia" ended "The 30 Years' War," marking a noteworthy cultural shift from Christianism to nationalism, in which religious orthodoxy was renounced in favor of objectivity and rationalism, science, and free investigation. As such, German took the place of Latin, lectures replaced the canonical texts, and elective courses were offered that prompted a certain degree of professional freedom for students to pursue knowledge in personally reflective manners (Ford, 2002, 27). Essentially, the curriculum at the University of Halle, and others soon following, was designed to train German officials and bureaucrats to lead and train others for secular improvements, and the people of Prussia. Interestingly, the University of Halle is infamous for also granting the first professional PhD (medicine) to a woman in 1754. Largely under the influence of the powers of Kantian reasoning, and other modern thinkers of the times, the nationalistic universities of the 17th and 18th centuries marked the beginning of the practical and scientific purposes of university education for all of Europe, and the cessation of theology as *the* center of the institutional mission.

Prior to the 1800s, knowledge was largely categorized and filtered across the seven liberal arts domains (arithmetic, geometry, astronomy, music, logic, grammar, and rhetoric), and changes in the "English College" replicated curriculum were slow to materialize (Lattuca, 2001, 5). In the 1820s, the University of Virginia and Harvard University were the first American institutions to develop academic departments, a sign of things to come for higher education in an intellectually young nation. Meanwhile, Benjamin Rush and Noah Webster have been identified as being instrumental in pushing this more objective and practical notion of the modern university in the United States by gradually diversifying the curriculum at schools like Harvard, but it wasn't until a certain revolution took place that their visions of a nationalistic university would firmly take hold. The dawn of manufacturing, commerce and engineering that arrived with the industrialization age in the United States, and the passage of the Morrill Land Grant Act in 1862 led to the opening of the Rensselaer Polytechnic Institute, the first college for science and engineering in Troy, NY, in 1824 (29). The Morrill Land Grant Act promoted the utilitarian mission that changed secondary education by making way for the many land grant institutions that now dot our country's landscape, which primarily focused on agriculture and the "mechanic arts."

In the decades between the Civil War and World War I, the newly instituted "elective system" of the American universities allowed higher education institutions to better respond to the advanced in occupational training and technology; or in short, to transition from "general universities to "research" universities (Lattuca, 2001, 7). From this point forward, higher education in the United States became more economic, personal and commercial as disciplinary specialization and organization gradually became the desired operational mantra for the University. But it wasn't until the middle of the 20th century that secular, state supported schools focusing on practical education became the *dominant* form of higher education in the new west. Eventually, World War II, and the subsequent passage of the American GI bill led to major curricular transformations, as our country's leaders worked to address the military, scientific, and economic shortcomings of post-World War II America by "scientizing" and economizing our various educational models (Ford, 2002, 36).

Today, the modern university (Ford's 3rd stage) is best represented by the penultimate example of a neoliberalist-based institution at work, the for-profit University of Phoenix (Ford, 2002, 32). Representing the primary organizing principle of contemporary society, the University of Phoenix was founded in 1976 as a for-profit institution, obligated by law to maximize their profits for its investors. Thus defined, the curriculum of the economy-based institution is predominately developed by faculty and industry together for "industrial usefulness." In this day and age, practical education now means learning that can be "reinforced the next day on the job" and the emphasis of most if not all curricula has now been shifted towards the production of human capital to meet the needs of local, regional, national and now, global economies. Although the University of Phoenix, and other for profit institutions like it, certainly represent what may be argued as the extreme example of the economization of the university, many other secular universities in the United States have incorporated the University of Phoenix capitalistic mantra into their operations; an observation also articulated in the various works of Stanley Aronowitz, Henry Giroux, and Bill Readings, most notably.

Disciplinarity Becomes Formalized

In returning to the conversation regarding the evolution of the disciplines, Ford's inquiry also identifies one additional historical occurrence that, in his view has had a major impact on modern, career-oriented universities and their hyper-reliance on specific disciplines for their economic identity and sustainability. According to Ford, in 1910 the University of Berlin began the tradition of organizing knowledge in terms of academic disciplines in an attempt to improve "conceptual clarity" of the various knowledge domains and intellectual pursuits.

> Because academic disciplines function as independent units, free from the findings and operative assumptions of other disciplines and free from the facts of the real world, their "truths" cannot be contradicted or modified by the truths uncovered by other academic disciplines or by the events of the world itself. (2002, 40)

In other words, it might well be argued that the exponential development of specific disciplines of study so that "a few intellectually talented individuals could pursue knowledge as a means of spiritual realization" at the University of Berlin has led to the subsequent proliferation of myriad schools of specialized and technical thought and professions. Although this may be viewed as a "pro-postmodern" development because it appears to avoid/prevent the formation of one central and authoritative meta narrative, this perception is actually an opaque one that holds credence only if subversive elements of power, legitimation, capitalistic economics and authority can be effectively removed from their particular discourses, and subsequent modes of inquiry. In the modern University, save for the few remaining critical and inventive interdisciplinary and postdisciplinary programs of study that are shaped by permeable boundaries, the highly comminuted and disciplined disciplines are not readily utilized or visualized as being equally valuable or revealing "pieces of the puzzle" for the developing of subjective ontologies and epistemologies. In Julie Klein's assessment, the University of Berlin's innovative efforts bequeathed us disciplines shaped and constrained by "impermeable boundaries," that are "generally associated with tightly knit, convergent communities, indicating both stability and coherence of intellectual fields" (1993, 188). Each modern discipline has thus been formally and historically disciplined to compete for authority, power, legitimation, public admiration and resources (both material and financial) in vain attempts to exert multiple and competing modern meta narratives of "truth"; each expressing valid and often scientific claims to metaphysical reality and practical utility. Again, Ford's account proves effective at describing the double-edged (performative) sword that haunts the various specialized disciplines.

Academic disciplines, although not without their virtues, function today in ways that are harmful to the earth and to human communities. The university of the future will have to organize scholarship and teaching in some other manner. (2002, 40)

In the modern Dysacademic university, each discipline strives and exists for the right and the opportunity to discipline its disciples in its ways of thinking, seeing, and of being; all at the expense of other, different ways of knowing that might allow for a free and open transcendence of being and thinking. Almost every academic major on campus today has a highly structured, closed, and predetermined curriculum that students must follow on their path to "intellectual enlightenment." The classes that comprise these highly specialized and ordered curricula (often designed for economic purposes) are taught by myriad specialized professors in a fragmented and partitioned manner, with little attention paid to vertical and horizontal coherence, critical analysis, and cross comparison of the various elements, knowledges, and theories contained within the curricula. Pedagogies are even altered to "match the course," and infrequently have the opportunity to see, think and discuss how the various knowledge fields connect, disconnect, and challenge each other.

To Steven Fuller, "disciplines mark the point at which methods are institutionalized," and the accompanying disciplinary boundaries that mark off territory and inhibit traveling amongst the various spaces, "provide the structure needed for a variety of functions ranging from the allocation of cognitive authority and material resources to the establishment of reliable access to some extra social reality (1993, 126). In a nutshell, this sentiment embodies Serres' passionate concern for our natural world and underlies his call for a "new contract" capable of resituating ourselves in Earth's grand scheme of things (1995b, 35). I for one, do not see the University's comminuted identity as an example of a critical and transformative postmodern fragmentation of disciplinary thought and episteme that can challenge established hierarchies of power and knowledge; but rather, that the modern University has multiple, disconnected, and predatory meta narratives of thought adjacent to, yet separated by prophylactic and impermeable barriers that prevent and hide points of entry, all competing for "the center" of the educational discourse, and for meta narrative dominance. Because higher education now seems to rely largely upon a quasi-scientific, compartmentalized disciplinary and foundational model (behaviorist psychology, curriculum guidelines, accreditations standards & objectives) fueled by neoliberalist initiatives and ideology to essentialize knowledge, truth and reality, it is my observation that the contemporary customer of the educational factory that is "higher education" is being duly denied her/his epistemological and axiological rights, human potential, and ultimately, a free, critical and personal existence.

In brief, disciplinarity embodies the potential and real effects that the inorganic (the institution) can have upon the organic (the self situated in the inorganic Dysacademia). For Foucault, the "organic structure" I am calling Dysacademia can be characterized by an internal "transformation of structure into character" in which disciplinarity disciplines the knowing self into a disciplined disciple of a certain knowledge set and practice (1970, 227). And as Aronowitz, Ford, Readings, Giroux, and others have duly pointed out, the reproductive cycle that "is" disciplinarity is typically waged on the playing fields of economic and material security, advancement and productivity for both the sovereign and individual subject(s) alike. This point has been introduced before, and will be taken up for further discussion in subsequent sections. Thus duly noted, we now turn to the archaeological and genealogical analysis that Michel Foucault has provided regarding the discourse of disciplines, and our subsequent disciplinary sustenance.

In *Discipline & Punish,* Michel Foucault introduced his readers to the "political technology of the body," or for brevity purposes what he called, "biopower" (Foucault, 1977, 137). To Foucault, biopower represents a pattern of governance whereby the subject is no longer governed by something outside the self, some "other"; but rather, is now governed by the psychologically regulated expectation to exercise the power that governs the self, most often at the subconscious level.

> Discipline is no longer simply an art of distributing bodies, of extracting time from them and accumulating it, but of composing forces in order to obtain an efficient machine. (164)

Primarily using the modern judicial and penal systems to articulate his conception of biopower, Foucault also makes many direct and discrete references to the presence of this corrective dynamic at work in the military, hospitals, and even in schools. In contemporary American schools, it can without doubt be argued that the state's biopower over the "educated" student is no longer external, no longer an extension of a supreme and open sovereignty; but rather, a type of internal power that is characterized by the subjects (students) governing themselves through self-surveillance, behavior normalization, and passive ontological receptiveness. In setting the stage for their critical discourse concerning the discipline of accounting, Hoskin and Macve amplify and extend Foucault's ideas on discipline in order to identify the various institutional practices that "engender a disciplinary way of seeing" (1993, 29). In particular, Hoskin and Macve pay particular attention to the binary meanings of discipline that I have provided at the beginning of this chapter, in order to "play with" the difference between discipline as a form of knowledge, technology and power, and also with the Foucaultian notions of biopower and political technology of the body in order to explicate the inherent and subversive connections found between power and knowledge, and the discursive connection that the knowledge-power relation has to educational transformation.

In expanding upon the performative and binary capacity of *discipline*, Foucault differentiates between discipline's biopower over/on the subject, as has already been discussed, and the evolution of a much more profound and more metaphysical affective quality of discipline that permeates most, if not all levels of our society. Here, Foucault differentiates between the physical, negentropic and solitary locality of discipline associated with the prison-industrial complex, and the subtler, yet also more commanding disciplinary mechanism that he calls the "disciplinary society" (1977, 209). Inherent in the development of our disciplinary society, are several subaltern dynamics that have profoundly impacted the formation, utility and the social roles of the various academic and professional disciplines. By introducing the "functional inversion of the disciplines" Foucault contends that as our society has moved away from the more corporeal practices of discipline, the central purposes of the disciplines have evolved from negative/corrective purposes (like neutralizing dangers, or fixing disturbed populations) to more positive roles designed to increase the possible utility of individuals. In short, the disciplines gradually began to function as techniques for making useful individuals; and so they emerged from the outer, excluded margins of society and gradually took their place as more essential and industrial functions for the overall good of society. In linking the economies of power with disciplines, and thus with subjective utilities of those that the disciplines *discipline*, Timothy Lenoir's account enlightens Foucault's discourse concerning discipline.

> Disciplines are dynamic structures for assembling, channeling, and replicating the social and technical practices essential to the functioning of the political economy and the system of power relations that actualize it. (1993, 72)

Furthermore, Lenoir is quick to point out that discipline has both inorganic and organic effects, that it is not merely about institutions and professionalization, but above all else it is also fundamentally and urgently about human bodies. Disciplines produce knowledge…disciples (bodies) learn that knowledge in a disciplinary fashion…becoming disciplined in seeing, thinking, speaking, and dreaming about other forms of knowledge and invention…thus further contributing to the perpetuation of the disciplinary ways of knowing that started the cycle.

> Disciplines are institutionalized formations for organizing schemes of perception, appreciation, and action, and for inculcating them as tools of cognition and communication. At the same time, as embodied practical operators, disciplines are political structures that mediate crucially between the political economy and the production of knowledge. (72)

In using an archaeological approach to investigate disciplinary power found in our own higher educational systems, Hoskin and Macve argue that "the first institutions that were 'disciplinary' in this double sense were elite colleges in the late eighteenth century, where the power-knowledge innovation lay in bringing together for the first time three educational practices: constant rigorous examination, numerical grading of examined performance, and an insistent presence of writing by students and around students" (1993, 29). According to Hoskin & Macve, top-level institutions of learning in early 19th-century America took their disciplinary and pedagogical leads from West Point, which in turn, had copied the methods and curriculum employed at the *French Ecole Polytechnique*. In 1817 Sylvanus Thayer, the fourth superintendent of West Point, returned from a research trip in Europe concerning current educational trends and brought back with him enlightened "ideas" that have since effectively altered the educational history, character and landscape in the United States. Specifically, Thayer returned with the notion that a scientific curriculum and a disciplinary pedagogy, based on "the constant deployment of writing, examination, and grading" were needed for educational improvements and reform. Upon his return to West Point, Thayer began to use numerical marks to grade all aspects of learning, and at the same time added a powerful managerial dimension that he didn't find in France—a CEO like presence at the head of the school system that kept track of behavior and grades from behind closed doors. Specifics aside, Hoskin and Macve argue that Thayer's pedagogical and curricular imports were directly responsible for the evolutionary change in "how" education was perceived, and thus carried out at institutions following his lead.

> Such institutions disciplined students to learn in a new systematic way, under constant examination for grades; but also they prove to be the sites where new disciplinary forms of knowledge were pioneered, forms that constitute the basis for the modern explosion of academic disciplinary knowledge. (1993, 29)

Today, one need not look very hard or far to see the influences that science and technology have had upon our various curricula and its central emphases, the proliferation of specialized academic majors, and economic initiatives and ideals that characterize our social times—science and technology rule. Perhaps more disturbing for critical pedagogues and those concerned with the current state of learning, standardized outcomes, and objective visions of truth and knowledge that now dominate our educational landscape concerns the role and power that educational psychology now has in much of our educational endeavors. Social science has been "naturalized" over the last century (Abbott, 2001), and thus gradually accepted as a standard, core foundation of all things that are educational.

Concomitant with the development of specific disciplines designed to construct "useful individuals" for the economic engine of the state, came the double tendency to increase both the number of disciplinary institutions and to discipline the existing apparatuses into unique and specialized professional entities (Foucault, 1977, 211). Following WWII the burgeoning capitalistic opportunities associated with the advancement of science and technology worked in concert with Cold War politics and economics, and the increasing desire of the social sciences to gain more credibility by becoming more "empirically objective," to induce profound social and cultural effects on the purpose, identity and utility of higher education in the West (Abbott, 2001; Ford, 2002). The net effect of this industrio-social transformation can be evidenced by the gradual fragmentation of the primary disciplines into many secondary and tertiary ones. Suddenly, the 20th century college/university student had a plethora of professional occupations to pursue, mostly under the guise of an academic major designed to meet certain economic-professional interests, or perceived socio-political needs. Disciplinarity was thus born. No, correct that, disciplinarity was now fully-grown.

Neoliberal(ist) Disciplinization of the Citizenry

The inherent and inescapable developments (the functional inversion of the disciplines and the increased number of disciplinary institutions and professional entities) that have contributed to the evolution of what Foucault has described as a "disciplinary society" (Foucault, 1970, 1977), and thus to our comminuted and *dyscratic* pedagogical condition, are also inextricably and undeniably linked to another major cultural phenomenon that now shapes much of the contemporary University's identity and operative functions. The increasing proliferation of capitalistic and vocational influences upon the University's mission over the last century that have been expertly described in the writings of Giroux (1999, 2003), Readings (1996), Aronowitz (2000), and Ford (2002) has dramatically altered the utilitarian intention, visionary focus, and thus the pedagogy and curricula of many postsecondary institutions in the United States. Together, the various and complex interconnected genealogical factors involved with the cultural, social and political transformations associated with the fragmentation of the disciplines and neoliberal influences have worked to drastically alter the values and purposes of higher education today by shifting the emphasis towards disciplinary expertise and specialization, specific job training, career mobility, economic performativity, and legitimacy; and thus away from intellectual transcendence, democratic and social urgency, and authentic personal freedom. Stanley Aronowitz incorporates a structural analysis of the shifts in the contemporary University's function that reflect the sentiments expressed herein.

> The wider social role of the University is now up for grabs. It is no longer clear what the place of the University is within society nor what the exact nature of that society is, and the changing institutional form of the University is something that intellectuals cannot afford to ignore. (2000, 2)

Perhaps the convoluted and enfolded discourses surrounding discipline, disciplines, disciplinarity and their inherent connection to Dysacademia can best be represented with Lyotard's contentions that "in the context of delegitimation, universities and the institutions of higher learning are called upon to create skills, and no longer ideals," and "the transmission of knowledge is no longer designed to train an elite capable of guiding the nation towards its emancipation, but to supply the system with players capable of acceptably fulfilling their roles at the pragmatic posts required by its institutions" (1984, 48). Added to this sad and counterproductive industrial based development is Norbert Wiener's observation that the pursuit of higher education is no longer driven by a "deep impulse" to transform and grow intellectually, but rather by the desire to attain a certain "social prestige" (1954, 133). In short, the disciplined disciplines' disciplinary training of subjects in higher education, and the subsequent production of highly trained and disciplined objects of human capital represent the penultimate example of *performative subjectivity*.

According to University of Chicago sociologist Andrew Abbott, as American colleges continued to follow the techno-industrial and consumerist model of growth, academic disciplines gradually developed as social constructions designed to support geographical and cultural initiatives (2001, 125). The reasons for this evolution are many and complex, but include the sheer number and decentralized nature of American universities and colleges, the rapid expansion of faculty positions to staff the institutions and run the myriad academic majors that have proliferated in the Post-WWII era, and the increasing trend for professional schools to require arts and science degrees as prerequisites for admission. In time, the gradual blending of graduate and undergraduate programs (on the same campuses), the need for schools to have comparative advantages (different, specialized programs for recruitment of top students) for economic viability, the development of professional subsystems (organizations, meetings, journals, languages, etc.) led to the eventual disciplinary *fractilization* of the disciplines into separate and disparate fields of study. Abbott takes this evolutionary growth a step further by positing that in effect, a *dual institutionalization* was started whereby the specialization and alienation of discipline subsystems led to special doctoral training programs, which in turn, led to highly specialized undergraduate degree programs that had strong economic ties. This, the college major, according to Abbott is "the most consequential single disciplinary structure—in terms of extent and impact" (127). Ironically and amazingly to Abbott, this reflection has never been the subject of serious pedagogical debate amongst scholars critiquing our higher education system. Of course it is not very hard to imagine what the primary driving force behind this process might be—the technico-scientific thirst of the ruling corporate and political classes, and their well rooted financial connections to major degree programs and other higher education initiatives (Apple, 2001; Giroux, 2003).

Foucault's second point regarding the evolution of disciplinary societies concerns the idea that as the disciplinary establishments increased in number, their operational mechanisms had a tendency to "de-institutionalize"; or rather, to fragment into smaller, more flexible methods of control by increasing the number of disciplinary institutions, each with unique and specialized professional identities and utilities (1980a, 211). Sometimes, these new, specialized and fragmented disciplines, although remaining closed to blatant external control, added to their internal and specific function a role of external surveillance in an attempt to increase their mobility, adaptability and credibility to those outside the disciplines. Thus, as each specific "neodiscipline" gained momentum and credibility, they also created their own degrees, experts, and codes of behavior, professional associations, academic journals, research paradigms, and languages. In short, they created their own professional identities, replete with specific inclusion and exclusion criteria for anyone who desired entry, or access to the sought after knowledge. Naturally, the creation of a neodiscipline also necessitated the development of some structural control, a hierarchy that recognized leadership, and a mission that summarized its own particular meta narrative; yet this needed to be done without sacrificing the intellectual and professional autonomy of the infantile association. This actuality may best be evidenced by the extreme proliferation of local, regional, national and international professional societies, academic journals, and accreditation agencies (especially in the natural sciences) that now exist as separate and disparate entities underneath the larger umbrella of academia; a discourse that will be taken up for further analysis in subsequent sections of this text. As a direct result of this Foucaultian recognition of disciplinary proliferation, the resultant secondary disciplines that have been spawned are now well defined and shaped by their own particular languages and codes of behavior that together, embody the construction and survival of Foucault's disciplinary societies, and their revitalizing systems of "truth."

Defined as "a system of ordered procedures for the production, regulation, distribution, circulation and operation of statements," Foucault's "regime of truth" conception is a discursive formation that illuminates the body of practices and the presence of discourses that a certain society constructs, perpetuates and accepts as true (1980a, 133). For as Foucault has reminded us, "there can be no possible exercise of power without a certain economy of discourses of truth which operates through and on the basis of this association. We are subjected to the production of truth through power and we cannot exercise power except through the production of truth" (93). Or in Lenoir's interpretation, the inherent and recursive connections that exist between knowledge-power-discourse-discipline imply that "disciplines are essential structures for systematizing, organizing, and embodying the social and institutional practices upon which both coherent discourse and the legitimate exercise of power depend," not only in negative/repressive fashion, but also in positive/constructive ways that offer potential for new truths, and thus for new discourses, as well (1993, 73).

Foucault's third historical point that has shaped our disciplinary society involves the redistribution of state-control of the mechanisms of discipline (Foucault, 1977, 213). Although blatant sovereign control was gradually waning throughout the 17th and 18th centuries, specifically in France and England, control was not being lost altogether, it was merely being redistributed and reconstituted to different divisions of the state, via different mechanisms like schools. Specifically, Foucault argues that the transition from the King's army to the organization of a centralized police force by the state was the next step in organizing various branches of local and state control, which of course was still controlled by the ultimate magistrates, the Kings. In this manner then, "all the radiations of force and information" spread from the center outward, towards the circumference and into the various localities under the guise of local control. The major difference that this aspect of the evolving disciplinary mechanism brought was the increasing concern for detail that the newly created police force developed. No longer was the state merely interested in large, gross acts of felonious behavior (murder, tax evasion) or revolution (political dissension), they were now more interested in 'everything' that happened among their subjects on a much broader scale.

> It is an apparatus that must be coextensive with the entire social body and not only by the extreme limits that it embraces, but by the minuteness of the details it is concerned with. Police power must bear 'over everything...it is the dust of events, actions, behavior, opinions—'everything that happens'; the police are concerned with 'those things of every moment', those 'unimportant things'. With the police, one is in the indefinite world of a supervi-

sion that seeks ideally to reach the most elementary particle, the most passing phenomenon of the social body. (1997, 213)

Perhaps more problematical than the topographical splitting of
the various knowledge fields into disciplines that Foucault and Ford
described, is the discursive relation between power and knowledge
that have resulted from of our disciplinary practices. For Lyotard, the
concurrent development of language games and specialized discourses that have surfaced in modern times as the various fields have
become more advanced, more special, and thus more powerful is a
thorny and complex political issue that bears attention (1984, 8). To
Lyotard, language games thus become responsible for the construction of hypomobile (less than normal movement) and impermeable
barriers keeping those not in possession of the appropriate language
apparatus "out" of the game; which subsequently leads to the "occidental" (knowledge and power being two sides of the same question)
development of the "knowledge-power" duality that dictates "how"
knowledge is generated, "what" knowledge is worthy, and "who"
gets to make knowledge decisions (9). In effect, "power seems to be
what changes or maintains disciplinary boundaries, thus advancing
or preventing new knowledge production" (Messer-Davidow et al.,
12). Inevitably, the postmodern awareness that power and knowledge
are inextricably linked to each other, and are thus largely constructed
and controlled by socially constructed disciplinary practices leads to a
concomitant recyclable production and regulation of knowledge and
authority that parasitically feeds off of various language games. Timothy Lenoir elaborates further on Foucault's "discourse as a political
commodity" as it pertains to disciplinarity by connecting elements of
structure, control and discipline into a coherent exposition of his analytical purpose.

> It is this aspect of control and policing, not in an external or repressive sense,
> but rather through the internalization of patterns of discourse, structures of
> knowledge, and modes of practice to which I want to relate the present dis-
> cussion of discipline. If my interpretation is correct, disciplines are essential
> structures for systematizing, organizing, and embodying the social and insti-
> tutional practices upon which both coherent discourse and the legitimate ex-
> ercise of power depend. (1977, 73)

Hoskin & Macve have analyzed the meaning and roles that disciplinary language has had upon the practice and learning of disciplinary knowledge, and thus upon the formation and sustenance of the
related discourses that shape and characterize the disciplines and
their disciplinary professionals. In their analysis, two principles are
always at work in modern power systems. The first, *Grammatocentrism*, conveys the fact that "power and knowledge become increasingly exercised through writing," while the second, *calculability*, infers

that everything is subject to constant examination and grading (1993, 32). In a disciplinary society, both inorganic institutions and organic subjects are grammatocentric, or centered on writing in a world where the written word takes precedence over the spoken word. J. H. Miller has elaborated upon the inherent power of the written *mark* to create a communicative force, a notion that resonates strongly with Foucault's disciplinary body and with grammatocentrism. According to Miller, written marks have the performative effect of creating a secret transference from meaningful marks to a physical force, an event that has the double power to constrain and invent (2001, 90). Constraining in that the written word too easily becomes accepted as an authoritative utterance, or "T"ruth; and inventive in that it offers the potential to also open up new thoughts, words, and expressions of "t"ruth for the person making the mark.

In returning to disciplinary grammatocentrism, adolescent and established disciplines make their marks by exerting their truths, their versions of reality, and their "T"ruths in myriad media, texts, accounts, analyses, evaluations, budgets, and other objective forms that serve as the center of the educational endeavor designed to reproduce disciples of the discipline. And as Lenoir states, the performative aspect of discipline can indeed be positive if new utterances, voices, and visions are allowed to sprout from within the scope of disciplinary practice. This (sprouting) can often occur on various levels and in various places; but it is more common and recurring for the negative power of discipline to dominate the discourse by preventing and preempting the open invention of new, creative modes of thought, being and action.

Managerialism Takes Over the Ivy Towers

Regarding our current educational institution, the increasing disciplinary "quality" of our system can be viewed as part and parcel of a complex and bothersome dynamic at work in the halls of our schools and universities. That is, the increasing influence that the social sciences have had upon our pedagogy and curricula has worked in concert with this disciplinary migration to construct the idea of *calculability*. Calculability, the cloak that hides the invisible technology of the mark, doesn't "just put a number on performance; it puts a value on you, the person," it provides a measure of success, of objective change, and theoretically of learning (Hoskin & Macve, 1993, 32). In this regard then, the central question for the disciplined self, as well as for the various disciplines becomes "how does one prove him/herself"? With the performative power of accountability...by performing well and often...by being objectively evaluated and documented by those in control, and of course, by the self. Thus is born *managerialism*, an amalgamated expression of grammatocentrism, calculability and accountability that is most often carried out as "action at a distance." In primary and secondary school settings, this spectacle can be readily seen in the form of the Federal "No Child Left Behind Act," but perhaps is not so visible in our postsecondary institutions of learning. Managerialism's subsequent effects on the fundamental educational utility of the University have been elaborated upon in great detail by Bill Readings (1996), Stanley Aronowitz (2000), and Marcus Peter Ford (2002), the central points of which have been presented in previous sections of the current text, but the poststructural underpinnings of this concept require further scrutiny.

Managerialism is grammatocentric in that it is perpetually accomplished with a continual and ordered set of written directives, truths, and languages that shape its discourse and associated meta narratives, and it observes the notions of calculability and accountability because it is always concerned with examining and grading the subjects and objects of its production (student tests, papers and reports, and presentations, manuscripts and teaching of the professorate). Obviously, grammatocentrism brings to mind the poststructural analysis that Foucault and Derrida have performed on language, the games they work to construct, and the overall structure of signs that shape and define our knowledge and interpretation. In *The Order of Things* (1970), Foucault spends a great deal of time and effort attempting to explicate the connections that have evolved between the sign and the signified, and between the different levels of language that history conceals. According to Foucault, the 17th century initiated a change in the way the language was both used and understood, because prior to this point the arrangement of signs was a binary process and thus defined as the "connection of a significant and a signified." Leading up to the Renaissance period, language was understood on three interrelated and discursive levels, all based upon the single being of the written word, 1) in its raw and primitive being as a written expression of marks, a unique and absolute layer of language, 2) commentary, "which recasts the given signs to serve a new purpose" and exists "above" written language, and 3) the text, "whose primacy is presupposed by commentary to exist hidden beneath the marks visible to all" (42). However, the end of the Renaissance snuffed out this complex interaction of elements because of two evolutionary events that would shape the formation and dissemination of knowledge for years to come, and forced the knower to ask, "How a sign could be linked to what it signified?"

> Because the forms of oscillating endlessly between one and three terms were to be fixed in a binary form which would render them stable; and because language, instead of existing as the material writing of things was to find its area of being restricted to the general organization of representative signs. (1970, 42)

The classical age of the 17th and 18th centuries thus saw the disappearance of the "profound kinship of language," and language became nothing more than representation or signification, the seen and the read were no longer interwoven. Things became simpler, more ordered, and more rational during these times; "the eye was thenceforth destined to see and only to see, the ear to hear and only to hear" (Foucault, 1970, 43). During the Classical Age, in which science and Cartesian thinking dominated the intellectual landscape, language only had value as discourse, and mystical uncertainty was frowned upon; representation meant everything, and everything had its place in a rational order of things, language gave signifying functions to things, not knowledge (59). As language continued to be constructed through disciplinary modes of inquiry, and as science continued to exert its epistemological dominance on other forms of knowing, the social construction of knowledge began to become increasingly fragmented as each discipline gradually and separately constructed their own discursive language games, signifiers, signs, and eventually, separate and competing regimes of truth. Timothy Lenoir summarizes this historical process and connects it to the current exposition of our disciplinary society, by describing it as a "discursive formation" in which the "historically conditioned system of representation" can be best understood with the realization that objects and concepts were socially coproduced in discourse, and did not have an *a priori* existence that defied language (1993, 74). Thus noted, the Classical Era's penchant for creating essential signs and marks with an assumptive historical and natural pre-existence provided the foundation for our understanding of a natural and ahistorical world of knowledge. Naturally, the move by modern age Universities to promote and promulgate disciplinary specific knowledge only made matters worse, as multiple languages, discourses, and metalanguages burgeoned and competed for political power and epistemological authority in the Western world. And, as Foucault points out, this *a priori* assumption of knowledge and truth had (has) an extremely commanding effect on the construction of knowledge, the intellect, and eventually the self.

> This…delimits in the totality of experience a field of knowledge, defines the mode of being of the objects that appear in that field, provides man's everyday perception with theoretical powers, and defines the conditions in which he can sustain a discourse about things that are recognized to be true. (1970, 158)

In effect then, grammatocentric managerialism founded upon language games and discursive formations have taken over the Academy and its disciplines on many interconnected and interdependent levels—most notably, the design of the curricula, the production and advancement of scholarly knowledge (whose knowledge, what knowledge is of most worth, what counts as knowledge?), the teaching and learning experiences (just what are "best practices"; when is learning complete?), and the performance appraisals of the professoriate (just what is "effective teaching"?) by dictating the language and marks used, and by setting a certain order of things. Or as Hoskin & Macve suggest in their piece on disciplinarity in the field of accounting, the explicit materialization of managerialism in the Academy today has led to what they call *grammatocentric panopticism*; an apt Foucaultian extraction that effectively describes the political commodity that shapes and characterizes the modern University, and a term that will be taken up for further analysis in the next chapter on control societies and accreditation procedures.

> By extension of the simple originating practices in administrative coordination, managerialism can know and control the furthest reaches of organizational space and actively construct new scales of organization complexity and size; at the same time, it penetrates every tiny corner of organization. (1993, 33)

The Capitalization of Knowledge

Obviously, the precise depth and breadth of disciplinarity's effects have/will/do vary between, and amongst the various disciplines of the academy. In general, and I say this with sincere humility, the natural, technological and harder "social" sciences have experienced the most pronounced neoliberal-disciplinary effect(s), while the arts, humanities, and "softer" social sciences can arguably be seen to have been less affected. That presumed, Etzkowitz & Webster's articulation of the academy's "2nd revolution" bears inclusion into the current discourse because of its pertinence to the performative and neoliberal arguments being made currently (1998, 21). According to their analysis, the medieval University's first large-scale evolutionary change occurred in the post-WWII days when government sources became the primary means of financial support for the Academy. Today's University, however, is undergoing its "second revolution" in which "academic-industrial relations and the growth of commercialization of academic science have become major items on any science policy agenda." In a nutshell, the 2nd revolution has built upon the first revolution and can be represented by the translation of research findings into intellectual property, marketable commodities, and economic development initiatives—the capitalization of knowledge. This synoptic statement in the *Introduction* of *Capitalizing Knowledge* highlights their central thesis, one that resonates strongly with the current articulation of Dysacademia, as well.

> In particular, universities and firms have become more alike in that both are involved in translating knowledge into marketable products, even though

they still retain their distinctive missions for education...These relations, formerly the special interests of a small coterie of academic institutions and firms, have formed the basis of a general model of how to create knowledge and wealth simultaneously in the late twentieth century. (1998, 8)

To be clear, Etzkowitz, Webster, and Healey are not arguing that this revolution is new, or that it can be pinpointed to a specific time or place in our historical chronology, but rather, that the critical issues requiring a deconstructive discourse now reside in the recognition of the "intensification of this process" and the "increased reliance of industry on knowledge originated in academic institutions" (2). In fact, the authors go on to say that because the stakes are so high with the corporatization of knowledge, that its effects and manifestation have now become so prevalent and diffuse amongst the various types of institutions, that even liberal arts professors and administrators have become part and parcel of the game. In what was once considered a "linear model" for the flow of knowledge, academic scientists produced knowledge for the distribution and consumption across the various niches of society, including the private/corporate sector. Now however, the model can be seen as one being more "spiraled," with a reverse flow from industry to academia. This drastic change in knowledge production roles thus induces an iterative effect in which "industrial innovation opens up new basic research questions, suggesting academic involvement in industrial innovation enhances the performance of basic research."

Although some data appears to suggest that academics with industrial connections publish more than their peers without like support and resources, the spiral models of academico-industrial relations are much more complex and multifarious than they appear on the surface. Specifically, the myriad influences that industrial and corporate America have had upon the University have combined with the ever decreasing public support from governmental sources to produce debilitating, conflicting and compound effects on the mission of higher education, and thus, its social and cultural utilities. Academic scientists' efforts and workloads are now regularly and acceptingly centered on foundation work, patent development, consulting, product R & D, and other economically based initiatives for the production of knowledge deemed valuable and vital by private, outside forces. Perhaps most notable among the secondary, domino-like effects of this revolution, at least as it pertains to the current discourse anyway, is the increasing specialization required by "capitalized academics" in order to meet the economic and technological needs of corporate America (in contrast to the social, ethical and cultural needs, which are typically not as linear and disciplinary specific as product development). For Etzkowitz, Webster, and Healey then, *Capitalizing Knowledge* is intended to convey the economic and symbolic processes that now govern the modern Neoliberal University and its constituents.

> It refers to the translation of knowledge into commercial property in the literal sense of capitalization of one's intellectual (scientific) assets; more generally, it refers to the way in which society at large draws on, uses, and exploits its universities, government-funded research labs, and so on to build the innovative capacity of the future. (1998, 9)

Specialization No Longer Special

In *Chaos of Disciplines* (2001), sociologist and academic scholar Andrew Abbott discusses and analyzes the specific history, development and current condition of the social sciences, and then applies his discourse to the relative state of other academic disciplines. Chiefly, Abbott lays blame on the fairly recent development and reliance upon the specialized PhD—academic major reproductive cycle, and the standard emphasis on academic majors and all of their financial and administrative underpinnings as being the primary disciplinary structures responsible for preventing a true, interstitial, or consilient curriculum (2001, 127). As such, it can quite easily be argued that many of today's college graduates merely symbolize a departmentalized, specialized and highly technocratic "product" that has been sold a bill of goods, an object that has been subsequently duped into believing that they have paid for, and received in full the tools and knowledge necessary to create a substantive and critical ontological and epistemological foundation. A foundation that has traditionally been intended to provide the means necessary to transform all participants into active and productive citizens in a democratic, postmodern society, rather than a foundation of critical and open epistemological and ontological awareness and invention. In arguing for a more postmodern and poststructural approach to the production and dissemination of knowledge, Julie Klein notes the effects that fragmented disciplinarity has upon the "higher educated masses."

> As disciplines have differentiated into increasing numbers of autonomous subunits that train practitioners and provide specialist identities, goals, and techniques, only a few departments now claim to represent fully the range of specialties categorized under a single disciplinary label. (1993, 189)

Abbott, a self-professed "eclectic," uses his professional experiences wherein he has attempted to eradicate the intellectual boundaries between interpretative and positivistic work in sociology and kindred fields as his central theme for the *Chaos of Disciplines*. Although largely based on sociology and the other social sciences, Abbott's work regarding the history of American academia and its industrial, economic, intellectual and social roles in our society shed considerable light on the current status of today's academic utility. In Abbott's words, the aim of this particular text is more general than sociology in and of itself.

> While a principled defense of eclecticism and indeed of a certain form of relativism is the personal aim of the book, understanding recent develop-ments in sociology is its substantive one. (2001, xii)

Abbott is clear to elucidate that he's not intent on challenging the foundational uncertainties of epistemologies ("there is indeed not one sociology, but many"), and seems to intentionally avoid an immersion into the development and/or perpetuation of the grand meta narrative argument, but does set out to challenge the way scholars in his field interact (4). In his view, too many sociologists betray a common pat-tern, or a "universal knowledge upon whose terrain the local knowl-edges wander," and it is this behavior Abbott contends, that prevents meaningful and productive epistemological cohesion or mutual un-derstanding. To be clear, Abbott is not advocating a marginilization of sectarian sub-disciplines or alternative epistemologies, he is merely calling for his colleagues to pay more attention to the larger, but im-plicit framework that such local knowledges end up making together. Knowing this, it is easy to see how Abbott's interests concur with those of the philosopher of science Steve Fuller, as he works to decon-struct the disciplinary boundaries that constrain and define science. For Fuller, "social epistemology" characterizes the paradigm he works out of because of his fundamental contention that "disciplines mark the point at which methods are institutionalized, or, so to speak, the word is made flesh" (1993, 126).

Thus said, Fuller, like Abbott, studies the construction, mainte-nance, and deconstruction of disciplinary boundaries because they provide the performative structure needed for "a variety of functions ranging from the allocation of cognitive authority and material re-sources to the establishment of reliable access to some extra-social re-ality" (126). Academic disciplines and their offspring, professional associations, have all been socially and historically constructed and formed by cognitive authority, language games, marks, and rules of order that govern the production and dissemination of knowledge, the legitimation of the discipline, and the perceived economic utility of the respective disciplinary/professional production. Foucault looks at history and its role in "giving place" to analogical organic struc-tures like disciplines, and rather than looking at history simply as a linear occurrence of happenstance, identifies it as "the fundamental mode of being of empiricities, upon the basis of which they are af-firmed, posited, arranged, and distributed in the space of knowledge for the use of such disciplines or science as may arise" (1970, 219). In situating science (in particular) as a discipline *sans* an ahistorical essence then, Fuller suggests that the strategy for subverting existing disciplinary structures is to "show their long-term lack of discipline," their ahistorical essence, and lack of "natural" foundation. Likewise, it is Abbott's contention that any discipline can actually be represented by self-similar fractal patterns and chaos, and that there is actually much less to disagree about amongst, and between the different disciplines that are competing for meta narrative authority. Or in Fuller's terms, since philosophy has shown that "there is no epistemically privileged way of conferring epistemic privilege," the provinces of possibility are open for subsequent deconstruction and reconstruction of knowledge (127).

Presented from the ground up then, from the perspective of the individual disciplines, Abbott calls for a curriculum that has less boundaries and one that illuminates the existing fractal connections between different types of knowing; an idea that will be extended in detail in later sections of this text. For Julie Klein, the ability to engage in "boundary work" is a pre-eminent theme in the studies of disciplinarity, and as such represents the opportunity(s) to cross, deconstruct, and reconstruct the boundaries that artificially separate one discipline from another (1993, 186). By "permeating" across and through the margins that have fragmented disciplinary groupings, taxonomic categories, and larger institutional constructs, the wandering and permeating self can render inoperative the power that discipline has on the social production of knowledge, and thus work to re-write and fragilely reconstruct the various disciplinary histories and the status of discipline as a category of knowledge. By recognizing and accepting the poststructural contention that disciplines "don't really exist" in the natural world, or in some pre-compartmentalized *a priori* natural history, disciplinarians must also accept the idea that all disciplines are in Lenoir's words, just a "discursive formation" that changes over time. Viewed as such, cross/inter/post disciplinarity works from the premise that there exist multiple spaces within and amongst the various disciplines for "cracks, blurring, and crossing" (Klein, 1993). Accepted as such, the disciplined disciplinarian must also realize the paradoxical nature of the disciplinary structures that govern the production and dissemination of knowledge in the various academic and professional fields. Klein addresses this point directly in asking, "What counts as a discipline?"

> Close scrutiny of epistemological structures reveals that most modern disciplines embrace a wide range of subspecialties with different features. Unidisciplinary competence is a myth, because the degree of specialization and the volume of information that fall within the boundaries of a named academic discipline are larger than any single individual can master. (188)

In like fashion, Abbott subtly plays with the dilemmas associated with postmodern debate by calling for the development and progress of alternative voices and knowledge (local and smaller knowledges) on the one hand, while simultaneously cautioning against knowledge becoming, in effect "re-disciplined." Because Abbott feels that a divergent and fragmented epistemology risks losing sight of any relation to the bigger, larger framework of our social and human conditions, his arguments for a more chaotic yet quasi-connected approach to knowledge can be seen to effectively mirror the consilient notions put forth by Edward Wilson.

> My interest in that larger implicit framework is both theoretical and practical. On the one hand, I feel that an understanding of it will clarify the relations between various subsets of social science and sociology. Knowing the framework simplifies—perhaps even explains—those relations. (1998, 5)

As Andrew Abbott has articulated, the economically induced proliferation of specialized and myriad PhD programs in the last 20 – 30 years has only compounded the evolutionary fragmentation of specialized disciplines, and their offspring micro-disciplines, even further. When combined with the various ingredients that have given rise to disciplinarity and the metaphysical restraints associated with disciplinary boundaries and the discipline, a profound "stasis" can be witnessed in the Academy. This stasis then, is a direct result of the disciplinary practices that form the discourse of disciplinarity, and as such, often and readily prevent the disciples from moving into new, unexplored and unmarked spaces that may prove advantageous for the production of new non-disciplinary knowledge and being. Sadly then, the disciplinary nature of this disciplined stasis gradually becomes synonymous with safety, security, and comfort; a state of consciousness that often precludes one from venturing outside the space for fear of losing the original space. Michel Serres captures this paradoxical moment best by informing us that although invention and wandering may best represent the definitive exemplifications of intelligence, and thus the true path to authentic learning, he also points out that when one vacates one's space and gets too far away from the center, he/she is doomed to lose one's space (1997).

The Discursive Power of Space

Thus perceived, drifting away from the center space that is accepted, normal and disciplined knowledge brings with it the risk of being excluded from the safe space that is already being occupied (within a discipline); of not being considered, being ignored by those who subsequently hold or take the space. Only the brave and foolish leave the sacred space that "is" disciplined already, only the erudite.

Of course, the sacred spaces that the various disciplines occupy require the continual perpetuation of the discourse that has allowed them to originally take and hold the particular authoritative spaces; the various meta languages, codes, marks and meta narratives that have worked to define and shape the discourse must be reproduced. The power-knowledge connection must be continually reconstituted with the production of new, useful knowledge that further legitimates the discipline that produced the knowledge. And too, the occupied space(s) must be legitimated, credible, and accountable for the meta narratives it possesses and disseminates. How better to remain connected to the center than by having a certain level of "external surveillance," membership, and belonging that legitimates not only the professional positions that occupy the space, but the disciplinary infrastructure that supports the respective professions, too. New and existing disciplinary associations like schools and professions, generally don't desire to be overtly controlled by sovereign forces representing them, for it will inevitably squelch the disciplinary production of disciplined knowledge, yet they don't necessarily want to set themselves adrift on the margins of society either, and risk losing their occupied space. Thus recognized, the maintenance of a disciplinary society also requires "some" element of control—grammatocentric panopticism.

In the discursive process that governs the economic production of knowledge then, disciplinarity can be seen to marginalize the potential "internodal" inquiry and mobility that Abbott (2001), Klein (1993), Wilson (1998), and others call for, while simultaneously preventing unique, local and personal constructions of knowledge that are capable of providing a material contextuality, subjectivity and partial objectivity for each individual consumer/practitioner. From a disciplinarity perspective, "the genealogical insight offered here is that knowledge does not grow naturally but is selectively produced in order to realize socially defined goals," and that "disciplines, as arising from and involving material practices, are contingent organizing schemes that distinguish knowers, knowledges, and truths" (Messer-Davidow et al., 1993, 7). In the end, perhaps the Lyotardian language games best systematize and organize our society; while at the same time also characterizing and perpetuating the disciplinary fragmentation of knowledge that started in the Classical Age. If this is true, and it is obviously my intent to present the case that it is, the disciplinary comminution of knowledge will inevitably lead to an intellectual ineptitude of sorts, one that renders E. O. Wilson's higher education challenge a formidable obstacle for educators and those concerned with our social and cultural well-being alike.

Lyotard has deconstructed the innate connection that he sees existing between science and cultural power by reminding us that scientific knowledge "does not represent the totality of knowledge," but rather it "exists in conflict and in addition to other narrative ways of knowing" (1984, 7); a notion reinforced by Timothy Lenoir in his piece on "The Disciplining of Nature and the Nature of Discipline" (1993). In considering Western culture's hyper-reliance and blind faith in scientific knowledge in combination with the perception that other forms of knowing have been marginalized and repressed because of their perceived subjectivity and minimal economic value, one might wonder where this situates our current society. Lenoir pins the source of this dilemma on the power of discursive formation.

> The discursive formation is, accordingly, a historically conditioned system of regularity for the coexistence of statements. Configuration, coexistence, and grouping of statements are crucial to the discursive formation. In Foucault's terms, it is not through reference to some object anterior to the discursive formation that statements acquire their meaning. Objects and concepts are coproduced in discourse. (1993, 74)

As is the case between many contemporary professionals and academics across the disciplines that have become specialized experts in their respective fields, the *everyday* educated person is thus both an object *and* a concept produced by the discourse that is disciplinarity. Being denied a more meaningful episteme and understanding of the world's chaotic culture, its many structural and organizational complexities, and its many interconnected nodes of significance and interpretation both within and outside the various scientific disciplines, the contemporary educated elite has been coproduced by the combined effects and affects of disciplinarity and neoliberalism. If this notion that nature is indeed constructed by the disciplines and by those that work within them is to be embraced, then knowledge must be viewed as more than just information, more than objectively testable material, and much more than mere fragments or sound bites from the various fields that purport to have the objective version of reality. In a Lyotardian vein then, perhaps we must more critically embrace the sentiment that since we *are* living in postmodern times, we must therefore address knowledge in a more complimentary postmodern manner.

A "university as corporation" discourse can thus be seen operating as a conglomeration of effects working dioptrically between society and the university, in which corporate/neoliberal influences have combined with academic and professional disciplinarity, and the promulgation of a Foucaultian disciplinary society to result in Dysacademia in the Ivy Towers. Understood as a direct sequelae (unintended complication) of neoliberal machinery that characterizes our postmodern economic, social, cultural and political conditions, and seen as a condition that feeds openly off our current disciplinary structure in order to meet the "supply and demand" needs of our economy, Dysacademia has become its own discursive formation.

Henry Giroux's analysis of the neoliberalist agenda, and its techno-cratic effects on higher education, the student-consumers, and thus society at large sympathetically reflects the concerns put forth by other scholars concerned with our social coherence.

> In the neoliberal era of deregulation and the triumph of the market, many students and their families no longer believe that higher education is about higher learning, but about gaining a better foothold in the job market. Colleges and universities are perceived—and perceive themselves—as training grounds for corporate berths. (2003, 167)

One evolutionary by-product of the disciplinary-neoliberal discursive formation that can be found in contemporary academic institutions has been the gradual and pronounced production of *educational technocrats* (itself a modernist concept) that values specialized expertise and technique over a broader, wiser and more holistic approach to knowledge and life (Doll, 1993, 24). In contrast to our "uniquely powerful and powerfully unique" disciplinary system (Abbott, 2001, 128), European university systems developed intermediate institutions to help structure the larger interactional fields of the university because they realize that most complex interactional fields tend to break up into clusters of entities that develop internal identities. This recognition thus provides a better small framework-large framework platform for students, who are then able to see and connect the two frameworks with a more consilient perspective and understanding. Even Albert Einstein expressed concern with the growing trend towards overburdening our young students with specialized knowledge. To Einstein, highly specialized and technical education, if not countered with diversity and depth, would preclude a more well-rounded and harmonious enlightenment.

> I want to oppose the idea that the school has to teach directly that special knowledge and those accomplishments which one has to use later directly in life. The demands of life are much too manifold to let such a specialized training in school appear possible. The development of general ability for independent thinking and judgment should always be placed foremost, not the acquisition of special knowledge (64)...It is essential that the student acquire an understanding of and a lively feeling for values. He must acquire a vivid sense of the beautiful and of the morally good. Otherwise he—with his specialized knowledge—more closely resembles a well-trained dog than a harmoniously developed person. (1982, 66)

In my admittedly limited personal experiences, I have noticed that far too many of the college and university students I have encountered in my local space(s) are relatively ill-prepared to carry out the meaningful analysis and problem solving skills needed for confronting the critical social, scientific, and political issues that define and characterize our post-human condition in inventive and creative manners. With reference to Lyotard's observations on the dualistic purpose of higher education, I am concerned that today's academy may not be producing enough of the second type citizen that he mentions—the type of educated elite capable of maintaining the "internal cohesion" of our society. Rather, my collective experiences and observations have led me to the impression that too many general university students today enroll for specific job training skills and knowledge, and inevitably, the associated lure of economic and social security that higher education *promises*.

In fact, a recent study conducted by *The Chronicle of Higher Education* supports Norbert Wiener's "social status" claims, and Giroux's corporate-neoliberalist claims by reporting that 92% of the public sees higher education's most important role today as "preparing undergraduates for a career" (Selingo, 2003, A10). Additionally, this fairly inclusive study shows that 90% of all respondents consider higher education to be principally responsible for "providing education for adults to qualify for better jobs." Ironically, respondents also urged universities to focus less on research and economic development, and to focus more on general education, teacher education, leadership and responsibility, indicating a paradoxical understanding of just what university education is "for." How universities should reconcile the public's perceived need to *decrease* initiatives designed to spur local and regional economic growth, educate students *more* for the economic work place, *and* to focus *more* on civic, social and personal responsibilities and general intellectual growth at the same time, is a very interesting and complex social impression that begs further research and analysis.

Take for example the recent and complex hyper realities associated with our current post 9/11 society. How many of the thousands of "educated" university students entering the work force each year are truly capable of critically analyzing and genuinely understanding the complex, multifaceted, and nebulous factors associated with this horrific and mind boggling event? My intent here is not to essentialize the modern college graduate into an intellectual or social midget, but the standard responses I received during those days, weeks and months following the events of 9/11 can essentially be reduced to simplistic, fairly juvenile, monolithic, and in their minds at least, "rationale" causes that place the blame for the events of 9/11 on "psychotic," "ignorant," and "jealous" Middle Eastern terrorists. Not only do these responses reflect a bothersome lack of cultural and political sensitivity, and an ignorant, biased essentializing of the evil "other" that brandishes all Middle Eastern peoples as threats to our national security, but also a critical lack of awareness regarding relevant current and historical world events, politics, power, and global interrelations. Most undergraduate students that I encountered during these times have either, never given any real consideration to world events outside our local, regional, or global barriers up to the moments immediately preceding the events of 9/11, or were effectively incapable of understanding, or even entertaining the role(s) that our nation's foreign and economic policies (both overt and covert) might have on "non-Western" cultures. As a result of this "cultural ignorance," many of my students perceived any attempt at a discourse surrounding these factors as "unpatriotic," "unbiased," or "flaky"; and perhaps just as important for the discourse at hand, they couldn't see the purpose of having these discussions in one of our major classes.

Another relevant example involves the issues pertaining to global economic expansion, ecological sustainability, and our [post] human futures. Many, if not most of the students and young adults that I have been involved with assume that recycling their beer bottles and newspapers is "all that is needed" by our society to counter the hyper-consumptive appetites of the Western economic machine that is gradually devouring our natural resources. As such, those who actually do recycle their waste containers are inclined to think that they are doing "their part" to solve this complex and multifaceted problem (which, ironically is actually seen as simple and exaggerated in their eyes). Inextricably bound as cogs in the apparatus of consumption and its associated free market policies, much of today's citizenry (including those with higher education degrees) are unqualified to critically deconstruct their respective roles, impact and eventual effects in/on our current neoliberal society dominated by consumption, production, and the mythical American right to material acquisition. Bigger. Better. More. As long as I can afford it…it's my American right!

In effect, far too many undergraduate students of today's University are not academically capable of inventing the knowledge necessary to deal with the issues that we, as a historical society/culture, have left for them to confront; they either don't have, or aren't allowed the opportunity to live, work and exist from within, or without a Thoureauvian consciousness. Global capitalization and the associated diminishing natural resources and increasing pollution/contamination of our ecosphere; post cold war and pre - postmodern war (terrorism and the "Axis of Evil") plutonium propagation; the human genome project, cloning and stem cell research; the ecological, social, economic and health complications associated with worldwide rain forest deforestation; and the scientific and technological invasion upon all forms of culture, including the impending development of artificial intelligence, pre-determined sex selection, and autopoietic robots are just a few of the extremely complex and pressing knowledge issues facing our current and future generations. Discussing, participating in, or attempting to develop resolutions to these contemporary problems, as well as various others, requires both breadth and depth of knowledge; it requires a transdisciplinary and transideological approach that embraces multiples, heterogeneity, complexity and invention. Contrastingly, it *is* inhibited, thwarted even, in the contemporary modern university governed by myriad disciplinary societies that are increasingly being fragmented and (dys)altered by state and external sources of control. In this light then, contemporary college graduates of the neoliberal-disciplinary discourse may be (are) ill prepared to demarcate and clarify the various knowledge claims that philosophy, science and art (on a more global level, inclusive of the humanities, music, etc.) construct of our world, and thus may not be inclined to think openly, critically and reflexively about issues requiring a certain "chaoplexic" approach (Arnott, 1999, 49). By "chaoplexic," Arnott is coalescing the properties and principles of chaos and complexity theories into a postmodern appreciation for the notion that as things appear to get more chaotic, they actually show deeper signs of complexity and organization.

Perhaps more disturbing is the awareness that not only are many of today's university subjects ill equipped to deal with critical issues such as our post 9/11 society, or our ecological sustainability, but that many of them are also fundamentally and apathetically detached from the reality of our present and future ecological, social, cultural and political complexities that we/they will encounter. They have been disciplined in other ways, towards other means, and for different utilities. If this observation proves to have any merit whatsoever, the internal cohesion of our society that Lyotard is concerned with, may indeed be in for a long bout of turbulence and misery. The epistemological and ontological transformations that do occur in far too many students today, is actually not a transformation at all, but rather a continuation of the docile process initiated in earlier educational experiences. This "atransformation" (signifying "lack of") that does occur can be denoted by what Foucault's biopower; a subconscious power that transforms the curious and free thinking subjects into objects of (self) disciplinary technology, a mass marketed and commodified product artistically crafted to operate in today's self-centered, neoliberal, and materialistic society; and most likely, one that inaudibly subverts students to the "hidden curriculum" of higher education elaborated upon by Henry Giroux (2003), Eric Margolis (2001), and others. In short, the perceived "hypomobile" and "acritical" (meaning in this sense, a lack of critical mass) condition of the contemporary student ought to be problematical for all those concerned with our contemporary posthuman condition, our collective and individual political and social futures, and the ethico-ecological sustainability of our kind. For Wilson, a truly effective and consilient-like curriculum that disciplinary scholars argue for, should allow every college student, public intellectual and political leader to be capable of answering a complex, yet simple and critical question.

What is the relation between science and the humanities, and how is it important for human welfare? (1998, 13)

Thus said, the disciplinary hyperfragmentation of the University curriculum coalesces with performativity for excellence, a competitive and exclusive homogeneity of ideas and values, and neoliberal-corporate influences to effectively and drastically alter the inorganic makeup of the University institution, and its organic constituents. According to Aronowitz, the particular role shift that our modern University has undergone is due specifically to the decline of our nation's cultural mission; a mission that revolves around economic productivity and the global proliferation of *Amerocentric* market initiatives, a mission that will inevitably have even further impact on our culture with the advent of the European Union, the WTO and the WMF (2002, 3). Further still, the culturally stimulated inorganic transformation of both the structure and role of the modern University, have compounded and exponentially proliferated their effects to produce profound and subsequent affects, or *sequelae* for the organic constituencies of both the University community, and society at large. Dysacademia has produced the dysacademic. Specifically, the application of Michel Foucault's genealogical and archeological analysis of disciplinary societies to the fragmentation and authority of discipline specific knowledge and authority (1970, 1977), and Lyotard's notion of performativity (1984) regarding educational excellence, legitimacy, and the ongoing and increasing corporatization of the University can be seen as etiological factors in the production of dyserethesia, dysgnosia, and dyslogia in the organic elements of the University. In effect, modern academic disciplines are disciplining our citizenry according to disciplinary practices that are fundamentally influenced by neoliberal initiatives and ideologies, largely put forth by corporate and governmental America. The dysacademics sit on our school boards, teach our children, lead small and big business, run for Congress and other elected public offices, operate on us and prescribe us medicine, produce the television shows we watch, and print the newspapers we read.

Surveillance, Control & Censorship in the Ivy Towers

One can envisage education becoming less and less a closed site differenti-
ated from the workplace as another closed site, but both disappearing and
giving way to frightful continual training, to continual monitoring or
worker-school kids or bureaucrat-students. They try to present this as a reform of the school system, but it's really its dismantling. In a control-based
system nothing's left alone for long.

—Gilles Deleuze (1995, 175)

The more classification there is, the less evolution there is, the more classes
there are, the less history there is, the more coded the sciences there are, the
less invention and knowledge there are, the more administrating there is,
the less movement there is…Parasitic growth has brought everything to a
standstill.

—Michel Serres (Serres & Latour, 1995, 94)

Controlling the Discourse

As I listened to NPR one recent morning, I happened to catch the tail
end of a story concerning higher education that troubled my sluggish
and slowly emerging consciousness. After contacting the local public
radio station, I learned that Congressman Jack Kingston (R-Georgia)
had introduced a bill to the state legislature designed to "ensure fair-
ness in higher education and protect college students from one-sided
liberal propaganda." Specifically, Rep. Kingston wrote an "Academic
Bill of Rights" to safeguard a student's right to "get an education
rather than an indoctrination" (Press Release, October 22, 2003). According to Kingston's myopic and philistine logic, "College is a time
when you form your own opinions about the issues that effect our so-

ciety...if our students are not shown the whole picture, they are being cheated out of a true education. University professors should be teaching our kids how to think, not what to think." A deserved and "true" education (whatever "true" may mean) is indeed desirable for all parties involved at all levels of education. In this sentiment there is not much debate or consternation, but for those interested in more meaningful, liberal and critical education a further analysis is warranted.

As highlighted in the introduction of this text, more recent developments surrounding this discourse demonstrate that Rep. Kingston is not just an isolated maverick speaking out of turn. Disturbingly, Kingston's rhetoric is now of more dire concern for the academy as it has gradually been the recipient of increasing momentum and attention by those in power. A very recent article in the *New York Times* demonstrates just how far Kingston's earlier propositions have come, as news of an official federal commission empowered to study higher education outcomes and effectiveness became more public (Arenson, February, 9, 2006). Motivated by the financial outlay that the federal government provides to most public and many private institutions of learning, the neoliberal underpinnings that guide most, if not all of our nation's foreign and domestic affairs, and the reported "successes" of the No Child Left Behind Act in improving primary and secondary education quality, the Bush administration has created The Commission on the Future of Higher Education to examine whether standardized testing should be expanded to higher education in order to prove that students are learning, and to allow easier comparisons on quality. Perhaps even more interestingly, is the confession by the Bush administration that the impetus for this movement is based on the economic and technological challenges confronting us in the 21st-century (United States Department of Education, 2006). These initiatives are further indications of the increasingly neoliberalist and technocratic nature of education in the United States.

Headed up by Charles Miller, a Houston business executive and past head of the University of Texas Regents (where he directed the system's nine campuses to use standardized tests to prove student learning), the Commission has been charged with generating an August 2006 report on issues relating to accountability, cost and quality. According to U. S. Secretary of Education, Margaret Spellings, "The new commission is charged with developing a comprehensive national strategy for postsecondary education that will meet the needs of America's diverse population and also address the economic and workforce needs of the country's future" (United States Department of Education, 2006). Obviously another biased partisan government entity with pre-existing ties to the testing craze, the Commission includes Kati Haycock, the director of the Education Trust in Washington who has long supported standardized testing; Jonathan Grayer, the chief executive of test-coaching company Kaplan, Inc.; and Robert Zemsky, a professor of educational policy, management and evaluation and co-author of *Higher education as competitive enterprise: When markets matter*, a text focusing on how colleges and universities, in a world increasingly dominated by market forces, can be both mission-centered and market-smart (Arenson, 2006, 2). Challenging the notion that colleges and universities have historically and problematically asked the public and government sectors to "trust us," Miller and the Commission are motivated by the belief that postsecondary testing "would be greatly beneficial to the students, parents, taxpayers and employers." Miller's challenge is to get the Commission to agree on the various skills that college and university students "ought" to be learning, like writing, critical thinking and problem solving, and then test them in standardized formats. In a feeble attempt to appease the skeptics amongst us, Miller is quick to point out that he does not "envision a higher education version of the No Child Left Behind Act"; a paradox that should be highly transparent at this point. Standardizing critical thinking? Standardizing writing? Standardizing problem solving? Most universities have well over 120 different degrees (technocratic specialization)—just how does one develop and grade standardized tests for critical thinking, writing, and problem solving? Looked at another way, exactly how do the economic and technological educational "needs" (and thus, the test results) for a successful and vibrant neocolonial 21st-century connect to, or compete with the testing of critical thinking, problem solving and writing in the many disciplines not connected to technoeconomics? For Miller and his Commission, certain "levers" are needed to make such an undertaking possible and real, "and maybe the accreditation process will be one. Or state legislators. Or members of congress" (Arenson, 2006, 1). Yet even more control over the Academy.

Disturbing evidence for what may lie ahead if standardized tests are extended from our primary and secondary schools, and college admissions tests into higher education can be found in recent reports concerning scoring errors for thousands of high school students taking the college entrance litmus test—the SATs (Arenson & Henriques, 2006). All who've entered college are acutely aware of the cultural capital that SAT scores promise to aspiring college students. Receive a high composite score and admittance to the most prestigious schools and attractive financial aid is almost guaranteed; receive scores anywhere below the top 90% and second- and third- tier schools become the only options. As highlighted in Jonathon Kozol's disturbing but gracefully written *Savage Inequalities*, statistics bear out that wealthier, suburban and white students do much better on these standardized tests that purportedly measure math, reading and writing abilities because of their ability to afford private tutoring and exam preparation classes, and their socioeconomic status provided largely by their educational heritage and higher income zoned schooling (1992). In contrast, students of color, from low- to middle- class households, and those from rural and inner city conditions are at a significant preexisting disadvantage from the start. Typically from poorly performing schools with substandard curricula, technology, and other educational opportunities, performance on standardized tests of all varieties (including SATs) is an uphill battle for even the most ardent and motivated students trying to gain the cultural capital necessary to break their cycle of poverty and despair. Obviously, from where one graduates has a lot to do with the subsequent opportunities for graduate and professional school admittance, and for attractive and prestigious possibilities on the open job market—a powerful cause and effect reproductive cycle that is difficult to break for those not in possession of the cultural capital needed to be included. As if educational bias were not bothersome enough, there now seems to be wide spread problems with how SAT results are score, graded, and reported to institutions of higher education.

As Arenson & Henriques report, the company that handles SAT scoring (Pearson Educational Measurement) acknowledged that false scores were tabulated for 4,000 students who took the October 2005 test because of answer sheet moisture (due to improper storage), and faulty scanner sensitivity (2006). No small glitch, this latest gaffe found that test scores were off by as many as 400 points out of a possible 2,400 tests taking that month. This is not the first time that Pearson has been guilty of test score errors. In 2002 they settled a large lawsuit regarding 8,000 tests in Minnesota that prevented several hundred high school seniors from graduating and admitted to several more blunders in Washington and Virginia. Seeing as how the contract between Pearson and the College Board was just one of many awarded to this rapidly growing company since President Bush signed the No Child Left Behind Act in 2002, and that Pearson has worked for over 20 years in Texas on its state testing program made famous by Mr. Bush, one has to wonder what Mr. Bush will empower Pearson to carry out, and how accurate will the process be if higher education testing becomes a reality. Most notably, how many college and university students will receive erroneous test scores preventing them from graduating or going on to post-baccalaureate education? If test results are mistakenly reported as substandard, what will the implications be for the institution and faculty involved on those outcomes?

Perhaps the biggest "stone in the shoe" regarding control and censorship in the Academy however, is David Horowitz, a one time Communist conscientious objector in the twilight of the Eisenhower area of 1959, and now a major force for the right's culture wars on political correctness, leftist chicanery, and Marxist terrorism (Sherman, 2000, 1). The recipient of millions of dollars of conservative foundation monies, Horowitz was the brain trust that launched anti-affirmative action Proposition 209 in California, has been involved in efforts to create a conservative talk show on PBS, is a frequent writer of op-ed pieces on right-wing issues, is the architect of the Republicans' "political war" on Leftist Democrats, the author of *Hating Whitey* (2000), an outward attack on leading African American leaders such as Cornel West, and the current civil rights agendas, is a Republican Party theoretician supported by 35 state Republican Party chairmen and the Heritage Foundation (amongst numerous others), the benefactor of former House majority whip Tom DeLay's efforts to support his book on political war by providing copies to every Republican Congressional officeholder, and the guest of honor at a Washington, DC soiree hosted by Senators Arlen Spector, Rick Santorum, Sam Brownback, and a dozen other House members which raised $40,000 to support his right wing activities. But perhaps Horowitz is best known for his more extensive efforts as president of his self-founded "Center for the Study of Popular Culture," an escalating empire that produces a remarkable array of right-wing services and products, and has a budget of approximately $3 million that is mostly funded by conservative foundations such as the Bradley and Scaiffe Foundations (Sherman, 2).

Relative to the current discourse surrounding higher education is Horowitz's current lightning rod, the Academic Bill of Rights (ABR). His self-proclaimed ABR is, according to Horowitz "not about Republicans and Democrats," but rather "about what is appropriate to a higher education, and in particular what is an appropriate discourse in the classrooms of an institution of higher learning" (Horowitz, 2005, 1). In another piece published online in his "FrontPageMagazine," Horowitz bluntly states that universities in the last academic generation are not "themselves democratic" because they are effectively ruled by internal bureaucracies that ignore and protect radical and inappropriate professors who abuse individual student rights by controlling the discourses in their classrooms, silencing disparate voices, and grading with political biases (2002, 1). Furthermore Horowitz (without proof or data to support his claims) contends, the "academic hiring committees are elitist and self-selecting," in that they incestually hire their "own," ignore Republican candidates and insulate themselves from external scrutiny and opposing voices, and are hypocritical in that they defend and champion diversity, yet don't apply these values to a plurality of viewpoints. At this point, it should be fairly obvious that Horowitz's motivations are indeed about "Republicans and Democrats," a contradiction that instantly undermines his arguments and analysis of the University and its Democratic utility. Perhaps even more perplexing than the transparent flip-flop on his motives and true agenda, is the ironic fiber that constitutes his call for an Academic Bill of Rights based on purported leftist bias and exclusion of intellectual freedom by Democratic members of the Academy—he is advocating for one voice (the Conservative Republican) voice to trump the liberal (or, in his view Democratic) voice that is purportedly suppressing disparate voices. Ironic in that liberal education, as aptly expressed by Karen Halnon, a professor of sociology is exactly what Horowitz is extolling as the intended outcome of the ABR.

> Liberal arts education is intended to cultivate tolerance, respect for difference and diversity, critical thinking, the pursuit of knowledge and truth, and a sense of worldliness and civic responsibility...prizes freedom of thought and expression, and who makes principled arguments in favor of things such as equality and social justice. (2006, 2)

Halnon continues her attack on the ironic and censoring power of Horowitz's proposed ABR.

> As education leaders they may be countering and correcting for what they know is not "fair and balanced" in the media mainstream. If this is so, the solution is not censoring educators with intellectual and social conscience, but initiating broad society changes that will bring integrity to the meanings of liberty, freedom, and democracy. (2)

Today, Ohio, Georgia, Florida, Indiana, Maine, Massachusetts, Minnesota, North Carolina, Pennsylvania, Colorado, California, Washington and Tennessee have passed, or are seriously considering legislation and implementation of some form of an ABR designed to silence the liberal bias that "dominates" the nation's colleges and universities and deprives conservative students of "academic freedom" (Halnon, 1). There is a ray of hope however; the state system of New York condemned the ABR on the basis of its "Orwellian" and "McCarthyite" underpinnings that promised to encourage, amongst other things, Holocaust denial (deRussy, Langbert & Orenstein, 2006, 1). In May, 2005 Dick Iannuzzi, the New York state system's president reiterated his disdain for an ABR by commenting that it would be "an orchestrated and dangerous attack on academic freedom and a serious threat to the lives of our colleagues in higher education." Iannuzzi went on to label Horowitz an ideologue and that an ABR would "provide a forum for right-wing politicians and others who seek to impose a political agenda in the classroom."

Paradoxically, the paranoid and controlling bureaucrats following Horowitz's ABR initiative and Bush's call for standardized testing nationwide, and the polemical political agendas they push, ardently believe that controlling what academics say, teach and test within the walls of the Ivy Tower will ensure a non partisan, multi-ideological educational experience for all students; a higher learning experience that automatically awakens each student's political and social consciousness from its currently repressed and comatose state of being. After all, the political partisanship of liberal and democratic thought that predominates the halls and classrooms of academia by its resolutely liberal professorship (as Horowitz sees it) is in addition to being a widespread problem, "an abuse of students' academic freedom." As such, Horowitz sees his *Academic Bill of Rights* as a necessary vehicle to "take politics out of the university curriculum" by putting an end to unequal funding of student organizations that host guest speakers with biased liberal perspectives, and instituting hiring quotas policies based on party affiliation. Interestingly, another inclusion in the ABR states that "the quality of education should not be infringed upon by instructors who persistently introduce controversial matter that serves no pedagogical purpose" (deRussy, Langbert & Orenstein, 5). Skeptical academics take comfort, supporters of an ABR assure us that their particular vision of academic freedom, convoluted as it is, is not supposed to "dictate any academic curriculum" but rather, to "challenge Universities to voluntarily adopt ideologically-neutral hiring processes and academic policies." So much for the inclusion of pedagogically "useless" discourses surrounding evolution vs. intelligent design, the legality of secret government surveillance, the exorbitant profit making of the U. S. pharmaceutical industry, or the existence of global warming as elements of a higher education initiative. Can anybody say "control"? Censorship?

A University in Ruins?

Widespread budget shortfalls, increasing private and public partnerships between universities and the corporate world, the renewed pleas from conservatives to squelch academic freedom and eliminate tenure, and the increasing neoliberal fragmentation and technocratization of the curriculum--these are just a few of the many current challenges that threaten to destabilize the historical, intellectual, ethical and socio-cultural missions of the American University. In *University in Ruins*, Bill Readings goes so far as to say that, because of the decline in our national cultural mission, the wider social role of the University as an institution is "now up for grabs," and thus that both the place and nature of the contemporary university are now nebulous and awkward for those intellectuals vested in our academic and social futures (1996, 2). In short, it is Reading's critical contention that the University has fundamentally and resolutely succumbed to the capitalistic demands associated with the Western neocolonial globalization project, and thus, it no longer participates in the historical project for humanity that once served as the original legacy of medieval Enlightenment, that being "the historical project of culture" (5). This "university as corporation" discourse candidly operates as a chief feature of the neoliberal machinery that now characterizes our postmodern economic, social, cultural and political conditions.

As such, a critical discourse surrounding the modern university has been constructed from multiple fields in an attempt to maintain a counter-discourse of hope and restitution that honors the original and critical missions of higher education (Apple, 2001; Aronowitz, 1998; Ford, 2002; Giroux, 1999 & 2003). For Giroux, higher education's "hidden curriculum" symbolizes the "creeping vocationalization and subordination of learning to the dictates of the market, a phenomenon that can now be seen as an open and defining principle of education at all levels" (1999, 16). As the modern University continues to become increasingly corporate in its acceptance and production of a consumer culture, a perceptible similarity can now be seen between those dynamics of control and surveillance (standardized tests, certified outcomes, objective quality, teacher deskilling) that define our public schools, with comparable processes now operating across many levels of postsecondary education. To be more specific, the University's increasingly open love affair with school and program accreditation, educational standards of excellence, the production of quality "educated objects," and the various forms of internal and external control that work to define and characterize the modern educational system have made it increasingly difficult to differentiate it from primary, middle- and secondary-school education.

(Dys)Affecting the Intellect & the Senses

In blending various critical discourses put forth primarily by Michel Foucault and Gilles Deleuze that deconstruct the social mechanisms of discipline, surveillance and control, it is the intent of this chapter to address the various bureaucratic and industrial mechanisms of power and control that the inorganic Dysacademic University now relies upon to discretely survey and control the various organic academics and professional disciples it houses. In effect, the controlling University operating as the penultimate example of what Hoskin and Macve call "grammatocentric panopticism" (1993, 33) can thus be diagnosed as the primary etiological factor for the production of "dysgnosia" (abnormality of the intellect), and/or "dyserethesia" (impairment of sensibility) in its objects (primarily, the professorate). Secondarily, this chapter will also examine the resultant affects and effects that the power-control mechanisms associated with grammatocentric panopticism have on the reproduction of technocratic and ideologically limited objects of desire—the students, or what Stanley Aronowitz has called "techno-idiots" (2000). In extending the previous discourse concerning disciplinary societies into the current one, centered on the Deleuzian transition to a "control society," Foucault's analysis of disciplinary societies provides a seamless segue for the theoretical transition I intend. In recalling that disciplinary societies have been characterized by Foucault by 1) a functional inversion of the disciplines for political and economic utility, 2) an increase in the number of disciplinary institutions for unique and specialized professional entities, and 3) a redistribution of state control mechanisms of discipline from overt sovereign manifestations to more subtle and local means (Foucault, 1977), and that Hoskin & Macve's grammatocentric panopticism relies upon accountability, calculability and managerialism (1993). I hope to set the stage for my current contention that academic accreditation has become the ultimate Deleuzian control mechanism for the 21st-century University.

Accreditation as a Recursive Formation

In deconstructing the discourse surrounding educational excellence and pedagogical value, I intend to show how contemporary higher education's self-reliance upon accreditation as the marker of quality and excellence mirrors, and even in some cases duplicates Foucault's articulation of disciplinary societies. And because of the close theoretical and practical proximity, I also aim to demonstrate how the accreditation process symbolizes academia's conversion from a *Foucaultian disciplinary society* to a *Foucaultian-Deleuzian control society*; replete with complex and connected apparatuses of surveillance, external and internal control, performativity and legitimacy, and of course, discipline. In so doing, I will briefly highlight the historical, administrative, and contemporary trends associated with general, institutional accreditation in American higher education; and then attempt to weave these events with current university initiatives to accredit myriad specific programs of study with external agencies designed to "improve educational quality and professional preparation." Lastly, I will intersperse some of my own particular experiences with undergraduate accreditation in athletic training education, as they appear to be relevant and capable of strengthening the central arguments and may provide readers with an opportunity for a comparative analysis.

Central to the analysis of the complex and multifarious mechanism that is the modern university, is the increasing organizational reliance that is being placed upon program and institutional accreditation processes. Long thought of as just a minor nuisance by many academics with little to no "teeth, accreditation initiatives increasingly dominate the current vernacular and consciousness of many University administrators, particularly in the myriad service professions and techno-science fields. For administrators interested and vested in "educational excellence" and the external perception of educational quality and economic value, program accreditations have become very powerful and telling markers that now perform substantial roles in public relations, marketing and annual reviews of most if not all institutions of higher education in the United States. Essentially, a program that is accredited by an external agency has been automatically deemed to have reached a certain level of effectiveness, excellence, credibility and thus also professional and economic value in the eyes of department chairs, deans, provosts, presidents, and now even, the public consumer. Witness the utility and expansive "reach" that the Council for Higher Education Accreditation (CHEA), a private, nonprofit national organization that coordinates accreditation activity in the United States, has over 3,000 college and university members (February, 2003, 1). According to CHEA, they are *the primary advocates* for "voluntary accreditation and quality assurance to the U.S. Congress and the U.S. Department of Education," and the "primary national voice for voluntary accreditation to the general public, opinion leaders, students, and families." One may find it ironic that, although they are a "voluntary" external service that legitimizes educational quality by providing authoritative data and information regarding various accrediting agencies, they also "report" to the U.S. Congress and Department of Education. The CHEA also informs us that although its accreditation services are indeed "voluntary," educational institutions must be accredited by some externally accredited, accrediting agency if its students wish to be eligible for Federal Title IV financial assistance. Although, accreditation "may be voluntary," membership in the accredited club is fairly inclusive and it appears as though non-membership doesn't pay as 6,421 institutions and 18,713 programs were accredited in the United States, as of their August, 2003 report (2003, 1). Thus noted, the discursive formation that "is accreditation," and its power to control and survey the Academy begs for a poststructural analysis capable of revealing its inherent connections to disciplinary and control societies.

Readings' "ruing of the University" contention may be better appreciated by scrutinizing the momentum taking shape with the increasing formal regulation of academic programs, specialized disciplines, and professional degrees. Otherwise known as accreditation, the move to standardize, regulate and control the content, pedagogy, future outcomes, and overall "quality" of various higher educational programs has become increasingly fashionable amongst educational administrators, disciplinary professionals, local and regional policy makers, and student-consumers alike. Indeed, Readings' cynical prophecy has been fulfilled today when one realizes that powerful accreditating agencies like the Southern Association for Schools & Colleges (SACS), which rather mandatorily accredits all institutions of higher learning in the Southern United States, now requires *every* academic program to produce a "quality enhancement plan"(QEP) in order to document its relative excellence and utility (2003). Although most of the research published on accreditation refers to state and regional accreditation processes that are involved with colleges and universities (like SACS), otherwise known as "general accreditation," much of the theory, philosophy, and practicality of the accreditation machine can also be applied to specific degree accreditation processes that are now extremely popular for educational administrators and public policy pundits. Invented by, and still somewhat unique to the American academy, general and disciplinary accreditation has been part of higher education regulation for over one century in the United States with roots in the American desire to "privatize" higher education, with external, non-governmental control (Blauch, 1959; SACS, 1963; Selden, 1960). Ideologically, it was thought that American universities could escape the sovereign control that European universities suffered by excluding the central government from the administration and shaping of the academy by using non-governmental influences to monitor and control educational quality.

Ironically, the early advocates of accreditation thought that this non-sovereign process would also free them from political and ideological interests of the state, thus providing them a certain degree of freedom and neutrality (Blauch, 1959). Accreditation it was thought, was the responsibility of "qualified educators" not statesmen, and so it was important for all involved in higher education to be aware of the meaning, purpose and effects of accreditation (Commission on Colleges, SACS, 1963, 2). Because accreditation was presented as "a symbol of respectability in the academic world," it was deemed that everyone associated with the university must in effect be both conversant in, and supportive of the apparent positive goals and benefits of achieving and maintaining accreditation. In fact, CHEA even reports that their standards are "developed or changed through a process of public consultation involving, e.g., faculty, administrators, students, practitioners in specific fields, governing boards, and members of the public" (February, 2003, 3); a well-meaning and comprehensive ideal for sure, but realistic and actual as a praxis of utility remains to be seen. Interestingly, some of the explicit "roles" of accreditation listed by the SACS report (1963, 1) provide fertile ground for the creation of a hierarchy of "school quality" that will help students and parents with their selections, and future employers select employees based on the "quality" of their university training; sentiments that have since been reinforced by CHEA. After all, if "qualified reviewers" do not formally accredit a school, how can it be any good at delivering quality education to the masses? If a particular discipline fails to produce and write a quality QEP that demonstrates and dictates its utility of excellence, how can it be of any educational value? How can a particular program or institution adequately and effectively prepare citizens for the industrial work force, if not first validated by external sources empowered to judge quality and value?

In a 1963 report printed by the Southern Association of Colleges and Schools (Commission on Colleges, SACS, 1963), entitled "General Accreditation in Higher Education," accreditation was initially defined as "the recognition accorded to an institution which meets criteria or standards of achievement established by a competent agency or association for educational activities of the nature and level being offered by the institution" (1). Updating this definition a bit, CHEA has described accreditation as "a process of external quality review used by higher education to scrutinize colleges, universities and educational programs for quality assurance and quality improvement," and proudly note that "institutions and educational programs seek accredited status as a means of demonstrating their academic quality to students and the public and to become eligible for federal funds" (2004b, 2). According to Blauch's synoptic, yet authoritative and Ralph Tyler like work, a fully developed accrediting procedure includes four steps; 1) establishment of standards or criteria, 2) inspection of institutions by competent authorities to determine whether they meet the established standards or criteria, 3) publication of a list of institutions that meet the standards or criteria, and 4) periodic reviews to ascertain whether accredited institutions continue to meet the standards or criteria (1959, 3). Conceptually, accreditation was deemed necessary for demonstrating the respectability and soundness of educational programs by a) discovering and propagating good educational practices, b) improving the overall educational process, and c) strengthening the educational institutions themselves (Commission on Colleges, SACS, 1963, 1). In updating the ideological mission of accreditation, CHEA's recognition standards now include 1) advancing academic quality, 2) demonstrating accountability, 3) the encouragement of purposeful change and needed improvements, 4) the employment of appropriate and fair procedures in decision-making, and 5) a continual reassessment of accreditation practices (August, 2003, 2). Aside from one stated foundational CHEA principle regarding the desire to maintain core academic values central to higher education and quality assurance, noticeably absent from these rather vague, extremely subjective and contextually sensitive "missions" and standards of accreditation are any authentic references to the individual student, society, civics education, intellectual transformation, critical democracy, or cultural advancement. Incidentally, these omitted or overlooked critical issues and entities have historically embodied the more authentic roles and purposes of higher education from the Enlightenment era to modern times (Readings, 1996).

One text that did provide information beyond that of state and regional general accreditation was Lloyd Blauch's *Accreditation in Higher Education* (1959), a text that painstakingly chronicles the nature and evolution of state, regional, and various professional accreditations in the United States. Blauch's manuscript includes specific chapters on the historical processes involved in the accreditation (with the year the accreditation process started) of such fields as Bible college education (1947), education for design (1948), forestry education (1933), journalism education (1946), landscape architectural education (1920), library science education (1926), music in higher education (1928), religious education (1946), just to name a few of the more interesting professional specialties. For the record, the oldest known educational accreditation process known in the United States belongs to the field of osteopathy, beginning with six accredited programs in 1897. Predictably, the highly specialized and disciplined professional fields of law (1900), medicine (1904), and dentistry (1916) followed shortly thereafter; while fields more representative of the social sciences like teacher education (1927), social work (1932), and psychology (1947) lagged behind considerably (Blauch, 1959, 224). As of this writing, the college that I teach in (one of six in the university) currently has 19 different program accreditations that purportedly "validate" the quality and effectiveness of the professional pedagogy of those who teach in those respective programs, to those outside the university with an interest in the various events and phenomena occurring inside the Ivy Towers.

Accreditation as a Disciplinary Organism

Using Foucault's analysis of disciplinary societies then, it can be asserted that the subtle and historical mechanisms that bolster a disciplinary society can also be seen in operation amongst the accreditation processes of many, if not most higher education programs; a contention confirmed by Blauch's early text on accreditation in higher education. Foucault's first point, regarding the 'functional inversion of the disciplines', can thus be seen in the incredible proliferation of sub-disciplines and highly specialized professional degrees that most institutions now offer to their consumers (students). The fragmentation of the curriculum into myriad majors and academic programs of study can be viewed as an industrial side-effect of our modern infatuation with the processes, knowledge and advancement of technoscience and all of its wondrous capitalistic potential, with a concurrent de-emphasis on the less marketable and practical humanities and social sciences. Viewed as economically viable and thus valuable to all vested parties, accreditation serves as the primary agent for professional and economic legitimization in the modern university. Viewed as such, it can thus be logically surmised that accredited knowledge can be readily and easily converted into capitalized knowledge—ready for delivery and pickup by the consumer when needed. If the academic discipline is economically valuable and marketable to the public (job market) and corporate sectors (highly trained potential employees), it must then be validated as a quality educational program that disciplines its students in the ways of the disciplinary professional field.

In its 1966 report on its organizational "Role and Function," The National Commission on Accreditation (NCA) report specifically reinforces this notion, "the development of new professions goes hand in hand with the increase in knowledge and the advancement of technology" (NCA, 1966, 49). As more advanced and specialized programs of study were gradually borne in our post-WWII Disciplinary University, the opportunity for accreditation control also proliferated as a necessary means of regulation, legitimation, and professional surveillance. A quick look at the mission and vision statements, various curricular programs, stated learning outcomes, and number of accredited programs of most modern universities and colleges in this country reflects this contention wholeheartedly and thus can be seen as evidence of growing neoliberal control and influence in higher education. Accreditation thus assumes its legitimating role in the various academic disciplines by certifying the quality of both the instruction and curricula of the academic (professional) discipline, and by guaranteeing specific and objective value-laden learning outcomes for all of its students. Approved and surveilled Quality Enhancement Plans, which in turn are designed to ensure academic quality and excellence, have thus become the biblical blue print for guaranteeing educational performativity.

The 1966 NCA report also addressed the perceived emergent need and pressure to expand from the present 28 professional education-accrediting agencies (48). This historical recognition clearly brings to light Foucault's second issue—"the swarming of disciplinary mechanisms". In short, along with an increase in the number and type of "new knowledges" came a perceived need to qualify these new professional fields, or rather, it was felt that it was necessary to provide external surveillance in the guise of accreditation in order to authenticate the new programs of study. According to the authors of the NCA report, the increasing pressure for recognition of new professional accrediting agencies stemmed from two sources: "1) the steady growth in the number of groups rightly recognized as professions and 2) the extension of professional programs in the direction of supporting technical occupations and the extension through the graduate level." It was also a consensual thought at that time that as new professions emerged outside the realm of teaching, so too did the need for some type of external, quality control by respected authorities; "as the disciplines prepare persons for professional work other than teaching, their professional societies become more conscious of the advantages of accreditation" (50). As the CHEA proudly reports in its August, 2003 "Fact Sheet," this dream has since become a reality as there now exist 18,713 specialized accredited programs in the United States, and "engendering employer confidence" remains one of four fundamental "purposes of accreditation" (2003b, 2).

The state-control of the mechanisms of discipline, Foucault's third factor of disciplinary societies, is perhaps most relevant to the current discourse regarding the recursive nature of accreditation. Originally, one large central agency, the National Accreditating Agency (NCA), actively worked to perpetuate the purpose and function of accreditation to other non-teaching fields as 'required' evolutionary steps, necessary to ascertain quality and credibility. Today, other "non-governmental" agencies like CHEA and SACS have somewhat diluted the NCA's hegemonic hold over educational control, but organizational competition hasn't lessened the bureaucratic processes associated with accrediting endeavors; in fact, it has probably accelerated it somewhat. Ironically, the NCA's concern for increased surveillance and control (a.k.a, quality assurance) was seen to be even more pressing when it came to degree programs that served as feeder programs for government and industry; even admitting that, "pressures may actually be exerted by the employment agencies" in its 1966 report (49). In the preface to his 1960 text entitled *Accreditation: The Struggle Over Standards in Higher* Education, author William Selden explicitly confirms accreditation's role in the struggle for control over academic standards in higher education by comparing it to the like struggle for control and influence in civil government (1960, x). Indeed, CHEA advocates itself as "the primary national voice for voluntary accreditation and quality assurance to the U.S. Congress and Department of Education," and professes to serve as "the authoritative source of data and information about regional, national, and specialized accreditors" (February, 2003b, 1). This "big brother watching" view was also brought to light in the 1963 SACS statement on accreditation in higher education, as it attempted to distance the accreditation process from governmental watchdogs. Ironically though, SACS effectively treaded on its own proverbial tongue in this paradoxical passage that shouldn't go unnoticed by those concerned with the discursive power of external surveillance.

> At the same time there is no inclination to protect the spread of obnoxious ideologies, which might occasionally fan across institutions. Policies governing the teaching of communism or related dogmas, and procedures for applying them are determined by governing boards. These matters are not normally within the province of the Commission on Colleges. However, in the final analysis it is ingrained in the philosophy of the Commission that we must "stand ready to protest in the name of academic integrity when the educational effort is hampered by political interference, stifled by authoritarian fiat or in any way menaced by those who would subvert the search for truth." (1963, 4)

Ironic indeed, perhaps even paradoxical that SACS would operate under the premise of "protecting truth" by subverting political interference, while simultaneously exerting another purported "truth," all in the name of "academic integrity." As will be demonstrated over the remainder of this particular chapter, this historical precedent can be seen simply as one political interference replacing another. Today, SACS requires that institutions "place primary responsibility for the content, quality, and effectiveness of its curriculum with its faculty" (2003, 9), a reversal of policy that ostensibly supports academic freedom, but one that has somewhat and simultaneously undermined the standards and guidelines associated with many of the 18,000+ specialized program accreditations that govern the various curricula and pedagogies of the myriad academic disciplines (a consideration that will be revisited later).

Certainly then, the sense of urgency and pressure expressed by the NCA in their 1966 report, coupled with the sociocultural proliferation of highly specialized and fragmented disciplines (now made for and from accreditation molds) can be seen as Foucaultian operations of the 'swarming of a disciplinary mechanism', and also as a variegated form of 'state-control over the mechanisms of discipline'. In fact, all four declared "purposes of accreditation" put forth by the CHEA in 2003 reinforce the tendencies of accreditation to be based on elements of state control, discipline and neoliberalist policies. Looked at through the lens that refracts accreditation as a discursive formation then, the CHEA's "purposes" of accreditation can all be deconstructed to reveal minimal to moderate levels of control and surveillance, depending upon the position of the viewer: 1) assuring academic quality for students and public (just how is quality measured across the various disciplines? How does one qualify/quantify compassion, critical consciousness, ethical behavior, sociological and civic connection, or interpersonal respect?), 2) access to Federal funds as the accreditation of institutions and programs is required in order for students to gain access to federal funds (if accreditation is "voluntary," why are federal funds tied to it then? Political interference comes to mind), 3) easing transfer for students among colleges and universities (the codes that are needed to be deemed "acceptable" come in the name of credits from accredited agencies, automatically ensuring "quality," and 4) engendering employer confidence when evaluating credentials of job applicants and providing financial support to current employees seeking additional education (the corporate interests are obvious here, but it is indeed ironic that many corporations still complain that they have to retrain many of their new employees and that far too many of them lack creativity and critical thinking skills) (August, 2003a, 2).

In effect, accreditation's discursive power works to create a discourse that defines and calls for a commitment to certain meta languages, codes of thought and behavior, and ultimately meta narratives that produce disciplinary truths and realities that in turn, shape the subsequent discourses. With a discerning eye then, one can see delicate examples of a Foucaultian biopower at work in the microphysics of the accreditation discourse, as it inevitably exerts a conspicuous hegemonic authority over students' professional identity formation and awareness, over the actual pedagogical process used and evaluated, and ultimately of course, over the specific curriculum itself. For example, the accreditation discourse that I operate out of for athletic training education requires teaching a very specific, detailed, and comprehensive list of over 1,500 cognitive, psychomotor and affective competencies and clinical proficiencies deemed necessary to become a qualified "entry-level athletic trainer." Included in this exhaustive list, which by the way must be documented and recorded in numerous painstaking and pedantic ways for each student, are such qualitative and esoteric skills and abilities as the ability to communicate with patients, think critically, and act professionally. Just how does one evaluate and document proficiency in qualitative domains such as these?

So dominant, so powerful, so subversive is accreditation induced Foucaultian biopower that very few objects in the system (students and teachers) actually have the opportunity to discover what it means to experience genuine ontological and democratic freedom, to explore life's many complexities and contextual, non-essential realities, or to invent their own worldly knowledge and phenomenological understanding. Perhaps most importantly though, overbearing accreditation standards and outcome evaluations can severely hamper the power and freedom of those involved in carrying out the accredited program—the program directors and teachers who become disciplined and controlled by the respective accreditation standards and guidelines. Jack Kingston's "Academic Bill of Rights" then, can thus be seen as a type of accrediting biopower that exerts epistemological, ontological and axiological authority over its subjects; so much so in fact, that university subjects inevitably become objects of hegemonic discipline and control. Where's the academic freedom in that, I wonder?

Consequently, state regulating agencies, local school boards, and disciplinary societies in custody of such authoritative biopower (accreditation standards) can effectively survey and control their subjects by determining normal, standardized, and acceptable modes of behavior, knowledge and even subjective identity (Foucault, 1977, 136). Even though SACS, for example, mandates that the primary responsibility for the content, quality, and effectiveness of its curriculum lie with its faculty, the specialized accrediting agency that governs certain educational programs (teaching and athletic training, for example) often circumvent, undermine and supercede most of those principles by dictating the majority of the tasks required and expected of program directors and faculty members via various "standards and guidelines" deemed necessary to "produce excellent entry-level professionals." In effect then, the particular viewpoints, experiences (both didactic and practical), knowledges and philosophical inclinations that each highly trained and expert faculty member brings to the process are largely decentered and marginalized by the authority that is accreditation.

The Functional Reduction of Educational Bodies

This "functional reduction of the body" (of the program directors, teachers and the students) that accreditating processes exert can thus be seen then to exercise a complex psychosomatic authority over the *subjects* (those "subjected" to the authority); one that limits the ability of the *objects* (subjected long enough, one becomes an object in the discourse; unable to remove him/her self from the objects under analysis in the discourse) to think, to question, to interpret, and to live their own, independent professional and personal lives (Foucault, 1977, 164). The functional reduction of the body diminishes, limits, and ignores the local and contextual dynamics of practicality that are involved with both the teaching of, and the practice of the various disciplines especially as it relates to the various disciplines within the allied health field, where the essential goal revolves around the competent and compassionate delivery of health care services. And, as it regards professional preparation, the duly accredited director/teacher is often forced to teach his/her students how "to do" the profession (become an object), rather than how "to be" the professional (to maintain oneself as his/her own subject). As Lyotard has prophetically stated, the "death of the professor" becomes actualized in that instructors no longer need to be subjectively involved, they only need to serve as objects in the discourse, as pawns in the game, as remedial interlinkages between the authoritative source and the passively, receptive students (1984). Although directed at the hidden curriculum found in primary, middle and secondary public schools, Julie Webber's expansion on this concept can rightfully be applied to the rigid and overly standardized processes that structure the discursiveness of accreditation in higher institutions of learning, as well.

> School policy only recognizes the objectivity of its curriculum, and these contradictions force students to conform to rote discipline in unrealistic ways. There is an overwhelming emphasis on "knowing" in the cognitive sense, but not "believing," so that "doing" becomes a worthless, repetitive gesture on the part of students who can see nothing in education that speaks to them as people. (2003, 13)

In context with my experiences with a contemporary program accreditation in a technical, specialized and disciplined allied health field, I often feel as though my primary duties are to teach my students how to "do athletic training," how to become "effective objects" for the disciplined profession. As such, it has become increasingly difficult for me to teach my accredited, disciplined, and controlled students how "to be athletic trainers," how to be competent, local, contextual and critical subjects of their own volition with compassion, energy, and commitment to lifelong learning, the perpetual expansion of thought and skill, and the indispensable nature of health care service provision. A subtle difference illuminated only by semiotic distinctions perhaps, but seasoned professionals who have worked in real world healthcare settings with a compassion and commitment to helping people in need, or those who have supervised or educationally mentored shallow, technocratic and materially focused young emerging professionals/students, will acknowledge that a very powerful and meaningful peculiarity exists between "doing" and "being." In extending this discourse beyond my own particular discipline, I imagine that teacher educators working under the similarly controlling auspices of NCATE accreditation constraints feel similar frustration when it comes to the complex and largely qualitative processes that make up teacher education. Teaching future teachers how to "be" teachers is much more important and challenging than merely teaching them how to "do" teaching; a process that invariably must be made more exasperating and complex by the standards and guidelines that teacher accreditation requires and institutes over its practitioners. In short, this powerful aspect of the "hidden curriculum" that accreditation induces and mobilizes becomes a powerful and central characteristic of Dysacademia; and eventually it colonizes the individual identity and epistemological foundation of its organic constituencies. Over time, repeated subordination to the disciplinary "exercises" of those in power constructs a self-surveilling subject that no longer requires the physical presence of the authority figure in order for the hegemony and repression to continue (Foucault, 1977, 161). Accreditation in this sense then can be seen to cause the dysbulic (weakness of the will) and dyserethetic (abnormality of the intellect) object to operate under what Foucault calls a "technology of the self" (220). As such, the subjects of such a discourse are held hostage and prevented from seeing, experiencing, or reaching any sort of meaningful and distinctive self-appropriation, thus becoming objects of accreditation's discursive formation

In my field (athletic training), merely teaching students how "to do" athletic training potentially and typically translates into young professionals who, although they may prove highly capable of rote and mechanistic demonstrations of knowledge and skill, also demonstrate extreme difficulty analyzing intricate clinical problems, gener-

ating sound clinical reasoning skills, and inventing their own technical and clinical rationales for effective intervention. In short, the accredited production of specialized technocrats in athletic training are
accustomed to, disciplined to, and thus amenable to memorizing
"cook book recipes" for evaluation, treatment and rehabilitation
strategies, and not very capable of understanding the deeper and
more critical "why" and "how" issues that are involved with the actual delivery of healthcare services. Although these comments and
observations are specific to my field of athletic training and sports
medicine, I do not believe that other similarly accredited academic
programs are immune to this pedagogical problem. Just how does
NCATE, for example, assure that its like-disciplined future teachers
can adequately deal with the complex psycho-social-cultural-political-
economic issues that they will face every day in the classrooms of
America's heterogeneous populated schools? How do justly disciplined and accredited physical education teachers (also accredited by
NCATE) learn to deal with the many complex postmodern issues relating to gender identity, class, and sexuality that they habitually see
and experience with their students in the gymnasiums of our nation's
primary, middle and secondary schools? To Michel Serres, such
"standardization through control" critically hinders the student from
demonstrating what he calls the only true intellectual act; that being
"the ability to invent" (1997, 92-3). Simply stated, the more required
competencies and proficiencies there are, the less time and space
there is for invention—for both teacher and student. William Reynolds elaborates further on Foucault's "governmentality" concept by
unequivocally connecting pedagogy and curriculum to the discourse
of power, self-surveillance and technology of the body. Here, Reynolds' analysis of self-surveillance is worth quoting at length because
of its obvious relevance to the discourse surrounding the biopower
that accreditation exerts over its subjects.

> Instead of inflicting pain, the new techniques instill controlling habits and
> value-sustaining self-images, the intent was/is the increase of universaliz-
> able, efficient subjugation and control. These techniques proliferate in all in-
> stitutions involving the management of large numbers of people: the
> convent, the school, the barracks, and the university…The aim of this tech-
> nology is not mere control, as in the effective impositions of restrictions and
> prohibitions, but rather pervasive management gained through enabling as
> well as restrictive conceptions, definitions, and descriptions that generate
> and support behavior-governing norms. (2003, 35)

In his critique of those responsible for the current pedagogical
travesty we call education, Noam Chomsky uses the term *specialized
class*, to represent the power sources that control and operate an
"education for domestication practice"—the state (2000, 22). Typically, this specialized class includes a small group of privileged peo-

ple (politicians, policy makers, school administrators, curriculum directors, and, of course teachers) empowered to make very important and complex decisions for the benefit of the respective community, including those repeatedly excluded from membership in the specialized class. The economically stimulated technical hyper specialization of the disciplines previously described, has combined with the more recently popular perception of pedagogical necessity for program and degree accreditations have pushed the Tylerian-Behaviorist paradigm of education even further into the consciousness of university educators, program directors and administrators, alike. So, not only are higher educators involved in the most "industrial" and marketable fields now told "what" to teach ("whose knowledge?") for each discipline, but also they are now being told in large part "how to teach" (being disciplined). As it regards accreditation then, those "authorities and qualified educators" who formulate the standards and guidelines that accredited educational programs are required to pursue can be seen as representing the "specialized class of higher education," the authoritative sources of knowledge, truth, and value. In harmony with Foucault's biopower, Chomsky implies that the state is subversively and directly complicit in the production of "docile bodies," who because of their participation in a "pedagogy of stupidification" (22), are largely incapable of invention, independent and critical thought, and/or reaching a state of self-actualization; or what Foucault called "subjectification" (Foucault, 1977, 138). In the current discourse, disciplined accreditation of the technically specialized disciplines propagates a pedagogy of stupidification that subjects unknowing students to Dysacademia. Dysgnotic (abnormality of the intellect) athletic trainers and dysgnotic teachers of all varieties are thus *disciplined* as such, disciplined "to do" athletic training and teaching. Over time, this oppressive form of biopower steadily transform the disciplined subject(s) into dyscratic (weakness of the will) disciples that no longer see or feel the need to "do" anything different; or to "become" anything other than what they were disciplined to do.

Power, Control & Accredited Knowledge

In *Education and Power*, Michael Apple situates his arguments by boldly alerting the reader to the capitalistic reality and Marxist war cry that, "profit is more important than people" (1995, 4). As Apple articulates the inherent connection between power and knowledge, and the reproductive processes that our educational system perpetuates with the presentation and possession of "official knowledge" (41), by working under the assumption of a "neutral method of education" (11), and by reproducing "workplace resistance" in its objects of repression (23), he deftly constructs the deep and imbedded social roles of the school. Specifically, it is Apple's intent in this text to show

how schools naturally generate certain kinds of cultural, economic, social and political reproduction by maintaining the political hegemony of the ruling and industrial classes (38).

Central to this critical thesis is the notion that knowledge is actually a form of capital, and as such, that schools act as one of the primary modes of production of cultural commodities needed by a society (Apple, 41). Translation—this economically driven initiative and dynamical process has been instrumental in the post-WWII proliferation of the scientifico-technical knowledge fields in schools at all levels. By focusing on the production of technical knowledge in schools, especially at the postsecondary level, one can see how schools are complicit in maintaining a distinction between mental and manual labor. With the exception of "maintaining core academic values central to higher education and quality assurance," it is interesting and bothersome to note that direct or implicit references to social, cultural, natural, or humanistic endeavors are conspicuously absent from the Council for Higher Education Accreditation's stated purposes, recognition standards, or principles (2003). In short, if not in possession of the technical knowledge of a specific discipline, one can't move up the economic or social ladders of life, thus producing a hegemonic control over the cultural values and language that are perpetuated in school curricula. Witness the increasingly corporate influences over the various curricula, operating procedures, and expected educational outcomes of the modern University; prime examples of hegemonic control over the cultural capital needed for our neoliberal society. Resultantly, this corporately driven accumulation and control of technical and disciplinary knowledge also ensures that minorities, females, and the poor will get tracked into manual labor fields for the industrial labor force (46). In a perpetually hegemonic cycle then, state, corporate and most recently, educational leaders can be seen as socializing education and scientific research for capital and economic growth—especially at the postsecondary level. In the end, human and physical resources, significant monies, and other incentives and initiatives (increased faculty lines, teaching assistants, and high funded labs and schools) are being increasingly funneled into the academic research and service disciplines that can contribute to the "cultural capital" of the state, region and nation, while the disciplinary fields and professions that are not seen as being as culturally capitalistic are marginalized, reduced, and largely under-funded (read: humanities, arts and social sciences). Perhaps the most notable example of this trend can be seen in the increasing number of scientific labs named after high tech and biotech companies, and university business schools being named after wealthy private, or corporate donors.

As public primary and secondary schools across the nation come under increasing attack from state and federal education policy makers "to prove their effectiveness" under the No Child Left Behind Act, they have been forced to standardize their curriculums, their methods, and their evaluations in earnest attempts to objectively document the pedagogical outcomes that have been deemed necessary by the state. No longer is this phenomenon isolated to pre-university institutions. Increasingly, academic programs and higher educational institutions alike are being asked to objectively document specific learning outcomes in order to "justify" their pedagogical effectiveness, and thus their economic utility. Witness the recently formed Commission on the Future of Higher Education, headed up by Houston businessman and G. W. Bush crony Charles Miller, and its appointed task to examine whether standardized testing should be expanded into colleges and universities to "prove that students are learning and to allow easier comparisons on quality" (Arenson, 2006, 1). According to Mr. Miller, "what is clearly lacking is a nationwide system for comparative performance purposes, using standard formats," and the University of Texas' successful use of standardized tests to measure writing, analytical skills, and critical thinking is "proof" that it is possible to document real learning. To appease the faint of stomach though, Miller assures us that he does not envision a higher education version of the No Child Left Behind Act, because "there is no way you can mandate a single set of tests, to have a federalist higher education system." Interestingly, he then stated that he would like the commission to "agree on the skills college students ought to be learning...and to express that view forcefully." For those actually involved in higher education, this sort of "writing on the wall" means national standards, and national standards translate into a national curriculum. What's blatantly missing from this conversation and critique of higher education's performance are the various and complex sociocultural factors that play into many college students' ability to actually get through college and to become highly educated.

Most notably, the primary and secondary educational experiences, and the aforementioned motivations that many students possess for attaining a bachelor's degree can be seen to have profound and far-reaching effects on how a particular student navigates and behaves while in college. Thus appreciated, the No Child Left Behind Act has only exacerbated the dumbing down of the pool of qualified applicants by focusing more on standardized test results and the Western canon, and less on the arts, critical discourse, exposure to diversity and disparate viewpoints, meaningful writing, complex analysis, and the interpretation of complex phenomena. Additionally, it has been widely reported that the NCLBA has also directly contributed towards a radical and profound change in how teaching is "done"—teaching the test to ensure employment and advancement has become more in vogue, and critical pedagogy and "radical" approaches more dangerous.

Thus, the dramatic increase in formal ideological control and sur-veillance seen in our public schools can be paralleled with recent con-servative and neoliberal policies and initiatives designed to nourish and sustain our local and global economies, world position, and capi-talistic globalization efforts. And as disciplinary accreditation is largely found to subsist in the service, natural science and technology sectors of the academy, it can be seen then as a modus operandi that reinforces the neoliberal and corporatized nature of the modern Uni-versity that Aronowitz (2000), Giroux (2003, 1999), and Readings (1996) lament in their critical scholarship. Add to this the advent of standardized testing, and well-meaning and talented academicians will be further driven away from the business of the mind. Further evidence for the incestual connection between Aronowitz's meta-phorical "Knowledge Factory," and the importance placed on disci-plined and accredited majors of study can be seen in the significant expansion of specialized academic majors, faculty lines, and other material resources in the technology, science, and business fields, with a concurrent reduction in academic programs and support struc-tures that do not fit the needs, goals and functions of the 21st-century global economy landscape.

In short, classical and liberal educational programs that promote critical intellectual mass, epistemological flexibility, and ontological freedom, but contribute less readily to our economy have been largely marginalized in favor of more capitol-industrial degree programs. Lyotard viewed this as the "performativity of education," an insight that views education's primary mission to be one inherently con-nected with the local, national, and global economies (1984, 79). The silver lining in this situation, if there is one, is that very few if any formal disciplinary accreditation programs now exist for the classic liberal arts and social science based disciplines, a reality that academ-ics in those fields are delighted with, I'm sure. But, because SACS now requires a Quality Enhancement Plan outlining a specific plan for educational excellence for every academic program on a campus that it intends to accredit, the gauntlet seems to have been dropped on the humanities and liberal arts based programs, as well. As the University is becoming increasingly corporate in its acceptance and production of a consumer culture, a perceptible equivalent is gradu-ally evolving between the causes and effects that can be seen associ-ated with public school control, and the like processes gestating in postsecondary education as a result of its increasing love affair with program accreditation, standards and external control.

In *The Poverty of Postmodernism*, John O'Neill elaborates further on this sociological discourse—the social control described by Foucault, Chomsky, and others—by describing it as a "quasi-medical function," or more specifically as a "therapeutic state…whose function is to pac-ify clients, or to produce docile citizens" (1995, 40). Overzealous accreditation processes, in my field of athletic training for sure, can be charged with doing just this—producing book smart, grade producing, docile students; incapable of clinical reasoning, of inventing their own knowledge, or even of how to begin to construct knowledge in the absence of an "expert" (teacher) to dispense the necessary knowledge and insight. Walter Lippmann coined a descriptive, but bothersome idiom to represent what might be called a control society's citizens—the "bewildered herd." This expression, abounding with all of its visual and contextual robustness, does however effectively embody the converse of Chomsky's specialized class (cited in Chomsky).

> This specialized class carries out the "executive functions," which means they do the thinking and planning and understand the "common interests," by which they mean the interests of the business class. The large majority of people, the "bewildered herd," are to function in our democracy as "spectators," not as "participants in action." (2000, 22)

Of course, the specialized class also administers the various features of pedagogy and curriculum from within the paradigmatic constructs of existing ontological, political, economic, and ideological systems—in short, the political interference that SACS purportedly intended to prevent way back in 1963 with their initial mission statement. As postmodern and poststructural theorists have so eloquently pointed out, all systems are constructed with hidden agendas and ideologies, and all systemic language games, or texts seek to essentially replace another, an accreditation is no exception—it is indeed a socially constructed system wrought with political interference and hegemonic discourses. In deconstructing the accreditation system, it may be seen that many, if not most are infected more by the unknown than by political and economic ideologies. In short, attempting to consolidate and standardize all of the conceived cognitive, psychomotor and affective knowledge and skills necessary to practice a particular profession is a bit shortsighted, arrogant, and epistemologically dangerous. The discourse of accreditation then, denies the existence and exploration of what Serres calls the "multiplicity of multiples," specifically as it applies to alternative forms of inquiry, medical practice, professional behavior, and therapeutic intervention (1995a). To Foucault, this hegemonic dynamic represents a type of disciplinary power as it shifts analyses of power from the "macro" realm of structures and ideologies, to the "micro" level of bodies.

> In thinking of the mechanisms of power, I am thinking rather of its capillary form of existence, the point where power reaches into the very grain of individuals, touches their bodies and inserts itself into their actions and attitudes, their discourses, learning processes and everyday lives. (1980b, 39)

In other words, the parasitic reproduction of official knowledge, normalcy, class entitlement and the perpetuation of the social condition, lamented by Serres and others, are alive and well today, even in the various professional and academic disciplines, the latter of which were once thought to be "off limits" to such types of control (Serres & Latour).

> The more classification there is, the less evolution there is, the more classes there are, the less history there is, the more coded the sciences there are, the less invention and knowledge there are, the more administrating there is, the less movement there is...Parasitic growth has brought everything to a standstill. (1995a, 94)

In particular fields, this "parasitic growth" can often be evidenced when various accreditation requirements are put forth by a small band of policy makers (those in "power") with limited scope of practical experience, little to no knowledge of curriculum and pedagogy outside of the behaviorist paradigm, and perhaps even a bit "behind the times" with their own particular level of professional competence and proficiency(s). When this happens, those who set, dictate and evaluate the implementation and compliance with the various standards & guidelines required to attain accreditation hold a type of bio-power over those who actually "do" the teaching. Things become mechanized, routinized, in effect, standardized. Lost are notions of contextuality, individuality, intuition, and practical sensibility. Also mixed up in this complex web of power, political ideology, and reproduction is the intended focus of the educational process—students, teachers and ultimately, society itself. Becoming indoctrinated in this matter, with limited and ideologically motivated knowledge and a somewhat perverted notion of truth and democracy entitles the thriving herd member to the possibility of progressing onward—into the specialized class, or rather as a "quality" professional member of a discipline (Chomsky, 2000, 23). If one passes through the control mechanism called accreditation (provided he/she passes the subsequent state boards/exams which are built upon the accreditation module set forth), he/she can officially, and often legally, call himself or herself a teacher, or an athletic trainer. It is the same for physical therapy, medicine, law, etc.

Accreditation standards can not teach or direct qualified and energetic members of the academy how to prepare future clinicians, teachers and practitioners how to think critically, how to invent their own knowledge, or how to work towards a state of professional or personal subjectification. Accreditation guidelines cannot teach an athletic training educator how to "be" an athletic trainer educator, or how to teach students how to "be" or become an athletic trainer. It is just not that easy. Yes, competence begins with a mastery of the required psychomotor and cognitive skill sets relative to the field, but this is only part of the process. "Professional ontology" comes from real world experience that no one person, no organization can quantify, classify, standardize, or regulate for distribution to others. Being a competent and compassionate allied healthcare professional or teacher comes from caring about people, their problems, and their pain, from ontological and practical modesty, and from an insatiable desire to enhance one's professional and personal knowledge base. Learning how to be a professional derives itself from the ability and essential awareness of the need to continue constructing and inventing the knowledge needed to encounter unique and challenging medical and/or educational problems. Professionalism comes from process, from experience, and from wandering; not from product, standards, guidelines, and certainly not from a form, report, or other official pedagogical parchment of authority.

Nothing's Left Alone for Long in Control Societies

For anyone that's been enmeshed in the routine, the accreditation process is also historically renowned for its propensity to constantly "re-invent" procedures, standards and guidelines in an ever-present effort to be "progressive" in the name of quality assurance; in an effort to keep up with the latest innovations from behavioral and educational psychology, and from educational administration. Take note of principles number 2, 3, and 5 of CHEA's recognition standards for evidence of the need to continually "re-invent the wheel," or to what Hoskin and Macve have termed "calculability" (1993, 32): "demonstration of accountability," "purposeful change" and "needed improvements via ongoing self-examination, and continual reassessment of accreditation processes" (2003b, 2). Looked at differently, these procedural aspects of pedagogy and administration can also be seen as a manifestation of a Deleuzian control society in that, "In a control-based system nothing's left alone for long" (1995, 175). In accreditation, nothing's left alone for long either—new standards, new guidelines, new reports, new documentation, and new, *improved* ways of demonstrating quality assurance and teaching effectiveness. In short, the complex and stultifying process of academic program accreditation, and national standardized testing can be seen then as a *Deleuzian mechanisms of control,* in that it limits growth, heterogeneity, flexibility, locality, multiplicity, and individuality as it relates to curriculum, teaching, evaluation and administration.

Poststructural philosopher Gilles Deleuze gives credit to Foucault, the "father" of disciplinary societies and their principal technology, confinement, for being one of the first to recognize that we were actually in the midst of leaving disciplinary societies behind (1995, 174). As has been presented heretofore, disciplinary societies operate "by organizing major sites of confinement in which individuals are always going from one closed site to another, each with its own laws" (1995, 177). But as Deleuze points out, we have been gradually entering a society of control, one characterized by "new weapons," technology, communication, and varying other forms of social control.

> We're moving toward control societies that no longer operate by confining people but through continuous control and instant communication. People are of course constantly talking about prisons, schools, hospitals: the institutions are breaking down. But they're breaking down because they're fighting a losing battle. New kinds of punishment, education, health care are being stealthily introduced. (1995, 174)

Chiefly, disciplinary societies were confined by *molds*, while control societies are *modulated* by different ways of doing business, school reform, technological advancements, and other social transmutations that "never allow us to finish anything" (Deleuze, 1995, 178). Central to a Deleuzian control society are *codes*, or passwords that allow access to and rapid dissemination of digital information that inevitably work to provide the infrastructure of our society. In school settings these codes are everywhere, from student tracking data, grades, GPAs, standardized achievement tests, IQ tests, SAT scores, and other "objective" outcomes that purportedly signify learning, intelligence, ability and character. As in the business world, these control codes exist as commodities that are bought, sold, traded, and used as capital for advancement, and/or denial into the specialized class. Naturally then, the corporate University described by Readings, Giroux and Aronowitz qualifies as a Deleuzian-micro control society, a contention supported by Reynolds in his "Readingsonian" critique of the "ruined University."

> Schooling is being replaced by continual vocational education, and schools and universities are encouraged to compete for the 'best' results in terms of excellence. Many universities include the "techno-bureaucratic" notion of excellence on their logos. (2003, 91)

Accreditation agencies use codes too—outcome data like learning portfolios, graduation rates, national certification/licensing exam data, graduate and professional school placement, job placement are all essential parts of the codes that are routinely collected by accrediting agencies to evaluate and validate the external quality of an accredited program; codes of excellence. As such, accreditation codes serve as pivotal control modulators for the respective accrediting agency and help give shape and structure to the *grammatocentric panopticism* concept introduced by Hoskin & Macve (1993, 33). As such, proper administration, tracking and reporting of the requisite grammatocentric codes of quality and excellence can either help or hurt the respective program director who is inevitably responsible for management of the desired outcome codes needed to attain and sustain program accreditation. If the program director obediently follows the mandatory accreditation processes and edicts as a complicit and docile body, the students *should* be guaranteed a quality educational experience that meets the standards and values of the external judges. And of course, if the collected codes are deemed to be of acceptable *quality*, the students producing the codes will automatically become conscientious, reflective and critical practitioners in their respective disciplinary endeavors. However, as Deleuze prophetically pointed out, things in a control society are not that easy and predictable—things always change—accreditation standards and guidelines seem to be in a perpetual state of reform, always promising "best practices," and "continual quality assessment."

> One can envisage education becoming less and less a closed site differentiated from the workplace as another closed site, but both disappearing and giving way to frightful continual training, to continual monitoring or worker-school kids or bureaucrat-students. They try to present this as a reform of the school system, but it's really its dismantling. In a control-based system nothing's left alone for long. (1995, 175)

In addressing Herbert Spencer's age old and timeless pedagogical question, "what knowledge is of most worth?" (cited in Marshall, Sears & Schubert, 2000, 2), it is unquestionably the accrediting agency's knowledge that counts most in this repressive, mundane and predictably banal micro society that now relies on "credible" learning outcomes, measurable objectives and standards to control educational progress and effectiveness. The knowledge that counts in control societies can thus be seen as continual and restrictive modulators, or codes, that have been preferred by those in charge, those deemed expert enough to judge, and thus to accredit, control and discipline others. Those in power remain in power by enforcing what Lyotard calls their own *language games*, and by repressing the upstart entities by re-establishing and reverting to what are "normal" and acceptable operating procedures of the ruling class (Lyotard, 1984, 10). In accreditation processes, the powers of decision don't want to hear about what they have left out, what they may not know, or what the minority may think or know—they have the answers, the codes, and the language that is needed to assess and ensure quality.

In accreditation vernacular, these codes are expressed as "standards & guidelines," and usually include required "competencies and proficiencies" that have been deemed necessary for disciplinary expertise and practice. Together, the standards, guidelines, and various knowledge domains that the various accrediting bodies put forth construct the ruling and controlling language games that those seeking the ordained status of accreditation must meet and follow with utmost accuracy and compliance. Sadly, this directly implies that through language games, the function of our schools is to indoctrinate our students into becoming part of this self-serving and domesticated system, and thus to reinforce the two poles of control societies— *signatures* standing for individuals, and numbers or rankings standing for an individual's position in a *mass* (Deleuze, 1995, 179). Accredited programs provide the signature for the subjected and disciplined students by providing them with the necessary language games and codes needed to enter the respective specialized class. This signature typically comes in the form of a degree from an accredited institution, and/or academic program, which in turn, provides admission to the appropriate licensing, certification, or proficiency exam governed by the profession (athletic training certification exam, medical boards, teaching PRAXIS, etc.), while mass rankings are developed with the codes used by accrediting agencies to track the number of program graduates passing the respective entry-level competency exams (to externally assess the quality of the academic program). Foucault made similar observations about the functioning of disciplinary power in educational institutions.

> The activity which ensures apprenticeship and the acquisition of aptitudes or types of behavior is developed there by means of a whole ensemble of regulated communications (lessons, questions and answers, orders, exhortations, coded signs of obedience, differentiation marks of the "value" of each person and of the levels of knowledge) and by means of a whole series of power processes (enclosure, surveillance, reward and punishment, the pyramidal hierarchy). (1977, 218)

To improve upon this condition, and to lessen the impact of a potentially monstrous and socially debilitating bewildered herd, Chomsky challenges teachers to become intellectual seekers of the truth; to become more consilient in their knowledge base and understanding of the true complexities and objective interconnectedness of knowledge (2000). For disciplined instructors in specialized fields teaching at the university level, this means that they must be allowed to incorporate their real world, professional experiences (provided that they have any), with their own personal intuition; and that their pedagogy be allowed to adapt, to evolve, and to transcend as knowledge increases, and as social priorities change. For Deleuze, "our ability to resist control, or our submission to it, has to be assessed at the level of our every move…we need both creativity *and* a people" (1995, 176). In Serres' parlance, teachers must embrace the "third instruction," one which attacks the laziness, passiveness, and absurdness of "the center," one that embraces the synthesis of multiple forms of knowing and the uncertainty that accompanies the invention of new knowledge (Serres, 1997, 38). In effect, education at all levels should work to create an educational process that promotes a Freireian state of con-scientization, a Foucaultian subjectification in both personal and pro-fessional realms, or one in which students are allowed to "invent" their own knowledge base and to create their own identity and repre-sentation of their world. Subjectification in a Deleuzian sense is resis-tive and counter-controlling, it "eludes both established forms of knowledge and the dominant forms of power" (1995, 176). Thus situ-ated, authentic subjectivity may be the only constructive way to chal-lenge the status quo ideology, to attack the utter lack of true democracy that exists in our schools, and to restore hope and democ-ratic freedom for future generations.

To Chomsky, the state (policymakers, school boards, superinten-dents, principals) represents the specialized class, while teachers are the leaders of the bewildered herd. As it pertains to the current dis-course then, the specialized class can be seen as the accrediting agency and those who control it, while the program directors and in-structors working within the structure of accreditation are empow-ered to control the bewildered herd. In this type of hegemonic pedagogy, the bewildered herd simply needs to be controlled...to be kept in line...to merely be treated as spectators of knowledge and re-ality because they are too stupid to run their own affairs. Thus, the herd is in critical want of the specialized class to make sure that they won't have the opportunity to act on the basis of their "misjudg-ments" (2000, 23). In short, to play the game one has to play by the rules of the specialized class; they must learn the boundaries and terms of the discourse that accreditation has formulated, and subse-quently follow the accrediting agency's standards and guidelines for quality in order to be deemed "quality." In effect, they must become a binary part of the discourse of pedagogical control and surveillance that produces "students who are economically competitive but para-doxically monolingual (Reynolds, 2003, 74). As Reynolds points out in his articulation of "The Perpetual Pedagogy of Surveillance," it is ex-tremely ironic that "the trajectories being developed by the discourse in pedagogy are antithetical to the primary justification for the type of knowledge and thinking required by the global marketplace."

Becoming indoctrinated in this matter then, with limited and eco-nomically motivated knowledge and a somewhat perverted notion of truth and democracy entitles the thriving herd member to the possi-bility of progressing onward—into the specialized class, or rather as a "quality" professional member of a discipline (Chomsky, 2000, 23). If one plays this discursive game right, the bewildered herd member *may* move into the specialized class eventually; but success brings with it a compromise of sorts, as the now promoted herd member must be an accomplice in perpetuating the system that oppresses the remaining bewildered herd members. The specialized signature must now distinguish its mark on society by separating him/her self from those who are not members of the specialized class. In short, they must reproduce. In any case, one has to wonder just "who makes up the specialized class" that determines what knowledge, what methodologies, and what type of pedagogies are the best suited for achieving the "best outcomes" for the various accredited disciplines.

From this vantage point, it can be argued that any realistic desire to use the words "education" and "reform" in the same breath requires us to start with such a critical first step; that being to soften the effects from and reliance on the accreditation process as the ultimate judge of educational quality and credibility. We, the teachers, the pedagogues, must resist the administrative temptation to give into accreditation as the enlightening guide that will lead us to a simple and effective pedagogy. We, as a collective society must lighten the dependence and faith that we seem to have bestowed upon the accrediting process as the unquestionable "marker of educational quality." In short, educators, employers, politicians, and educational administrators must become better critical consumers of external control mechanisms, and the potential restraints and modulators that accompany their structure. In laying the responsibility for taking these steps squarely on the shoulders of the true pedagogical agents, the teachers, Chomsky acquiesces with this suggestion for a critical and democratic education.

> It is the intellectual responsibility of teachers—or any honest person, for that matter—to try to tell the truth. It is a waste of time to speak truth to power, in the literal sense of these words, and the effort can often be a form of self-indulgence. If and when people who exercise power in their institutional roles disassociate themselves from their institutional settings and become human beings, moral agents, then they may join everyone else. But in their roles as people who wield power, they are hardly worth addressing. It is a waste of time...A good teacher knows that the best way to help students learn is to allow them to find the truth by themselves. It is the obligation of any teacher to help students discover the truth and not to suppress information and insights that may be embarrassing to the wealthy and powerful people who create, design, and make policies about schools. (2000, 21)

After all, shouldn't all educators more fully embrace Serres' pedagogical contention that "the goal of teaching is to have teaching cease"? (Serres & Latour, 1995, 22). For those who believe in or adhere to Serres' educational philosophy, the question then becomes, just how can the formal, top down teaching that largely defines our current educational condition really cease when students are not taught how to "invent their own knowledge"?

As an athletic training educator and program director of an accredited program, I too am complicit in my own Foucaultian-Deleuzian control system—I am now forced to surveil and discipline my own pedagogy according to the system that I am now part of—an accredited educational program in the University. Whether I like it or not, I have become part of the discourse that is control, discipline and surveillance; I have formed the object of which I speak, and as such, I have become "attached to and retrospectively formed by the discourse surrounding it" (Pinar et al., 1995, 463). Logical and unavoidable, I had to become part of the discourse that is accreditation in order to better understand its discursive structure, and to gain access to the various language games that shape the discourse it has generated. Additionally, I have become acutely aware of the academic grim reaper that the accreditation discourse introduces, in that I am now profoundly leery of succumbing to Lyotard's "death of the professor." Because of my personal and professional attachment to the discursive formation of accreditation, I now realize that I must find constructive ways to avoid being "killed," to prevent the detransformation of my pedagogy, and to resist simply throwing out a cookbook curriculum with simple linear steps to disciplined success. At the same time, I must maintain my intricate connection to the discourse by preserving our program accreditation, while simultaneously honoring my professional commitments by continuously working to promote the various values, ideals and knowledges needed to practice athletic training. I must be an accredited disciple, yet I must also resist the necrotic spaces that control and discipline my mission, my self, and my consciousness. In borrowing the term "oppositional postmodernism" from Foster, Reynolds summarizes the complex and exhaustive challenges that discursive practices present to pedagogues.

> The problematic is to avoid totalizing theoretical positions yet at the same time amplify some type of viable oppositional discourse/practice. The question becomes, can we develop a type of "oppositional postmodernism" (Foster 1983) that doesn't' fall into a totalizing discourse, a new orthodoxy, or a fatalistic, nihilistic position? (2003, 83)

If along the way, the disciplined and controlled student (or leader) steps out of line, seeks critical change outside the controlled spaces, or "accidentally" becomes critically conscious, he or she will not make it through the game. He or she will remain one of the herd members. If I, as a program director, were to strongly and critically challenge certain aspects of my respective accreditation process to the specialized class who controls my destiny to a certain extent, I would be sure to suffer difficult and stressful repercussions when my next accrediting cycle arrives. For sure, I would be subject to increased scrutiny as my reviewers read (surveil) my self-study, annual reports, and the myriad reams of papers and documents that I must continually produce, reproduce and update, visit my sites, and interview my students, faculty, and clinical instructors. Therefore, I must fly under the radar of the surveilling accrediting agency, while at the same time holding true to my particular principles of higher education and athletic training education. I believe, as did Deleuze, that "subjectification, events and brains are more or less the same thing," and that "what we most lack is a belief in the world" (1995, 176). Educators must work persistently and tirelessly to find creative, promising and reconstructive ways to "precipitate events that elude control and engender new space-times ." If the academy genuinely intends to immobilize the technocratic intellectualism now paralyzing the academy, with its pathological production of dysgnosia and dyscrasia, it must find ways to counteract the discursive formation that is accreditation, and it must resist the increasing neoliberal-corporate influences that now define its character and mission.

So, whose knowledge and whose methods are of most worth in today's University? The knowledge put forth by specialized classes that rule the accreditation machines, of course. The state after all, or in this case the "external control that is not the state," has all the answers needed for teaching students how to "be" professionals. The state/specialized class has no need, or interest, in the various contextual localities and multiplicities that make both the teaching and practicing of athletic training exciting, open, and unpredictable, uncontrollable, *unstandardizable*. In summing up his complex and polymorphous conception of *discipline*, Foucault attempts to demonstrate that it is not something simple, something concrete, nor is it something unitary; while at the same time demonstrating how power and discipline can and do operate within the accreditation process.

> Discipline may be identified neither with an institution nor with an apparatus; it is a type of power, a modality for its exercise, comprising a whole set of instruments, techniques, procedures, levels of application, targets; it is a 'physics' or an 'anatomy' of power, a technology. And it may be taken over either by 'specialized' institutions, or by institutions that use it as an essential instrument for a particular end, or be pre-existing authorities that find in it a means of reinforcing or reorganizing their internal mechanisms of power. (1977, 215)

It is my contention that schooling, at any level must be based first on Serres' line of reasoning that invention is its central purpose, not reproduction and meaningless debate; and that it must be connected to the larger socio-cultural mission of education, regardless of what the chosen discipline is/will be. Disciplinary and professional development should be secondary and subservient to the self and socio-cultural inventive. In order to do this, to invent, students must be shown ways to myriad "third places." That is, all parties in the pedagogical relation, both student and teacher must be *allowed to* endure the pain, the discomfort, the uncertainty, and most importantly an open "boundarylessness of self" that accompanies a critical ontological evolution into the third place (Serres, 1997, 43). For this to happen, teachers, intellectuals, and administrators must reach out and interact with students as subjects viably interconnected with the purposes of education and democracy, rather than merely treating students as passive, economically oriented objects knotted within the disciplinary process of a controlled education. Teachers must of course possess and exhibit a profound and genuine level of professionalism relevant to their professional and academic fields, and they must surely adhere to academic and professional standards that subsume both the discipline's knowledge base with the teachers' professional experiences; but much, much more is needed at this critical juncture of our social and natural histories.

To be clear, I am not calling for pedagogical anarchy or professional nihilism in any manner, shape or form. Standardization of knowledge, of method, of delivery and thought is unethical, unprofessional, and counter-productive to the larger mission of the University writ large. And above all, university educators of all disciplines must be allowed and encouraged to teach students how "to be" citizens with varied professional lives and purposes, not just merely how "to do" their chosen profession. Young professionals must be critically and ontologically connected to the larger problems of society, and to what is required to live "in" a democracy, not just live "off" of a democracy. All educators, regardless of their impassioned field of study and particular scholarly specialization should take serious heed in their responsibility to help foster and develop what Berger calls a "sociological consciousness" in all students (Berger, 1963). Most educators do just this, they educate; but for those operating from within the restrictive framework of accreditation, this project is certainly more difficult and anxiety ridden. From this vantage point, it can be argued that any realistic desire to use the words "education" and "reform" in the same breath, requires us to start with such a critical first step; that being to soften the effects from and reliance on the accreditation process as the ultimate judge of educational quality, value and credibility. We, the teachers, the pedagogues, we must resist the administrative temptation to give into accreditation as the *enlightening* guide that will lead us to a simple and effective pedagogy. We as a collective society must lighten the dependence and faith that we seem to have bestowed upon the accrediting process as the unquestionable "marker of educational quality." As Deleuze says, "we must fight the "widespread progressive introduction of a new system of domination" (1995, 182). Rather, we ought to look to those professionals in the various fields that exude a true and genuine professionalism in all its various manifestations for guidance as to how to teach students how to "be." Better yet, we the members of the academy should embrace and seek out further and more complex professional experiences relative to our field of study, and to our society writ large as the central foci of curricular and pedagogical guidance. Technical competence and professional expertise are not enough; not for our society and its myriad challenges and problems, and not for what is required to "be" a professional in any disciplinary field.

In short, educators, employers, politicians, and educational administrators must become more critical recognizers, consumers, and resistors of external control mechanisms, and the potential restraints and modulators that accompany their structure. As William Reynolds puts it, we must all become more concerned with "wide-awakeness" by moving away from the habitual perception that long-term control and power have upon us as subjects in the system (2003, 66). To do this, to become more wide-awake, Reynolds suggests that we 1) actively "move towards a passionate engagement with social criticism," one capable of deconstructing the various myths, paradigms, and modes of thought that structure our consciousness, and 2) pay heed to the language games that we play, and more importantly are part of, and 3) become more engaged in a critical, transformative, and connected praxis of pedagogy. If academics want to maintain their rightful places as intellectuals in the academy, they must work to open up spaces of freedom, deconstruct boundaries that impede thought, and effectually challenge the various questions "swirling around the institution of standards and accountability." In laying the responsibility for professional and personal "wide-awakening" squarely on the shoulders of the true pedagogical agents, the teachers, Chomsky assents with those sentiments put forth by Reynolds, Readings, Aronowitz, Ford, and others for a critical and democratic education.

> It is the intellectual responsibility of teachers—or any honest person, for that matter—to try to tell the truth. It is a waste of time to speak truth to power, in the literal sense of these words, and the effort can often be a form of self-indulgence. If and when people who exercise power in their institutional roles disassociate themselves from their institutional settings and become human beings, moral agents, then they may join everyone else. But in their roles as people who wield power, they are hardly worth addressing. It is a waste of time...A good teacher knows that the best way to help students learn is to allow them to find the truth by themselves. It is the obligation of any teacher to help students discover the truth and not to suppress information and insights that may be embarrassing to the wealthy and powerful people who create, design, and make policies about schools. (2000, 21)

After all, shouldn't authentic educators fully embrace Serres' pedagogical contention that "the goal of teaching is to have teaching cease"? (Serres & Latour, 1995, 22). Then again, just how can formal teaching cease if the control, surveillance and disciplinary practices associated with much of our educational endeavors persist at their current levels? Furthermore, if the playing field and the rules for playing in order to "promote" the perpetual quality enhancement and outcome plans that "regulating" agencies such as SACS (now) and the federal government's commission to study higher education (future) mandates are constantly changing, just how will the academy overcome these hegemonic forces?

CHAPTER FIVE

Undisciplining the Disciplined

Writing has nothing to do with signifying. It has to do with surveying, mapping, even realms that are yet to come.

---Deleuze (1987, 4)

We have lost the world. We've transformed things into fetishes or commodities, the stakes of our stratagems; and our a-cosmic philosophies, for almost half a century now, have been holding forth only on language or politics, writing or logic.

---Serres (1995b, 29)

Thus far, I have been intending to pronounce and describe the various institutional, social, cultural and political forces that have historically interacted and contributed to a concept that I have called Dysacademia. In so doing, I have also attempted to illustrate various autobiographical links to this complex historical-cultural phenomenon in an effort to openly situate the local, contextual and subjective nature of this particular critique. Despite my personal biases, I also see Dysacademia as a prominent and far-reaching *epidemic* that exists beyond the personal realm, and one that merits considerable energy and thought by all those vested in the University and its utility. Thus, a systematic deconstruction of the University is required in order to develop and posit potentially effective prophylactic measures that may one day prove capable of preventing Dysacademia from mutating into a *pandemic* situation, with a life, energy, and reproductive capacity capable of long(er) lasting sustenance. If an effective intervention strategy is not devised and implemented soon for the postmodern University, those of us concerned with the fate of higher education face the dire risk of confronting a viral pathology with the very real potential to become resistant to any prescription, or treatment that may be cultivated. Thus situated, the current discourse will continue in the descriptive mode with an attempt to articulate the net effect(s) that Dysacademia has had upon the various constituencies of the University.

Dyskinesia, Dyslogia & Closed Space

As documented in Selingo's 2003 study on higher education in *The Chronicle of Higher Education*, there now exists an inordinately high percentage of students entering the college and university ranks with deep-seated industrial and capitalistic notions of what a college degree signifies, what the University's utility is, and what the primary goal of graduating from college should be—a good paying job, and the rightful entry into a higher social class. Yes, most colleges still have core requirements steeped in the traditional liberal arts curriculum that are designed to induce a certain level of moral, civic and critical awareness in our educated elite; yes, many colleges are experimenting with various pedagogical manifestations of interdisciplinary curricula in an attempt to hold on to the liberal arts and humanities; and, yes critical, transformative institutions of higher education still exist in this country, and they are doing their best to turn out critical and reflexive citizens for our democratic society. But the fundamental problem that describes and hampers the typical Dysacademic University lies in the bare fact that these positive and exemplary instances seem to be in the ever increasing minority, and the majority is now made up of general education institutions, online, virtual universities, and money making "degree stampers" who increasingly appear to resemble businesses more so than they do inventors of individual subjectivity, transformation and intellectual complexity.

I am not alone, nor am I original in this particular mode of thinking and level of concern, either. Derrida extended Immanuel Kant's 1979 concerns (put forth originally in Kan'ts *The Conflict of the Faculties"*) regarding the University by further lamenting the powerful and expanding censorship roles that developed secondary to the "Gewalt" disciplinization of the University, and the technology based, aphilosophical "non-teaching" culture that germinated when the state began to control and dictate higher education (2004). Additionally, Lyotard (1984) prophetically warned us of this pending development in 1979, while Giroux (1999, 2003), Readings (1996), Aronowitz (2000) and Ford (2002) are amongst those who have recently been loud and clear with similar concerns in the subsequent decades, and as such, have effectively helped keep this discursive exercise alive. In fact, The Carnegie Foundation for the Advancement of Teaching has taken up this cause in earnest by publishing research regarding American undergraduate education, and its failure to instill genuine moral and civic responsibility in its collective student body (Colby, Ehrlich, Beaumont, & Stephens).

> The consequences of this cultural climate include a growing sense that Americans are not responsible for or accountable to each other; a decline in civility, mutual respect, and tolerance; and the preeminence of self-interest and individual preference over concern for the common good. Goals of personal advancement and gratification too often take precedence over social, moral, or spiritual meaning. (2003, 7)

Central to the preceding theoretical exposition of Dysacademia lies an archeological and genealogical analysis of how neoliberalism, power/authority, disciplinarity, and control have all coagulated and interacted to affectively produce various states of "dys" (dysbulia, dyscrasia, dyserethesia, and dysgnosia) in the organic constituents of the University—the students *and* the professorate. Thus viewed, the end result (or "outcome") is that the Dysacademic University can metaphorically be seen as a *closed site* governed by disciplinary modes of thinking and seeing that is heavily controlled by authoritative and legitimate disciplinary and administrative practices and professional paradigms, and is predominantly shaped by neoliberal and corporate initiatives designed to optimize local, national and now international markets and modes of production. Together, these interconnected sociocultural/economic forces have (dys)formed higher education into a location designed primarily for specialized, technical and "legitimate" economic training. Each of these factors can be appreciated as intricately interconnected powers working cohesively to drastically alter the pursuit, production and possession of knowledge, and thus also, the construction and identity of the subjective and independent knower. Derrida is quick to build upon the concerns of Kant and F. W. J. Schelling (in 1969) by pointing out that any discourse, rhetoric or methods formed by the censoring state "in the name of knowledge according to the rhythm of techno-science" effectively excludes and marginalizes those types of knowing and being with little to no perceived performative value to the state (2004, 78). After all, what culture, what society, or what economy needs artists, writers, musicians and unrestrained thinkers?

Sliding into these marginalizing and exclusionary "epistemodic" spaces has also been a concern for Michel Serres as he considers the power, relations and irony that scientific knowledge has with law, reason, and judgment.

> Solitude slides so quickly toward inventive delirium and error that the site of knowledge production is never a relation between an individual and his object, but rather one between a growing body of researchers checking on

one another and a carved out specialty, defined and accepted by them. (1995b, 21)

In this segment of *The Natural Contract*, Serres goes on to communicate the "tacit and stable contracts" that bond the knower/learner to the disciplinary enterprise (in this case, science), and its particular discourse(s), and languages of authority. Serres summarizes the inherent connections that readily exist between disciplinarity, control, and performative neoliberalism in a rather lengthy passage that best illustrates the pathogenesis of Dysacademia, and its subsequent and authoritative affects on the knowing subjects.

> Let's just list the successive incarnations of this subject: beginning in infancy, the individual enters into relation with the community, which is already bound by this contract; well before starting to examine the objects of his specialization, he presents himself before accredited examining boards, which decide whether or not to receive him among the learned; after having learnedly worked, he presents himself once again before other authorities, who decide whether or not to receive his work into their canonized language. There can be no knower without the first judgment, no knowledge without the second. (1995b, 21)

Although he is referring specifically to the "business" of science in these passages, Serres' remarks can readily be applied to any discipline, or academic program of study in the Dysacademic University. In this vein then, it may be helpful to think of the *subject* as any college/university student, and the *successive incarnations* as the four, or five, year program of study typically undertaken in a modern University by the subject. To begin with, we are reminded that over 90% of all entering freshmen choose an academic major based primarily on job and earnings potential (Selingo, 2003, A10). Realized as such, "entering into relation with the community" can be seen to represent the choosing of, and immersion into a specific academic major that holds economic and social promise, and typically one that is also governed by a certain "disciplinary contract" that dictates and disperses the official knowledge, language, and truths associated with the respective disciplinary field. Derrida simplifies this notion by differentiating between "philosophers" and "mathematicians," whereby the inventive and reasoning learner embodies true philosophy (an "end" to "true education" found in the *Bildung* model of education), and the rigid, linear follower of content and law is the mathematician (a subject of biotechnological methods) (2004, 70). As subjects progress through highly structured and sequenced disciplinary curricula, the number and types of open spaces for philosophical, inventive and uncensored thought gradually and progressively begin to close down. Thus, each subject's successive incarnations become less, and less "spacious" as time passes on for each subject. In reflecting upon the historical and social factors that have led to this "space closing," Colby et al.'s analysis clearly reflects the central arguments presented herein.

> Science and scientific inquiry emerged as the dominant model for learning in college, including moral and civic learning. Free, open, and scientific inquiry would promote intellectual and social progress...Despite the considerable advantages of the new arrangements, the internal dynamics of specialized academic disciplines unintentionally created deep divisions in campuses, often isolating students and faculty into groups based on discipline, major, or school, with little opportunity for cross-disciplinary conversations. (2003, 30)

Ironically, this closing down of the disciplinary spaces can actually be seen to occur long *before* the subject "starts to examine the objects of his specialization" on his/her own terms, or subjective dispositions. In Derridean parlance, this means that systems that remain empirical, and thus are not based on reason, only provide a technical and not an architectonic unity; "know how" is just an order of human knowledge lacking rational architectonics and constructed by an institution regulated by profitable applications (2004, 58). Simply put, it is critically ironic that the more each subject progresses through the sequenced Dyscurriculum, the "less" space there is for each subject to wander, struggle, and invent their own subjective space and worldview; things have already been "figured" out for them to some extent or another, and so wandering off into other adjacent and distant spaces is largely viewed as a meaningless folly with little academic value. Students continue to marginalize other forms of knowing and being as a university student, they further focus on the socioeconomic prizes awaiting them at matriculation. In Derrida's terms, they become the "biotechnological" because they learn action and content relative to their chosen discipline, but not the critical reasoning skills needed to organize and coordinate the organic form of a system; something he calls "architectronics" (57).

Situating this problematic to my disciplinary field, a student in a highly specialized field like athletic training may in fact be learning more advanced and practical knowledges and skills relative to the field of athletic training in their later academic years, they are not typically encouraged or motivated to wander and struggle in the open spaces outside their major academic field. Because of the extreme technocratic and economic value now placed on one's chosen major field in the Dysacademic University, those "other" academic spaces capable of informing and transforming the subject in "other" cultural and social ways (i.e., the liberal arts courses that typically fulfill the "academic core" requirements at most institutions) have become marginalized, under-appreciated, and even ignored by our culture because of their perceived "antiperformative" value. As a result, subjective epistemological and ontological experiences and development in most "non-academic major spaces" gradually and progressively close down as subjects advance through their respective disciplinary college curricula.

In effect then, although the subject *may* be on the verge of becoming highly competent in his/her chosen field, he/she is simultaneously becoming habitually *subjected* to the affects of Dysacademia—he/she is gradually developing various states of "dys" subjectification. The subjects thus become *objects* produced by the Dysacademic system; in effect, they are *objected* to a dyseducation. Once the subject successfully passes through the disciplined, structured, and now typically accredited curriculum, he/she are then re-subjected to "accredited examining boards" in order to ascertain if they have become sufficiently, or proficiently "learned" enough to become a member the specialized *Chomskian* disciplinary class. If they have learned (been trained) well enough, they become entitled to the cultural capital that is so valued by today's neoliberal society—a well-paying job and esteemed position in a higher level of the social hierarchy. But in the end, one must wonder if all postsecondary graduates actually become *higher* educated? Are today's baccalaureates now citizens capable of dealing with the critical social, cultural and political issues that face our current and future generations? Or as Aronowitz laments, are today's baccalaureates merely "techno-idiots" trained to produce "something" that fundamentally and myopically works towards the enhancement of our nation's gross domestic product (2000)? Judging by the sentiments put forth by Colby, et al., there are grave concerns over what "is," and what "is not" happening on the campuses of America's higher education institutions.

> We are concerned with the development of the whole person, as an accountable individual and engaged participant in society—local, state, national, and global. Responsibility includes viewing oneself as a member of a shared social structure and as a fair target of evaluative attitudes, such as praise and blame. (2003, 18)

> Although some institutions of higher education are seeking ways to stimulate political engagement as well as other kinds of civic participation and leadership, we have found that this aspect of civic responsibility is less attended to in higher education, even among schools with strong commitments to moral and civic learning. (19)

Sitting Still & Paying Attention

By dictating who can and cannot enter the respective specialized class (by conferring degrees, awards, and honors), the disciplinary and control-surveillance based mechanisms of the University expressly take hold of the subject by functioning as disciplinary and professional "gate keepers." The control and surveillance mechanisms don't stop there however—depending upon the chosen disciplined field, the learned object is continually subjected to disciplinary scrutiny as his/her work is appraised for acceptance/rejection into the respective canonized language. In our current neoliberal epoch, the canonized language that Serres alludes to can be viewed as either the traditional canons associated with scientific/academic knowledge, or those canonized languages now generated by performative and economic modes of production (i.e., is it a valuable commodity or fetish?). This contractual recognition thus re-illuminates the significance of Herbert Spencer's timeless question regarding "whose knowledge is of most worth," while simultaneously illustrating the decentered position and space that the individual, knowing subject now occupies in the Dysacademic institution. Thus (dys) situated, the knowing subject paralyzed in a controlling and disciplinary structure of the University becomes ill with additional "dys" conditions, most notably "dyskinesia" (impairment of the power of voluntary movement, Miller & Keane, 1983, 348), and "dyslogia" (impairment of the power of reasoning, Miller & Keane, 1983, 348). The submissive and docile nature of disciplined pedagogy that induces dyskinesia and dyslogia is aptly captured by Serres' analysis of the contractual relationships our society has come to rely upon for disciplinary knowing and being.

> Thus experienced by the former individual subject, me or you, an obedient receiver or transmitter and a possible inventive producer of knowledge, the process of knowing runs from trials to cases to causes, from judgments to choices, and so never leaves the juridical arena. (1995b, 21)

In medical parlance, the care provider cannot merely treat the symptoms of dyskinesia and dyslogia, or else they will simply return, stronger and more robust than ever. Rather, the care provider attempting to extinguish Dysacademia must fully scrutinize and treat the root causes of these interconnected pathologies in order to resolutely purge the patient of its pain, discomfort, and eventually its various dysfunctions (symptoms).

If this is indeed the case that the socio-cultural role of the University has unashamedly shifted towards neoliberal principles of market value, commodification and technocratic expertise and away from intellectual diversification and maturity, then the majority of young citizens entering our complex, post-human/ modern /disciplinary /colonial /9/11 /structural world as professional policy makers, politicians, business leaders, educators, and eventually parents, are lacking a certain critical mass required to confront the immediate and long-term posthuman conditions staring the collective "us," right in the face. Something needs to change before the negentropic (negentropy in a closed system is dangerous due to the structural constraints that define and objectify the system) and closed University system self-implodes upon itself, and subsequently obliterates our civilization, our humanity, and our ecosphere in the process.

Impermeable Membranes, Language Games & Antiosmosis

In *The Postmodern Condition* (1984), Jean Francois Lyotard examines the status of science, technology and the arts, and the typical ways that knowledge and information are portrayed and shared in the Western world from a postmodern perspective. This landmark text centers on the development, implementation, perpetuation and deconstruction of knowledge, and their relation to power and authority, by way of what Lyotard calls a "meta narrative." In particular, Lyotard critiques the sociological and historical development of knowledge, language games, narratives & subsequent meta narratives, performativity, disciplines, modern systems theory, and inter-disciplinarity. In brief, Lyotard contends that language games, the base form of communication involved in truth assertions that drive all human communication (15), and knowledge, a pragmatic competency in playing a particular language game (53), are inextricably linked and coalesce to create small narratives that serve as authoritative bases for understanding reality (23). In time, the smaller, micro-narratives that persist and gain legitimacy merge to construct larger macro, or meta narratives that signify authoritative claims to truth and reality. Essentially then, the various languages and discourses that drive the constructed meta narratives function to circumscribe the epistemological contract that Serres analyzes; a phenomenon perhaps best epitomized by the hegemonic authority that science quietly enjoyed without distraction prior to postmodern and post-positivistic deconstruction of the meta narratives upon which it had been founded. Lyotard expands the conversation regarding our condition by exposing the postmodern delegitimization of science's modern meta narratives that has occurred recently, and in doing so demarcates postmodern science as being "discontinuous, catastrophic, non-rectifiable, and paradoxical" (60).

Within this context Lyotard expresses his somewhat paradoxical views on the disciplines, and their resultant effects upon the development and disbursement of knowledge in the various subjects of learning and inquiry. In one sense, he argues for a post-disciplinary structure whereby working at the limits of what rules permit in order to invent new moves, might allow the development of new rules and thus, new games, yet he simultaneously critiques and remains leery of any narratives that have the potential to turn into meta narratives (Lyotard, 1990, 100). In order for this to occur, one kind of inquiry would not be able to dominate others as the "way" to knowledge, and thus, the structure of research and curricula would be resituated in order to maximize the multiplicity of small narratives. For Michel Serres, classic epistemology in the "modern" sense is thus unattractive, unoriginal, and lazy because it merely reproduces and repackages old ideas and information with "ultra technical vocabulary that breeds fear and exclusion" (Serres & Latour, 1995, 24); and thus, an "authentic epistemology can be seen then as the art of inventing, the springboard for passing from the old to the new" (14). To Foucault, "the challenging of all phenomena of domination at whatever level or under whatever form they present themselves—political, economic, sexual, and institutional, and so on" represents the essential purpose and critical foundation of philosophy (cited in Bernauer & Rasmussen, 1988, 20).

In referring to that fragmented disciplinary and controlling University that I have previously described, systems scientist Ervin Laszlo comments on the awkward social and professional quandaries that can occur at the water cooler or copy machine, in simple terms that most professionals can appreciate with honest and candid reflection.

> The literary historian specializing in early Elizabethan theater may not have much in common with a colleague specializing in Restoration drama, and will find himself reduced to conversation about the weather when encountering an expert on contemporary theater. (1996, 2)

And as Laszlo points out, the consequences of this modern educational paradigm are that knowledge is largely pursued in isolation, thus presenting fragmentary and isolated pictures of our perceived reality, rather than being pursued in depth and integrated breadth, which would give us a more coherent and continuous picture of the various structures and organizational hierarchies of knowledge. Karin Cetina (1999) addresses this concern and extends the discourse surrounding it further, by positing that we live in an "epistemic culture" structured and organized largely around the production of expert scientific knowledge. If Cetina's assertion is indeed true, and I believe that it is, then knowledge must be viewed as more than *information*, more than testable material, and much more than fragments or sound bites from the various fields; while it must also be realized that "science" has effected the construction and sustenance of impermeable barriers that prevent the osmotic transfer of knowing, ideas, and information in and amongst the various knowledge domains. While we have previously articulated some of the genealogical and archeological factors that have influenced the fragmentary and solitary nature of today's academic disciplines, and thus the discourses that shape, constrain and define them, there are additional and deeply allied ingredients that must be investigated if we are to fully understand how academia can be seen as a closed space.

In extending this discourse beyond that of science alone, and into the economic and philosophical spheres Lyotard deconstructs the innate connections that exist in our modern society between science and cultural power by reminding the reader that scientific knowledge "does not represent the totality of knowledge," and rather that it "exists in conflict and in addition to other narrative ways of knowing" (1984, 7). In considering the typical consumer's strong hyper-reliance and blind faith on scientific knowledge, in combination with the perception that other forms of knowing are marginalized and oppressed because of their perceived subjectivity and minimal economic value, one might wonder just where this situates our current society and what "it really knows." In short, who really controls what counts as knowledge and what doesn't, and, how does one gain access to the performative and legitimized fields of knowledge that are deemed valuable and critical to society? Perhaps more importantly, does there not exist any sort of "middle space" when it comes to knowledge, its production, or its possession?

For Lyotard and other critical theorists, the topographical splitting of the various knowledge fields into specialized disciplines is not the central concern. Rather, the various language games, semiotic chains and specialized discourses that have concurrently been constructed to uphold and enforce notions of power and authority stand as the focal alarm point; especially with the socially legitimated economic and scientific fields that now dominate our social consciousness (Lyotard, 1984, 8). To Lyotard, disciplinary language games thus become responsible for the construction of hypomobile and "antiosmotic" barriers keeping those not in possession of the appropriate language apparatus "out" of the game; which subsequently leads to the "occidental" (knowledge and power being two sides of the same question) development of the "knowledge-power" duality that dictates "how" knowledge is generated, "what" knowledge is worthy, and "who" gets to make knowledge decisions. Inevitably, this postmodern actuality leads to a concomitant recyclable production and regulation of knowledge and authority that feeds off of various language games and marginalizes "internodal" inquiry and mobility, while preventing unique, local and personal inventions of knowledge that are capable of providing a material contextuality, subjectivity and partial objectivity for each individual consumer. In the end, perhaps Lyotard's language games best distinguish and perpetuate the disciplinary fragmentation of knowledge that now exists in our culture; a "comminution" of knowledge that will inevitably (already has?) lead to an intellectual ineptitude of sorts, and one that effectively renders E. O. Wilson's challenge for higher education a serious and formidable obstacle for educators and concerned citizens alike.

It is here specifically that Lyotard's theoretical position seems to comply with the poststructural approach I am presenting, but with one additional caveat—Lyotard seems to contradict his postdisciplinary views in other sections of *The Postmodern Condition*. Specifically, Lyotard seems to reject any interdisciplinary organization of knowledge, as it implies to him a "common measure"; or, the development of new language games and meta narratives, which of course, reifies existing narratives and eventually, meta narratives (Lyotard, 1984, 50). In "defining" a poststructural structure as "an ordered multiplicity of ordered multiplicities," Michel Serres' poetic thoughts can be seen to effectively soften Lyotard's extreme, and perhaps somewhat nihilistic poststructural concern with a more modest appreciation for the power and epistemological infinity of "multiplicities" and fragile syntheses of thought.

> The work of transformation is that of the multiple. (1995a, 101)

> It is not an everyday occurrence when there is a potential meeting between refined branches of knowledge, overt phenomena, and everyday language. We need to conceive the multiple as such…we need it in the social sciences and the humanities. (1995a, 103)

In my view, higher education ought to provide the same critical and philosophical foundation for all of its subjects; the ability to challenge, to deconstruct, to operationalize, and to appreciate multiple problematic perspectives should be endowed in all college and university graduates; regardless of their chosen field of study, or subsequent professional line of work. Or, as Derrida argues, higher education should be based on an artistic philosophy that is novel, unstable, unteachable and premised upon the knowledge of "the essential ends of human reason"; and this philosophical education should empower the student to transform their character, to develop aptitude to see the inanity of all finite knowledge" (2004, 71). But for this to happen, for higher education to become more philosophical and liberating, the history of academia and its power to reproduce must first be understood and appreciated as a chaotic, yet incestual process and system.

Andrew Abbott, a self-professed "eclectic," has attempted to eradicate the intellectual boundaries between interpretative and positivistic work in sociology and kindred fields as his central theme for the *Chaos of Disciplines*. Although largely based on sociology and the other social sciences, Abbott's work regarding the history of American academia and its industrial, economic, intellectual and social roles in our society shed considerable light on the current status of today's academic status. In Abbott's words, the aim of this particular text is more general than sociology, in and of itself.

> While a principled defense of eclecticism and indeed of a certain form of
> relativism is the personal aim of the book, understanding recent develop-
> ments in sociology is its substantive one. (2001, xii)

Abbott is clear to elucidate the fact that he does not challenge the
foundational uncertainties of epistemologies ("there is indeed not one
sociology, but many"), and seems to not want to contribute to the development and/or perpetuation of the grand meta narrative argument, but does set out to challenge the way that scholars in his field
interact. In his view, too many sociologists betray a common structural pattern, or a "universal knowledge upon whose terrain the local
knowledges wander," and it is this behavior that prevents meaningful
and productive epistemological cohesion or mutual understanding.
To be clear, Abbott does not advocate for a marginalization of sectarian sub-disciplines or alternative epistemologies, but rather he calls
for his colleagues to pay more attention to the larger, but implicit
framework that such local knowledges end up making together with
proper deconstruction and reconstruction methods and modes of inquiry. In short, Abbott is implicitly playing both sides of the modern-
postmodern debate by calling for the development and progress of
alternative voices and knowledge (local and smaller knowledges), but
without allowing them to become so divergent, so fragmented, that
they lose any relation to the bigger, larger framework; which in his
case, is the social and human condition. In Abbott's concise way, he
mirrors the consilient significance put forth by Wilson.

> My interest in that larger implicit framework is both theoretical and practi-
> cal. On the one hand, I feel that an understanding of it will clarify the rela-
> tions between various subsets of social science and sociology. Knowing the
> framework simplifies—perhaps even explains—those relations. (1998, 5)

According to Abbott, as American colleges continued to follow
the techno-industrial and consumerist model of growth, academic
disciplines gradually developed as social constructions designed to
support geographical and cultural initiatives (2001, 125). The reasons
for this evolution are many and complex, but include the sheer number and decentralized nature of American universities and colleges,
the rapid expansion of faculty positions to staff the institutions and
run the myriad academic majors that have proliferated in the post-
WWII era, and the increasing trend for professional schools to require
arts and science degrees as prerequisites for admission. In time, the
gradual blending of graduate and undergraduate programs (on the
same campuses), the need for schools to have comparative advantages (different, specialized programs for recruitment of top students)
for economic viability, the development of professional subsystems
(organizations, meetings, journals, languages, etc.) led to the eventual
disciplinary *fractilization* of the disciplines into separate and disparate

fields of study. Abbott takes this evolutionary growth a step further by positing that in effect, a *dual institutionalization* was started whereby the specialization and alienation of discipline subsystems led to special doctoral training programs, which in turn, led to highly specialized undergraduate degree programs that had strong economic ties. The college major, according to Abbott is "the most consequential single disciplinary structure—in terms of extent and impact" (127). Ironically and amazingly, and as pointed out by Abbott this observation has never been the subject of serious pedagogical debate. Of course it is not hard to imagine what the primary driving force behind this process might be—the technico-scientific thirst of the ruling corporate and political classes, and their well rooted financial connections to major degree programs and other higher education initiatives (Apple, 2001; Giroux, 2003).

Chaos & Consilience in the Disciplines

As is the case between many contemporary professionals and academics across the disciplines who have become specialized experts in their respective fields (see Lazlo's "water cooler" comments), the educated object of Dysacademia is also being denied a more meaningful episteme and deeper understanding of the world's chaotic culture, its many structural and organizational complexities, and its many interconnected nodes of significance and interpretation both within and outside the various scientific disciplines. In short, the modern University's dyskinesia is effectively inducing dyserethesia in far too many of the objects of Dysacademia. In a Lyotardian vein then, perhaps we must more critically embrace the sentiment that since we are living in postmodern times, we must therefore address knowledge in a more complimentary postmodern manner.

Based upon Wilson's courageous work regarding the disciplinary fragmentation of knowledge presented earlier, *Consilience* is one conceptual framework with the potential to resonate with the work of Lyotard, Serres, Derrida (Architectonic structure), & other critical theorists, and so I will re-present Wilson's theoretical argument here in order to explicate his educational implications, and in an attempt to exfoliate the "good" parts of his model that can be seen to partially support the present theoretical argument. But because Wilson calls for biology to serve as "the center" of all knowledge, and for reductionist thinking to be the dominant mode of inquiry for all knowledge domains, postmodern theorists can/will/have attack(ed) Wilson's translucent framework, accusing him of creating a new "meta narrative" that governs truth and objective reason. And, as I have previously articulated, its postmodern potential is/will be effectively diluted and disabled because of its meta narratives underpinnings. In the end then we need something more than Consilience...we need something else.

In recognizing this, I will then introduce and extrapolate the central tenets of open systems theory, chaos theory and cybernetics in an attempt to construct a postmodern framework for my alternative educational paradigm in hopes of articulating a thought and action process capable of rehabilitating Dysacademia, and its various sub maladies.

Why Consilience Won't Rehabilitate Dysacademia

In his controversial text, *Consilience: The Unity of Knowledge*, Wilson reintroduces *Consilience* as a term first presented by William Whewell in his 1840 synthesis *The Philosophy of the Inductive Sciences* (Wilson, 1998, 8). As reported by Wilson, Whewell describes Consilience as "a 'jumping together' of knowledge by the linking of facts and fact-based theory across disciplines to create a common groundwork of explanation." The author suggests that Consilience might actually be an intellectual spin-off from the *Ionian Enchantment* (an expression coined by physicist and historian Gerald Holton)—a belief in the unity of the sciences, or a conviction which is far deeper than a mere working proposition that the world is orderly and can be explained by a small number of natural laws (Wilson, 1998, 9). It is apparent to me that the word may have its roots in Webster's definition of the word *conciliar*, meaning, "of, relating to," or perhaps from *conciliate*, meaning, "to bring into agreement" (*Merriam-Webster*, 1997, 167). Whatever the source, Wilson has ambitiously developed a critical philosophy, or hyper-interdisciplinary position calling for the unity of all knowledge.

Drawing on the physical sciences and biology, anthropology, psychology, religion, philosophy, and the arts, E. O. Wilson demonstrates why the goals and accomplishments of the original Enlightenment era are surging back to life, and how they are again beginning to mold our exciting and profoundly complex world. Professor Wilson posits that the Enlightenment thinkers of the 17th and 18th centuries (The Marquis de Condorcet & Francis Bacon, in particular) were mostly right in developing scientific assumptions that contributed to a lawful world. In a strikingly parallel sentiment to those put forth by Doll (re: the scientific misapplication of Newtonian and Cartesian principles) in 1993 (Doll, 1993, 2), the author makes the point that the current and ongoing fragmentation of knowledge and the resulting chaotic status in the discipline of philosophy, are not reflections of the "real world," but are instead socially constructed by-products of human scholarship. The philosophy and scientific spirit of the great thinkers of the Enlightenment age actually promoted the intellectual engagement of the intrinsic *unity* of knowledge, not the separation and ultra-specialization that is so prevalent today (Wilson, 1998, 8).

In strong fashion, Wilson states that the greatest enterprise of the mind has always been, and will always be, "the attempted linkage of all the sciences and the humanities together" (Wilson, 1998, 9). Although this sentiment appears to be very modern and mechanistic, perhaps primarily due to his choice of wording (linkage), one could argue that a postmodern perspective exists here as well; one much like that presented by William Doll. What Wilson is really trying to say with this statement is that unless the humanities, the social sciences, and the natural sciences work with a strong sense of coherence and interdisciplinary urgency, the knowledge base and level of understanding of the world and human condition will continue to be nebulous, murky, and unresolved. In short, it is Wilson's contention that we need to collectively come to a better understanding of the workings of the human mind, the notion of consciousness, and the true meaning of knowledge before we can begin to constructively address the social and ethical illnesses of our current society.

> A balanced perspective cannot be acquired by studying disciplines in pieces but through pursuit of the Consilience among them. To the extent that the gaps between the great branches of learning can be narrowed, diversity and depth of knowledge will increase. (13)

In these latter statements Wilson uses *coherence* while concurrently shedding light on our current level of understanding of the world, while simultaneously expressing his scientific-empirical roots for truth and knowledge and us. However, Wilson is cautious and somewhat realistically reserved in stating the challenges, barriers, and delimitations of *Consilience*. He readily admits that the whole notion of *Consilience* is indeed a neo-intellectual entity that is currently embraced by only a few philosophers and scientists. Like other new theories and philosophical ideas, it possesses a certain vagueness and quality of the unknown. So new if fact, that the author categorizes his intellectual presentation as "...essentially a metaphysical worldview" (9).

Although many might consider the 4 domains that Wilson presents (environmental policy, ethics, social science, and biology) as being closely connected so that rational inquiry in one would trigger a chain reaction of reasoning in the other, the modern academic mind separates each domain so that they stand alone with their own practitioners, languages, modes of analysis, and standards of validation (1998, 9). In her exposition on the history of interdisciplinarity, Lattuca (2001) points out, that although problem based interdisciplinary research and curricular projects have been in existence for some time in the academy, "general systems theory and structuralist thinking provided the theoretical foundation" for much of the efforts, and so "structuralism and semiotics defied disciplinary boundaries in their search for underlying systems or forms that would unify theory in disparate areas" (9 – 0). The result of a structuralist based interdisciplinarity, or Consilience then is confusion; a confusion, or chaos that may be due in part to the evolution and history of the American academic institution and its subsequent economic dependence on majors and academic specializations (Abbott, 2001).

Wilson's way to avoid confusion, which Francis Bacon purportedly termed as "the most fatal of errors," is to unify the elements of the domains with a consilient approach to learning and inquiry. This, Wilson claims, is where most real-world problems exist and one in which fundamental analysis is most needed. The problem though, is that the modern academic fragmentation of information and concepts from the various specialized disciplines have left few concepts and maps available to guide us into interconnected, or interdisciplinary ways of seeing and thinking. Scientists have become too specialized, too focused on their own narrow worldview, and too reliant on the "objectivity" of the scientific method to genuinely see the consilient nature of their work. A new type of science is needed to overcome this modernist, anti-Newtonian and anti-Cartesian scientism that has dominated the intellectual and social landscapes of Western society for some time now. Doll seems to echo this sentiment by arguing that a post-modern curriculum should contain a "new version" of science; one that's more complex, indeterminate and more interactive than the classical version. This new science should, and will dominate the status quo and subsequently generate a new paradigm characterized by self-organization, dissipative structures, ecological balance, punctuated evolution and complexity (Doll, 1993, 12).

How does this all relate to education in the large scope of things; including, but not limited to, pedagogy, curriculum and higher education? Wilson addresses the plight of the current educational, intellectual and professional environment in his chapter on *The Great Branches of Learning*. His views on the state of education in our country are clear and succinct.

> In education the search for Consilience is the way to renew the crumbling structure of the liberal arts. During the past thirty years the ideal of the unity of learning, which the Renaissance and Enlightenment bequeathed us, has been largely abandoned. With rare exceptions American universities and colleges have dissolved their curriculum into a slurry of minor disciplines and specialized courses. (12)

Part of the causation for this movement can be seen in recent trends of college and university curricula. As reported but not referenced by Wilson, the percentage of mandatory courses in general education has decreased by more than fifty percent in U.S. colleges and universities, while the number of actual courses (major specialization) has doubled; and only one-third of the higher education institutions in the U.S. (in 1997) required students to take at least one course in the natural sciences (1998, 13).

Opening Knowledge & Knowing

One evolutionary effect of the previously articulated neoliberal shift in contemporary educational institutions has been the gradual and pronounced production of *educational technocrats*, or Derrida's "biotechnocrats" that values specialized expertise and technique over a broader, wiser and more holistic approach to knowledge and life (Doll, 1993, 24). In contrast to our "uniquely powerful and powerfully unique" disciplinary system (Abbott, 2001, 128), European university systems developed intermediate institutions to help structure the larger interactional fields of the university because they realized that most complex interactional fields tend to break up into clusters of entities that develop internal identities. This recognition thus provides a better small framework-large framework platform for students, who are then able to see and connect the two frameworks with a more consilient perspective and understanding.

In multiple and separate cases, even Albert Einstein expressed concern with the growing trend towards overburdening our young students with specialized knowledge (1982). To Einstein, highly specialized and technical education, if not countered with diversity and depth, would preclude a more well-rounded and harmonious enlightenment.

> I want to oppose the idea that the school has to teach directly that special knowledge and those accomplishments which one has to use later directly in life. The demands of life are much too manifold to let such a specialized training in school appear possible. The development of general ability for independent thinking and judgment should always be placed foremost, not the acquisition of special knowledge (64)...It is essential that the student acquire an understanding of and a lively feeling for values. He must acquire a vivid sense of the beautiful and of the morally good. Otherwise he—with his specialized knowledge—more closely resembles a well-trained dog than a harmoniously developed person. (66)

As Wilson, Doll and Einstein individually argue in their own manners, only when natural science, the social sciences and the humanities are all approached together with Consilience as the backbone to their scholarship and teaching, will a meaningful educational reform occur. As a measure of this advanced interdisciplinary frame of thinking, Wilson challenges the nature, content, and effectiveness of higher education by posing an edict for all college graduates. According to Wilson, a truly effective and consilient curriculum should allow every college student, public intellectual and political leader to be capable of answering a complex, yet simple and critical question.

> What is the relation between science and the humanities, and how is it important for human welfare? (13)

From a personal perspective, my own educational experiences at 2 very different institutions of higher education preparing to become a technocratically trained professional, and my subsequent eleven years in higher education can certainly attest to, and locally verify the insightful comments made by Aronowitz, Doll, Abbott and Wilson. It is my humble impression that this complex, multi-factorial and far-reaching question could serve as the foundation for curriculum development for many levels of education. Perhaps it could also provide an "addendum" to the theoretical framework of many postmodern curriculum theorists, thus providing a new angle, or a new approach to the discourse of educational substance and reform movements.

In many ways, the curriculum theory field may be seen as a microcosm of Wilson's notion of *Consilience*. Upon familiarizing themselves with the deeper underpinnings of Consilience, some theorists might agree that it just might be an effective and dynamic metaphor for curriculum reconceptualization. Except for one glaring, and modernism based fault that can be witnessed in Wilson's desire for a *unity of knowledge*, biology and the natural sciences serve as the central, binding discipline around which the humanities and social sciences interconnect. In using biology as "the" central node for the model (which, interestingly enough contrasts with Newtonian/Cartesian modernists, such as Bertrand Russell, who prefer to anoint a more mechanical philosophy—physics—as the center of all knowledge) Wilson violates one of the central tenets of postmodern theory. Ironically, or perhaps paradoxically, postmodern theorist William Doll agrees with Wilson concerning the use of biology as the center stone for a diverse and connected curriculum, citing biology's inherent hierarchical structure, complex organization, open system, and its connectedness to other natural sciences as the reasons for such a claim (1993, 58 – 68). Derrida, on the other hand believes that "metaphysics" should not be a centering force per se, but rather a counterforce capable of preventing any particular meta narratives from wrapping its metaphorical tentacles around a true and reasoned philosophy (2004, 63).

Doll certainly makes a strong scientific claim (he himself being admittedly "unversed" in the humanities as well as he would like) for the use of biology as the centerpiece of our curriculum (which of course, opens his stance up to considerable debate and disconcertment); but it is the metaphor of *biology for curriculum* that actually holds more interest and potential for education. In its most simplistic representation, Doll believes that curriculum and educational systems should be biologically oriented because humans are living, open systems (1993, 58). Doll continues to present his idea of curriculum as an open, biological system by arguing that such open systems are *transformative*. In direct contrast, Doll, presents the current, modernist and Tylerian curriculum as a closed, passive transmission system that excludes the student, the teacher, and the complexity of human thought from the center discourse(s). To further support this biological metaphor, Doll even ventures to say that physics (long considered the center of science) has excluded the concept of interaction and has thus had devastating effects on curriculum and student growth. Perhaps if Doll was more cognizant of the updated notion that open systems theory, chaos and cybernetics, and their many similarities and connected constructs, can (and are being) actually be applied to social systems as well as living systems, his articulation of a more biological curriculum might take on a different slant today.

Another common and central theme put forth by myriad postmodern theorists interested in opening up spaces for inquiry and development, is Herbert Spencer's age-old question pertaining to "what knowledge is of most worth?" (cited in Marshall, Sears, & Schubert, 2000, 1). A connected, consilient model for a curriculum's content could be imagined with input from the personal experiences, cultural diversity, ethnic heritage, "t"ruth and active democracy, gender and race issues, and so forth; all interconnected, coherent and interdependent, and "jumped together" in a way that promotes individual growth, creativity, intellectual honesty, and critical thought. Around these central themes are several dynamic and interconnected variables that must be included in a complete and realistic educational system. In this sense, one might propose for a *consilient curriculum* to be developed and implemented in place of the current modern-day educational curriculum structure.

One need not look much further than the table of contents in the cautiously comprehensive text edited by William Pinar and colleagues, to witness the desire that curriculum reconceptualists have for a more *postmodern, complex, heterogeneous, and consilient curriculum. Understanding Curriculum* (UC) is a text that chronicles and outlines a very multidisciplinary, yet central approach to curricular reconceptualization in an attempt to better "understand curriculum" (Pinar, Reynolds, Slattery, & Taubman, 1995). The various works in UC demonstrate the multi-factorial nature and myriad domains of consideration that are involved with a postmodern curriculum theory; ones that historically, have been marginalized, neglected, or not yet thoroughly evaluated. This text, like many other works in the field, includes considerable discourse and debate on issues ranging from politics, race, gender, phenomenology, arts, religion and internationalism. In considering the depth and breadth of this landmark text in curriculum, it might not be inappropriate to guardedly draw some parallels with Wilson's central arguments for the coherence of the many faces of social science, the humanities, and the natural sciences.

The critical difference between these two conceptions however, is that Pinar et al.'s vision has the student and the teacher firmly situated at the vortex of all educational endeavors, in the center of the

system shining like beacons in a foggy landscape; while Wilson's ideology is completely void of the personal self and its utility in the
learning process. The five domains of a metaphorical postmodern
consilient curriculum based on the tenets and arguments presented in
UC, would be psychological, personal, emotional, intellectual and cultural; all of which would interconnect and effect the true understanding, growth and development of the participles in the center—the
students and the teachers. Again, this metaphorical representation is
cacophonously similar to the open, biologically oriented model put
forth by Doll (and admittedly borrowed from Piaget) in his call for a
living, human centered, and self-organizing educational system (1993,
64). If we applied Wilson's explanation of Consilience to curriculum
then, the relative success of such an idea is dependent upon the relative state of knowing in each of the 5 core participles that Pinar et al.
have expressed in the reconceptualization of curriculum.

One could also easily extrapolate other sub components of the
five participles synoptically highlighted above, and continue the web
of connectedness across many levels, layers and fields, as Deleuze &
Guattari express in the articulation of their "rhizome" concept (1987,
7). In fact, if this were done for both student and teacher, imagine
what that would look like schematically! Considering the sheer magnitude of potential variables, or what Serres calls the "multiplicities of
multiples," that come into play with this modular expansion the potential is mind boggling, and perhaps even intimidating for some.
Doll echoes these sentiments with his curricular implications for
teachers and critical points for curriculum makers (Doll, 1993, 67). To
teachers, Doll suggests that they need to assess what performance and
operations have been learned at one level *and* (added for emphasis)
those that are in the embryonic stages of development. To do this
however, the teachers must be able to understand these varying levels
of knowledge and cognitive maturity themselves. In short, teachers
must be consilient in their knowing by having an understanding of
each student's position, disposition, experiences, understanding,
physiological and psychological states and maturity, AND know the
curricular content, its various levels of praxis and the myriad cognitive underpinnings that need to be taught. For curriculum developers,
there are 4 points that Doll feels are essential to creating a consilient
curriculum (my term for emphasis) (67):

1. Biology with its hierarchies, complexity, and network relations is heu-
    ristically a richer metaphor for curriculum.
2. Only available to those able to move to open framework.
3. Transformation requires perturbations.
4. Teacher awareness of multiple levels of operation is required.

Using biology as the center of a discourse surrounding interdisciplinary studies is very tempting since it does inherently represent the

"study of life". From a positive perspective, the ability to move to "open frameworks" imbibes a sense of open systems theory, perturbations are echoed in Serres' need for "turbulence" and discomfort, and "multiple levels of operation" exude a consilient and chaotic undertone that would make Deleuze, Guattari, Serres and other open systems thinkers proud. But because any center takes up "space", it thus represents a stagnant and paradoxical meta narrative by inhibiting "other" entities from using that same space, Wilson's idea must be resisted.

In these highly analogous and compatible models (Doll's and Wilson's adapted that I have been calling *postmodern Consilience*), the postmodern and effective curriculum connects the personal experiences of the teacher and student in a way that makes them a "multifarious one." The psychological state and emotional well-being of both teacher and students must be considered, and subsequently interwoven into the educational experiences and fabric to allow each participle to grow and mature in personal and truly democratic ways. Of particular importance in this view is the cultural diversity, background and perspective that each teacher and student brings to the classroom. Excluding the many cultural components of education and society, and their inherent interconnectedness will effectively undermine the perceptive notion we have of our "truly democratic and polyvocal society." The state, curiosity, capacity and well-being of students' intellects are generally considered to be the central pillar of the educational mission today. However, the consilient, reconceptualized curriculum includes the teacher and at least 4 other interdependent domains, without which, the task of culturing and developing the intellect becomes very difficult, if not impossible.

Noam Chomsky, author and professor of linguistics and philosophy at MIT, may be seen as a modern day consilient scholar whose works have influenced the diverse, yet connected fields of philosophy, political science, sociology, biology, and the cognitive sciences. In his recent text, *Chomsky on MisEducation*, he and editor Donaldo Macedo argue for a true democratic revolution in the halls and classrooms of our schools. Among other compelling arguments, they make the very poignant point that schools are by and large designed to support the dominant interests of our society—those with wealth and power (2000). The function of our schools currently is to socialize or indoctrinate, our students into becoming part of this self-serving system. Along the way, the *truth* is not taught or encouraged because this will cause a dramatic shift in the distribution of power in our social and political system. In reality, Chomsky argues, teachers in our current system teach myth, not truth, so as to safeguard the ideological yet often hypocritical doctrinal system of the United States.

As Chomsky and Macedo set up the foundation for their discourse on *MisEducation*, several consilient themes come to the surface and expose themselves as core philosophical tenets that the authors seem to rely upon. While discussing the need to teach *political clarity* (and thus help lead to the truth and a breaking out of the ideological and non democratic system of U.S. education), the authors allude to the need for teachers and students to be capable of linking different historical events if they wish to gain a clear understanding of reality.

> The inability to see through the obvious contradiction is part and parcel of the ideological manipulation that often produces a disarticulation of bodies of knowledge by dislodging observers from a critical and coherent comprehension of the world that informs and sustains them. This disarticulation of knowledge anesthetizes consciousness, without which one can never develop political clarity. (2000, 9)

With this in mind, Chomsky presents several historical examples describing how the typical American intellectual cannot truly decipher between political reality, and media and bureaucratic blurring of the lines (i.e., bombing of Kosovo to "ease human suffering," while failing to take the same action in countries that have similar unrest and injustice but provide us with strategic alliances, and or benefits). Developing or acquiring a "self-defense" for this forced ideology is only possible if we develop "a critical comprehension between the meaning of words and a more coherent understanding of the meaning of the world." This, Chomsky feels is a prerequisite for achieving what he calls "clarity of reality" (10).

Perhaps the strongest fibers of Consilience in this modern work can be found with Chomsky's comments on the need for scientific objectivism and the problems confronting the social sciences. Objectivity is something that should not be dismissed in education; rather it is something that should work hard to embrace in the pursuit of truth, regardless of a chosen academic major, or field of study. Furthermore, Chomsky elaborates on the inherent challenges associated with social science—that the constraints imposed on researcher by the outside world are much weaker. The complex problems confronting social sciences are harder to interpret, yet the understanding seems to be much shallower. In contrast to the nature of the social sciences, Chomsky supports the claims of Wilson that the natural sciences are more governed by the laws of nature, and thus experimental errors in their work can thus be easily exposed. Macedo also takes a postmodern, pro Wilson stance when he warns of the dangers of fragmented science and an over-reliance on abstract, anti-consilient empiricism by introducing a bit of intellectual prose from Paulo Freire with his own concern of "blind intellectuals" (Introduction to Chomsky).

> This social construction of not seeing characterizes those intellectuals whom Paulo Freire described as educators who claim a scientific posture and who "might try to hide in what [they] regard as the neutrality of scientific pur-

suits, indifferent to how [their] findings are used, even uninterested in considering for whom or for what interests [they] are working." (20)

In presenting these arguments, Chomsky challenges teachers to become intellectual seekers of the truth, to become consilient in their own knowledge base and understanding of the true complexities and objective interconnectedness of knowledge so that they can, in turn promote a different, more complex truth. This, he argues, is the only way to challenge the status quo ideology, to attack the lack of true democracy in our schools, and to restore democratic freedom to our future generation. In visualizing a consilient *Chomskiesque* curriculum that would center on the teachers and the students in a reconceptualized fashion, a slightly different conceptualization comes to mind that contrasts sharply with that of Wilson: Consilience = truth = democracy.

POST(ing) Up Thinking & Learning

In contrast to the "modern meta narrative in disguise" that Wilson's Consilience advocates, I am calling for an educational narrative that fills in the spaces...one that coalesces into a "fragile synthesis" (Serres & Latour, 1995, 119)...one that allows dissipation, autopoiesis...self-regulation to live in the middle...to flounder...and to ignite multiple and critical ontological transformations of the various independent subjects. As a poststructural argument, what I am calling for "denies all appeals to foundational, transcendental, or universal truths or meta narratives" (Pinar et al., 1995, 452), in that it freely promotes the wide open development of individual truths, realities, and subjectivities that liberally assemble themselves from underneath the deconstruction of knowledge, identity, politics, and language that constrain and define our cultural epoch. Thus situated, all knowledge domains in the postmodern condition, and not just those associated with modern scientific endeavors, can and should be appreciated as discontinuous and paradoxical. Or to exploit Lyotard's outlook, modern knowledge can be appreciated as "postmodernly conditioned."

In contrast to Lyotard's somewhat nihilist and relativistic perspective, a more practical and discursive approach is being called for presently; one that resonates strongly with Deleuze's & Guattari's contention that *some* element of order does indeed exist in life, that a little order in things and states of affairs indeed exists in our natural and social worlds (1994, 31). But for Lyotard, any attempt toward achieving consensus via a new grand meta narrative under the guise of rescuing humanity from the existing system is out of question, because such a project would invariably result in another oppressive system that inevitably perpetuates the same modern system he critiques. In reflecting this particular aspect of postmodern criticism,

Lyotard roundly condemns modern systems theory by claiming that it's merely another border developing meta narrative based solely on the substitution of another hegemonic language game that prevents and constricts multiplicity, multivocalism and local rules, contexts, and relations. In this view, it could be rightfully argued that Lyotard is thinking more of closed systems and not the open and undetermined systems that Laszlo, Bertalanffy, and Capra describe in their work; a type of myopia that if taken literally, can be translated as a rather nihilistic and far too relativistic perspective that offers little chance for hope, change, or reconstruction. In critiquing "systems" from a general perspective, it appears that Lyotard may not have been fully cognizant, or at least appreciative of the paradoxical differences between actual closed systems ideologies based on exclusion/inclusion, truth/untruth, and authoritative semiotic chains, and the more poststructurally oriented potential that open systems theory offered for epistemology and ontology; a foundational tenet that has been more commonly embraced by postmodern theorists like Deleuze, Guattari, Serres & Katherine Hayles, amongst others.

In contrast to an open systems based approach that can be appreciated in the philosophical compositions of Deleuze, Guattari, and Serres (of which, I will articulate in the upcoming sections), the closed systems that Lyotard is wary of attempt to rigidly control entropy (disorder) by enforcing linearity, absoluteness and objective predictability, while concurrently operating under a homogenous banner of exclusion and authority. Essentially and historically based upon socially constructed linguistic models, closed epistemological and ontological systems are to poststructuralists, not abstract or open enough; a perspective roundly supported by Deleuze & Guattari.

> They do not reach the abstract machine that connects a language to the semantic and pragmatic contents of statements, to collective assemblages of enunciation, to a whole micropolitics of the social field…A semiotic chain is like a tuber agglomerating very diverse acts, not only linguistic, but also perceptive, mimetic, gestural, and cognitive; there is no language in itself, nor are there any linguistic universals, only a throng of dialects, patois, slangs, and specialized languages…there is no mother tongue, only a power takeover by a dominant language within a political multiplicity. (1994, 7)

Perhaps thinking more practically than Lyotard, Serres wholeheartedly admits that parasitic and meta-authoritative knowledge can indeed be seen as "death," indicating that any time a new voice challenges or replaces another (which happens every time we speak incidentally) the other voice is eradicated in a violent death (1995b, 74). Respectful of the power of disciplined logocentrism, Serres intentionally uses simple language in his latter texts in order to perpetually change his conversational method. Although this strategy confuses and bemuses Bruno Latour, his interviewer and discursive partner,

Serres' methodology represents an earnest attempt to minimize "taking space," and to circumvent the willful and intentional creation of *other* supplanting meta narratives that will inevitably contribute to another type of death. Obvious in Serres' comments regarding this poststructural caution and apprehension, and likewise not readily apparent in Lyotard's *Postmodern Condition,* is the recognition and realistic submission that to some extent or another, we cannot avoid "killing" unless we remain absolutely silent (which ironically, is also a type of killing in its own right). Unlike closed systems, open systems embrace chaos, multiple associations, fractal networks, the existence and recognition of unknowns, reoccurring and disappearing patterns, growth & dissipation, reemergence, plastic organization, unbounded life and possibility. Thus viewed from a postmodern/poststructural perspective, open systems are constantly and perpetually working to deconstruct the various social, cultural and political semiotic chains that construct our "reality" and knowing.

It is in these apparently paradoxical and cautious thoughts expressed by Lyotard, that I see both support and critique for my particular perspective. I do not want to create a meta narrative that claims legitimacy, but yet I do want to allow for a dynamic and open intellectual diversification of inquiry and myriad way(s) of knowing that reflect the systemic, fluid, rhizomatic and interconnected nature of our existence; an open discourse that subsequently proves capable of treating what I have previously described as academic dyskinesia and dyslogia. An education characterized and anchored by the central tenets of open systems theory, and one interlaced with a postmodern sensibility capable of revealing structural tendencies and elements of power and authority is one compatible with the views on knowledge and being that shape the writings of Deleuze, Guattari, and Serres. Serres' various thoughts can be succinctly connected and characterized by a philosophy of multiplicities, and the process of knowing to Serres can be distinguished by fluidity and turbulence in that it is, and ought to be unpredictable, related, autopoietic, dissipative, self-organizing, chaotic, and most of all, open, unbounded, uncontrolled, and undetermined by any essential observer. Similarly for Deleuze & Guattari, "reality" and authentic knowing are constituted by "lines of articulation, segmentarity, strata and territories...lines of flight, movements of deterritorialization and destratification," that can perhaps best be described by the conceptual acceptance of "rhizomes" (1987, 3).

Using Serres' "fragile, liquid synthesis" and "amodern philosophy of prepositions," and the Deleuzian-Gauttarian notion of "rhizomes" as conceptual foundations for my discourse, I see in their work a recurring and intrinsic resemblance to what may be conceived of as *postmodern open systems theory (POST).* For me, *POST* represents a tenuous and open paradigm of inventive and multiple thought based more on postmodern comparativism, than on sequential linking; one based on the swift and fluid travels of Hermes, rather than one based on the modern, closed system consisting of solid constructions of deductive, reductionist, and modern rationalization (Serres & Latour, 1995, 73). A *POST* education has the potential to treat and rehabilitate dyskinesia by attacking the controlling boundaries and semiotic chains that disciplinarity induces on the thinking and knowing subject, thus allowing open and voluntary movement in, and amongst the various knowledge domains that inform our being. Like Serres' soccer goalie metaphor, a *POST* education will promote, allow, and even demand for a *hyperkinesia* that will command a complete and responsive freedom of movement.

> Relaxed, as if free, the body mimes the future participle, fully ready to unwind; towards the highest point, at ground level, or halfway up, in both directions, left and right; toward the center of the solar plexus, a starry plateau launches its virtual branches in all directions at once, like a bouquet of axons. (1997, 9)

Once freed from the disciplinary and hegemonic control that now defines our neoliberal based University, a *POST* education promises to eradicate dyslogia by offering the power to reveal modern, corporatized educational policies for what they really are—agents of human capital theory that possess little, if any meaningful epistemological and ontological potential for individual subjective growth and development. Thus accomplished, the rehabilitated subject is now free to move and think on "flat multiplicities of n dimensions," and to reason on open, undetermined, and postmodern terms that are fundamentally "asignifying and asubjective" (Deleuze & Guattari, 1987, 9). In order to articulate their "schizoid" approach to deconstructing modern reality, Deleuze and Guattari use "maps," or "diagrams" to represent the cartographic and folded sets of various interacting lines that constitute art, society and individuals (1995, 33).

In strong contrast to Lyotard's' overly cynical *logocentric phobia*, Serres has constructed a metaphor using a certain character from Greek mythology—Hermes—to define his idea of the "freedom of movement," an idea that aptly captures the prescriptive discourse being articulated herein (Serres & Latour, 1995, 64). Hermes, an "Agent of Rapprochements," is Serres' way to express the idea of a free mediator who wanders through folded time and establishes connections; an agent capable of inoculating the subject from dyskinesia; of describing spaces between things that are already marked out, or what he calls spaces of interference between methods, history, modes of inquiry and established knowledge. Hermes is a metaphorical agent designed to order disorder by holding on to a "connected intellection"; one capable of containing, not restraining chaos. In short, Hermes is the intermediary angel capable of passing through folded time in or-

der to making millions of connections between these maps, to trans-
verse the noise, to move towards meaning, to map out the potential
cartographies; and in an "amodern" sense, to explore and promote
the space between and amongst that characterizes Serres' "philosophy
of prepositions" (Serres & Latour, 1995, 127).

For Serres, inventing knowledge is the essential and fundamental
purpose of all education; a critical and practical ground still very
much unexplored my many educational theorists and pundits. For
Serres, the only way to truly invent knowledge (which is different
than information—that which is passed on, reproduced, "re"-
searched, reified over time) is to find and use an intermediary such as
Hermes, capable of effecting juxtapositions, of transporting modes
and means of invention, and of exporting and importing various
knowledge from all domains, from all the various levels of organization and networking that make up an open system, and from across
folded, non-linear and reversible time. The job of philosophy then is
"not only to invent, but to also invent the conditions necessary for the
future invention of knowledge" (Serres & Latour, 1995, 86). Derrida
would certainly comply with this contention, as he argues for a more
Kantian based philosophical approach to education based on reason
and inventive thinking.

> The philosopher, who teaches without learning, who teaches without teach-
> ing anything at all, teaches an action, not a content. (2004, 56)

In spirit then, I want to take advantage of Lyotard's ambivalence,
his paradoxical arguments, and *his postmodern condition* to argue for a
more comprehensive, critical, and meaningful exploration of knowledge and understanding; one based on undisciplined and reason
based action. The typical Dysacademic curriculum is based upon finite explanation and predetermined content that creates a legitimate,
centered, and fixed meta narrative (either intentionally or uninten-
tionally); a *POST* based curriculum in contrast, is founded upon a rhizomatic exploration that "connects any point to any other point...has
neither beginning nor end, but always a middle (milieu) from which it
grows and which it overspills" (Deleuze & Guattari, 1987, 21). In contrast to the ordered, decelerating, and finite effect that science (both
natural and social) has had on the open and chaotic nature of knowledge and our perceived reality, a *POST* education has an accelerating,
quasi-ordered, fractal effect on knowledge that is based on the action
of Kantian-Derridean notion of "philosophizing."

The concept that all knowledge consists of essential, or concrete
factoids that one can possess in totality is in direct contrast to a *POST*
curriculum that embraces the philosophical notion that philosophizing demands to be taught and developed in the individual seeking
"knowledge of the essential ends of human reason," but that philoso-

phy as a discipline should exclude teaching so as to not itself become the victim of essentialization as a cogent, finite and ordered system of knowledge (Derrida, 2004, 62). Or, as Deleuze and Guattari posit, a *POST* educational paradigm can be seen as one that preserves "the infinite speeds of chaos in the concepts that it creates and traverses" (1994, 118). In Lyotard's terms, "as long as the game is not a game of perfect information, the advantage will be with the player who has knowledge and can obtain information," or more simply the one who can traverse back, forth and between multiple spaces and can thus invent their own knowledge will have best views of what objectivity there is in nature (1984, 51). In short, the higher educated ought to be dually competent and cognizant of the knowledge needed to practice their chosen trade, and with the process and power of "how to philosophize" in order to invent and recognize new forms and shapes of knowledge. In a utopist world, such a curriculum might provide the canvas from which tomorrow's educated elite can seek, appreciate and invent new, creative and critical forms of knowledge capable of adequately and humanely addressing the problems and pitfalls of current and future societies.

I would like to now transition my current discourse regarding the "need" to change, to some prescriptive ideas concerning "how" to change by providing three germane comments from leading theorists that effectively relate the conceptual threads that exist between 1) the poststructural philosophy of Serres, Deleuze and Guattari, 2) curriculum reconceptualized in a postmodern manner, and 3) pertinent characteristics of open systems, information, and chaos theories. By introducing chaos and systems theory into the current discourse regarding a more postmodern education for the academy, it is my intent to demonstrate their inherent and vital connections to both my larger discourse, and to the subsequent alternative utterances forthcoming in the final chapter. Effectively, I intend to make a case for a *POST* higher education extended and informed by chaos and systems theories ideas; one that has the potential capacity to remedy the various ill effects that Dysacademia induces in its subjects.

> We are drilling holes in the wall of mystery that we call nature and reality on many locations, and we carry out delicate analyses on each of the sites. But it is only now that we are beginning to realize the need for connecting the probes with one another and gaining some coherent insight into what is there. (Laszlo, 1996, 3)

> The space between—that of conjunctions, the interdisciplinary ground—is still very much unexplored. One must travel quickly when the thing to be thought about is complex." (Serres, 1995a, 70)

> Conventional education in physics, biology, psychology or the social sciences treats them as separate domains, the general trend being that increas-

ingly smaller subdomains become separate sciences, and this process is repeated to the point where each specialty becomes a trifingly small field, unconnected with the rest. (Bertalanffy, 1969, 51)

CHAPTER SIX

Complicating Curriculum & Disabling Standard Outcomes

Since philosophy is everywhere, one must not reserve a place for it. Above all, one must not assign it a place.

---Jacques Derrida (2004, 63)

In *Chaos Bound*, Katherine Hayles presents her central thesis that "language's power to constitute reality and reality's power to constrain and direct language" as a testament to the poststructural and chaotic nature of all language, knowledge, and reality (1990, 3). In an attempt to generate a discourse around the challenges she sees central to literature and science, that being to develop methodologies that can illuminate convergences between disciplines while still acknowledging the very real differences that exist, Hayles sets the stage for her postmodern review application of the triangulation of chaos, poststructuralism and fiction. Following Henri Poincare's 1890 mathematical proof of the inability for Newtonian mechanics to explain how small perturbations in the moon's orbit would affect the sun and earth, that critics in other fields started to recognize and deconstruct the respective textual boundaries that confined their epistemological foundations. Newton's laws were not so impermeable after all.

Emerging from this newfound, anti-empiricist mode of thinking was "chaos theory," a paradigm of thought that embraced and sought out both the similarities and dissimilarities between various disciplinary fields, while also recognizing the effects and limits that culture and tradition had upon the respective fields, their scopes of knowledge, and their method of inquiry. As chaos theory gained momentum across many of the disciplinary fields, it gradually became apparent to those who embraced such a radical, postmodern idea that we were living in "a universe of discourse that is at once fragmented and unified" (Hayles, 4). In short, chaos theorists began to challenge the dominant modes of linear thinking by realizing that the more random and chaotic a message was, the more information it contained. To those unfamiliar with the scope and foundations of chaos theory, it was seen as a negative and nihilistic construct, one void of all meaning and content; but to pro-chaos scholars, chaos theory actually embodied the opposite of such cynicism. For chaos theorists, this new epistemological paradigm represented a more positive reflection on the nature and limits of humankind to completely grasp the fractal and complex nature of most phenomena in our natural worlds. In addition, the modern linear mode of thought that dominated our academic and scholarly culture up until the WWII era implied that order and structure inherently embodied a greater level of complexity and sophistication. But in chaos theory, order and quietness are believed to actually contain less information to interpret, less noise and distortion to decipher and comprehend, and thus non-chaotic entities were ultimately simpler. From this perspective came the notion, as contrary as it may appear, that as things (phenomena, concepts, etc.) emerge, and/or become more chaotic, they actually take on a more complex, organized, and dynamic nature that puts into question the limits of our understanding, perception and methodology concerning such phenomena. Inextricably tied to the central concepts of chaos and complexity is the belief that small fluctuations, or perturbations in the initial state or proximal extremity of a phenomenon can cause large, unpredicted changes in the latter, more distal extremities of the phenomenon under scrutiny. The classic example of this dynamical aspect of chaos theory can be seen in the potential effects that a butterfly flapping its wings in Florida might have upon the storm fronts and weather systems in Africa; or that very small changes in the earth's gravitational pull will dramatically affect the movement and behavior of the balls moving on a pool table.

Pedagogically, an example of the two sides of this perspective can easily be seen in the connection between learning and grades. From a linear modernist perspective (a.k.a., behavioral psychology), a student earning a grade of "D" on a project or exam is deemed to have failed to acquire at least 70% of the relevant material on the evaluation form used. From this data, a modernist would likely surmise, quite simply, that this student "has not learned" enough about the subject being evaluated, and so he/she requires remediation, is not a good student, or didn't prepare well enough. In short, a linear thinking, modernist pedagogue that uses standardized testing as an authoritative source of outcomes believes there is a firm, predictable and ordered relationship between student knowledge, performance, and the grade given. Teaching, learning and evaluation are closed sites, predictable, free from chaotic influences and processes, and immeasurable unknown entities.

In contrast, a chaos theorist would most assuredly look at this situation much differently by realizing that in all probability, there are myriad unpredictable, uncontrollable, and immeasurable factors involved in this student's performance and the subsequent evaluation. A "chaotic pedagogue" might be sensitive to myriad other, unaccounted for and uncontrollable phenomena that can, and usually do affect student learning: the students' mental and physical state of health on the day of the exam, the possibility that there do exist other, equally viable answers for many if not most of the questions on the exam, that the exam itself may not be "measuring what it is supposed to be measuring," that the teacher may have mis-taught, failed to express clarity during presentation, or even graded unfairly or incorrectly, etc., etc.

The central point of this example is that a chaos theorist is fully aware of and sensitive to the multiple possibilities that exist in teaching and learning, and to the limitations of all forms of measurement, among other things that can/do effect our social and natural worlds. Again, Derrida is on the mark here with his criticism of the bio-technological institutions and pedagogy, whereby systems that remain empirical, and thus not based on reason are only capable of providing an inorganic, technical unity, and subsequently acquired "know how" is merely an order of knowledge given shape by the performative institution (2004, 58). In contrast, Derrida argues in concert with Serres by positing that "teaching is non-teaching," and that the concept of architectonic pedagogy is a concept opposed to the traditional "conceptus scholasticus," whereby the system of knowledge is not scientific or logically perfect, but rather that novel education based on the art of philosophizing is artistic, inventive and transformative. Situated as such, it is this type of Kantian reasoning that distinguishes the philosopher from the mathematician, and is thus capable of liberating and transforming the character of those subjects who learn to philosophize and see the inanity of all finite knowledge.

Dissipative Structures: Curriculum & Subjects

Within the large domain of educational studies known as pedagogy, there are numerous examples of the dichotomous split between the two dominant paradigms of thinking about knowledge, teaching and learning; and it is towards some of these ideas that I will turn to more directly in an attempt to elaborate further on some of the intricate properties of chaotic systems. Hayles goes on to define, or perhaps categorize is a more appropriate term, the two general emphasis areas that have consumed chaos theorists over the years (1990, 9). In one school of chaos thought, scholars work from within the perception that chaos is order's precursor and partner, and that as such, there occurs a spontaneous emergence of self-organization from chaos even when entropy (state of disorder) production may be deemed as high. This school of thought was made more credible by Ilya Prigogine's work on the application of chaos theory beyond to all living systems, and can perhaps be best remembered as the "Order out of Chaos," or chaos produces order paradigm. Central to the order out of chaos paradigm sits the attempt to reconcile the "being with becoming" phenomenon, in which pre-existing, existing and future states of chaotic systems are seen to be continually changing, or becoming in dynamic and largely unpredictable manners—or what Prigogine called "dissipative structures" (Prigogine & Stengers, 1984).

Pedagogically, the order out of chaos principle can easily be applied to both the student and the curriculum by considering both the student and the curriculum as dissipative structures working in a chaotic state. Specifically, both the student and the curriculum can be viewed in this light and treated as open, chaotic, and dissipative systems, rather than the antithesis of such—closed, ordered, and self-limiting. Sadly, far too much of today's American education machine can easily be characterized as the latter—closed, hyper-ordered, and limiting—rather than one in which the self (the student) is allowed to find his or her own order amongst a chaotic sea of knowledge and realities, and one in which the curriculum is open, multifarious, polyvocal and thus, self-generating over time. In Prigogine's terms, the student and the curriculum can, and should be viewed as chaotic systems that focus more on the *becoming* aspect of learning, living and experiencing an authentic subjectivity, and less on the *being* which implies stagnation, closed order, and eventually death. As I see it, the pedagogical "being with becoming" reconciliation should center on the perpetual, self-organizing and open ability for subjects to construct an individual epistemology and ontology; as an opportunity to embrace a chaotic curriculum that allows *something* to emerge from the void of chaos, something individual that personifies an original and hyper-real epistemological and ontological subjectivity capable of real and meaningful deconstruction and reconstruction of experiences, phenomena, discourses, and knowledge.

The second important principle relative to chaos theory holds that a hidden order actually exists within chaotic systems, or more simply that despite their apparent disarray, chaotic systems inherently possess order already. Particular to this ordered system, and not found in Prigogine's idea, are deeply encoded structures called "strange attractors" (Hayles, 1990, 10). It is believed that these strange attractors, which are responsible for the inherent order found in chaotic systems, actually contract to a confined region and trace complex patterns within a particular structure's limits; much like the vascular and neural systems of the human body do as they expand and retract in response to physical and mental stress—undetermined, but with realistic boundaries of constraint that are defined by the system's structure, topology, or in the case of the human system, anatomy and physiology. In the case of the human anatomy and physiology, the neural and vascular networks that we are born with are, quite simply, not the same fractal patterns of physical mass with which we will die. As we exercise our minds and bodies, our internal circuitry and plumbing change accordingly, in both positive and negative ways. Vascularly, the more we exercise our muscles the more capillary growth (called "capillarization") we acquire in the working muscles in order to deliver the necessary nutrients and to dispose of the metabolic wastes that are part of exercise physiology. Chaotic in that there are no predetermined patterns in which the new micro capillaries lay down, but determined by the structure and topology of the muscles, fascia, bone, and skin etc. that limit the growth patterns somewhat.

Interestingly, the same is true of the neural networks that we create in our brains as we learn, experience, and process new sensory information and phenomena. It is thought that as we learn (used here in a larger more global and encompassing sense that includes all forms of intra and extra-sensory perception), our brain creates new neural pathways and connections between and amongst the existing neural network. This multi-level scaffolding like construction of existing nerves to create new pathways and networks in the mind based upon experience and learning, have been intricately defined by many terminological signifiers, but in essence is at least part of the theoretical constructs known either as "neural networks," "neurogenesis," and now "neuroplasticity" (Schwartz & Begley, 2002). What makes these "mind-brain-neuron" theories of consciousness especially compelling, if not even somewhat credible, is the networking, synapse firing experiences that one gets when playing the word association game—what do you think of/see/visualize, etc., when I say "dog"? As time passes, what other memories, thoughts, and/or visualizations come to mind that are connected with the original signifier "dog"? If enough time passes, the processor of this game could end up thinking of the most obscure, unrelated event, experience, or thought that started with the word "dog" (dog biscuits—biscuits and gravy—gravy and potatoes—French fries, France, wine, grapes, and so on) – open...fractal...chaotic...strange attractors.

Curricula, pedagogues and students alike, can all be viewed in this manner if chaos theory is appreciated as a very real element of knowledge formation and critical, reflexive ontological subjectivity. Pedagogically, the student can be viewed in this light as a chaotic system that has a hidden order; that being the neural networks that drive and substantiate their consciousness, their epistemology and their ontology towards a subjectivity that is unique, plastic, self-organizing, and limited only by the physical structures that confine them (the skull). These neural networks are undetermined, yet they are some-what confined. When nourished and stressed in a linear, modernistic fashion, they might be perceived to grow in linear, binary forms that are qualified by simple dichotomies of right vs. wrong, black and white, and truth vs. fiction. In contrast, when the neural networks are nourished in a more postmodern and chaotic fashion, they can be seen to grow in star like, laminar, folded and fractal patterns that have multiple synapses and cross bridges indicating greater depth, breadth, and heterogeneity and thus, the quantity of information re-ceived, processed and stored will be greater and richer. Over the course of a lifetime, the neural networks (and thus the mind) of the chaotic student will be much more complex, ordered, and saturated than will the networks of the linear student. In returning to Derrida's pedagogical concerns, philosophical reason is the thread, the glue, or more anatomically appropriate, the "connective tissue" that ties the mind's chaotic and plastic neural networks together in order to create an architectonics of thought and character. Irregardless of the aca-demic major or chosen discipline, the ability to philosophize would be the metabolic fuel needed to create and reform chaotic and dissipative networks and prevent the mind from becoming statically and necroti-cally disciplined.

Hayles summarizes four major characteristics that all chaotic sys-tems are thought to share in some respect, or another (1990, 11). First, and perhaps the most general and recognizable quality that chaotic systems possess is *nonlinearity,* a function opposite to linear and pre-dictable cause and effect systems because it is often distinguished by startling incongruities between causes and effects. Most often, nonlin-ear systems can be witnessed to have very large and pronounced ef-fects from very small, seemingly inconsequential causes (think, Butterfly effect, or the film *Pay It Forward*). Culturally, the concept of nonlinearity has shown to have a powerful influence in the postmod-ern challenge of the hegemony of Newtonian mechanics, and the clas-sical linguistic coding that has dominated modern epistemology in many disciplines, not just science. For Deleuze and Guattari, a rhi-zome captures the concept of nonlinearity perfectly.

> Unlike trees or their roots, the rhizome connects any point to any other point, and its traits are not necessarily linked to traits of the same nature. Unlike a structure, which is defined by a set of points and positions, with bi-nary relations between the points and biunivocal relationships between the positions, the rhizome is made only of lines: lines of segmentarity and strati-fication. (1997, 21)

A chaotic system's *complex forms* contribute the second shared charac-teristic, a feature that challenges the old, classical notions of scale as-sumed to be valid and unassailable in the modern paradigms of thought. Specifically, the notion of complex forms challenges a very strong modern assumption that all measurement forms are standard, objective and "multi-applicable." For example, although a standard ruler and its measurement values will do for measuring the length of a piece of paper, it will not suffice for measuring more complex forms, like the length of a coastline, the linear length of the human nervous system, or a rhizome. Thus, the modern assumption that measurement values and modes of inquiry reveal some sort of an *a priori* truth that is objective and strictly quantitative is directly challenged. Fractal geometry is perhaps the most recognizable off-shoot of chaos theory, in that it specifically addresses the notion of complex forms, fractal dimensions, and qualitative differences in chaotic systems.

Remembering that chaotic systems can have large-scale effects from small causes, a chaos theorist is fully aware that microscopic fluctuations in a system can send the system off in an impressive and undetermined array of different directions. Because of this quality, chaotic systems also share an acknowledgment of the *sensitivity to initial conditions*, the third common characteristic. Specifically, a chaotic system quickly becomes unpredictable unless the starting conditions of the system's structure, topography, or apparatus can be specified with infinite precision. In this sense then, chaotic systems can be seen to be both deterministic and unpredictable in that the observer may not ever be able to adequately ascertain the initial starting condition of the system under study, but is however able to observe that some sense of order and organization will eventually emerge from a chaotic system.

The fourth familiar feature of chaotic systems that Hayles presents, which ironically is also a major element of open systems, is called a *feedback mechanism*. As the theory goes, all living and social systems that are thought to be chaotic and open create loops in which output generated by the system feeds back into the system as input, thus having a perpetual and dynamic effect(s) upon the transformation and evolution of the system at hand. The resulting dynamics that occur of these continually working feedback loops are central to the process of system self-organization, and explain why complexity can eventually emerge in systems that have undergone small perturbations initially.

Open Systems Theory

The specialists concentrate on detail and disregard the wider structure which gives it context. The systems scientists, on the other hand, concentrate on structure on all levels of magnitude and complexity, and fit detail into its general framework. They discern relationships and situations, not atomistic facts and events. (Laszlo, 1996, 9)

The arrival, and subsequent popularity of general systems theory came about from the growing disentrancement with reductionist Cartesian science and logic that so dominated our modern era. Frustrated with growing criticism, failed results, and repetitive procedural redundancies, and suddenly acutely aware of the limits of atomistic and mechanistic paradigms of thought, 20th-century scientists (primarily biologists) and scholars (Gestalt psychologists) from many fields began to seek out a different lens from which to study their social and natural worlds (Capra, 1996, 17). This early postmodern paradigmatic flight of thought also spawned, or symbiotically emerged with the gradual development of other modern theories that began to shake the Cartesian and Newtonian foundations of rationality and objectivity. Although steeped in empirical methods and working from within modernist paradigms of scientific inquiry, Einstein's relativity theory, quantum mechanics, game theory, thermodynamics, and later, Norbert Wiener's communication theory all emerged from an evolving awareness of the incommensurability of certain, more complex phenomena with the perceived actualities of nature (Bertalanffy, 1969; Capra, 1995). As scientific knowledge progressed beyond the basic processes of organization, structure, classification, and functioning of simple systems that adhered to more straightforward laws and rules, and that could be understood with existent technologies, progressive scientists began to gradually see the inherent limits of modern science and the construction of a rational epistemology. In this sense, a postmodern sensibility seemed to begin to take hold in certain domains of science long before being given credit for such a movement. These activities subsequently contributed to the development of more comprehensive and modern paradigms of thought, most notably *systems theory*. Ludwig von Bertalanffy, long considered the modern father of systems science, quite simply defines a system as a living or social entity that consists of nonlinear characteristics with organized complexity (1969, 19), describes system science as a "general science of wholeness" (37), and differentiates an open system from a close system by pointing out that open systems (of which, all living organisms are) "maintain themselves in a continuous inflow and outflow...in a state of chemical and thermodynamic equilibrium."

Ervin Laszlo, who seems to have taken the systems theory beacon from Bertalanffy, expounds further upon Bertalanffy's definition by making it clear that each system has "a specific structure made up of certain maintained relationships among its parts, and it manifests irreducible characteristics of its own" (1996, 9). Simply put, the systems approach belies the mechanistic approach in that one cannot reduce a living system to its component parts, study them in a solitary fashion, and then hope to understand the complex and coherent function of the system itself either before, during or after "putting them back together." Laszlo goes on to clarify the openness and mobility of the systems practitioner by pointing out that the systems method "does not restrict the scientist to one set of relationship as his object of investigation," but rather that systems thinkers continually travel between relationships, levels, and depths in order to get a better, more global appreciation of the object under study. This point is an important one as it regards perspective, context and arguments centering on the local vs. the global, and as such, it will be an issue that we return to later. Today, systems theory is actively applied to myriad fields as diverse as economics, business management, information management, communication, ecology, weather, and yes, education.

In contemporary times, the systems theory torch bearers seem to be physicist, turned philosopher Fritjof Capra, and neuroscientists Francisco Varela and Humberto Maturano. Author of 6 books and one movie on, or related to the science, understanding and application of systems theory, Capra's life work now focuses on the application of open systems theory to ecology and our sustainable future(s). As such, it is in Capra's recent works that I find the most comprehensive, updated, and lucid explanations and material rationales for open systems theory; and although Capra is fundamentally referring to deep ecology with most of his energy, it also seems to me to provide an apropos fit for theoretically framing the pedagogical discourse centered herein.

> Ultimately these problems must be seen as just different facets of one single crisis, which is largely a crisis of perception. It derives from the fact that most of us, and especially our large social institutions, subscribe to the concepts of an outdated worldview, a perception of reality inadequate for dealing with our overpopulated, globally interconnected world...The recognition that a profound change of perception and thinking is needed if we are to survive has not yet reached most of our corporate leaders, either, or the administrators and professors of our large universities. (1996, 4)

Criteria of Systems Thinking

Since Capra more directly applies his discourse of living systems to all living and social systems (organisms, parts of organisms, and communities of organisms), and effectively expounds upon the many complexities involved with all such living systems, his account of the criteria and tenets of OST can be readily applied to the living system that is curriculum, as well as to the more obvious living system, the student. Because living systems can be viewed as a multilayered, multi-dimensional "web of life," they must be viewed and appreciated as series of networks exiting within other networks, much like the fractal, but ordered neural pathways that are believed to make up the brain's neurophenomenological physiology. Another strong, somewhat postmodern tenet of systems thinking is that, because of the complex "network within a network infrastructure" of systems, we only have approximate knowledge of a system, not "real truth" (Capra, 1996, 41). As such, the following criteria are deemed existent in all systems modes of thought: 1) a shift from the parts to the whole, 2) the ability to shift one's attention back and forth between a system's various levels, 3) a relational reversal between the parts and the whole, 4) that ultimately, there are no parts at all, only patterns existing in an inseparable web of relationships, and 5) epistemology has to be included explicitly in the description of natural phenomena.

If one were to take a little liberty with Capra's system criteria, apply a little critical postmodern flavor, and thus apply them to the pedagogical elements known as the curriculum and the student, the reworked criteria would look very interesting and compelling for critical pedagogues. Criterion number one, that pertaining to the part to whole shift, would mean that the curriculum would be looked at as a "whole entity," not as individual subjects mired in technocratic and highly specialized forms of inquiry. Problems and knowledge, to borrow Wilson's term, would be addressed and studied from a more consilient manner with a systems approach to curriculum; more than interdisciplinary, it would be transdisciplinary. For example, instead of addressing the deforestation of the rain forests simply from an environmental perspective, the social, political, economic, cultural and medicinal issues as they relate to the various critical tangents associated with chopping down acres of trees in order to grow more potatoes, graze more cattle, produce more French fries and hamburgers, increase cardiovascular disease amongst the Western consumers, increase pharmaceutical research and design for cholesterol reducing and blood thinning drugs, and so on, could be addressed from a systems approach that stresses the organizational relations of the parts.

The second and third criteria, the ability to shift attention back and forth within and amongst the various layers and fractal wings of the network, and appreciating that the relationship between the parts and the whole have been reversed, can be looked at together in the case of the curriculum and the student. Appreciating these two criteria would force educators to realize that a system's properties at all levels are emergent. Thus, educators might be inclined to see how ineffective the majority of tests and other evaluations of static knowledge are in measuring the overall intellectual, social, and emotional state of a student (a living system). Additionally, this criterion would compel educators to more fully see how little the various parts (outcomes, tests, objectives, etc.) of a curriculum actually and realistically connect to the whole—that is to the students themselves, and to the socially constructed world of their present and future existence. As the contemporary curriculum continues to become even more centered on capitalistic-industrial principles that will drive the market and world globalization (domination?) ideologies, students are becoming increasingly removed from the system they are thrown into (the curriculum). In short, the modern education paradigm fails to shift back and forth between the system's various levels that affect the central living system (the student), i.e., the outside world, the curriculum, the student, and the family. A systems approach to curriculum would amend this linear, irreversible flaw in the modern education machine and effectively address the local contextuality of each and every part of the system, in all directions, at all levels, and with an appreciation for the existence of only partial truth.

In an ongoing attempt to further challenge the paradigmatic constraints that have been bequeathed us from the Enlightenment era, criteria four and five can be condensed into the more postmodern pedagogical model being articulated here—that being that there are no separate parts nor essential objects, only interrelated, fractal patterns of relations; and also that epistemology must be included in the description of the natural world. Specifically, attention to these criteria would work to dispel the false, linear pursuit of absolute truths, essences, and absolute knowledge, and instead, embrace the concepts of chaos, limited order, fractals, and networks; while also allowing for the socially constructed reality of knowledge and truth to surface as legitimate concepts capable of rivaling our Eurocentric, anthropocentric logocentrism. This would introduce a strong notion of partial subjectivity and contextuality to the knowledge introduced and covered in a curriculum, while also placing students more in the center of the curriculum as opposed to their present position on the outside as "non-experts" of knowledge. Thus, students would be introduced to the very "real" notion that nature, for example, is not what we observe, but rather, what we socially construct which of course is a by-product of our methods of questioning and our current language and technology. Naturally, this requires a shift from an objective, Newtonian science framework to a more postmodern "epistemic science" that challenges the construction, reification and interpretation of all knowledge.

Building upon his explicit but overlapping criteria for systems thinking, Capra then presents several critical and interesting characteristics of open systems, that when deconstructed with a postmodern lens, can aptly be applied to students and curricula. Primarily through the amalgamation of the works of such renowned scholars as Ilya Prigogine, Alexander Bogdanov, and Humberto Maturana, Capra takes great pains to review and clarify these concepts as they were developed singularly, then following his criteria for thinking about systems, deftly connects them together in order to provide a well articulated, partially lucid, and partially nebulous view of the complexity and depth of living systems. Underpinning all of these characteristics is the notion that all living systems are nonlinear networks with intricate feedback mechanisms, designed to allow for sustenance and growth (Capra, 1996, 82). It is from this simple point that one may potentially see education existing as a large, open system; full of complex, fractal, and multidimensional layers or networks; and with multiple feedback mechanisms built in for checks, balances, and re-organization.

> Thus the community can correct its mistakes, regulate itself, and organize it-
> self. Indeed, self-organization has emerged as perhaps the central concept in
> the systems view of life, and like the concepts of feedback and self-
> regulation, it is linked closely to networks. (83)

In light of this "nonlinear network" representation of all life systems, self-organization eventually emerged as the central concept in systems thinking as a result of the early cybernetics work done by neuroscientists and mathematicians in collaborative efforts (Capra, 1996, 83). In contrast, today's educational system can in reality be seen as one big closed system, with linear progression (grades based simply on chronological age, standardized tests, "normal" knowledge, objective overemphasis, skill tracking, graduation tests, etc.), and the only sort of feedback provided is that of simple pen-paper, objective knowledge tests that portend to measure learning, skill and objective knowledge of the world. When speaking of our modern school, I think that it goes without saying that students "are not allowed to self-organize" anything in their respective curriculums, nor are they much allowed to self-organize themselves into autopoietic subjects. If however, students were treated as open systems, and the self-organization principle were allowed to operate unimpeded, ordered patterns would begin to spontaneously emerge out of the initial random state that young students represent upon arrival in the school. In short, self-organizing students would eventually turn chaos into order, and gain order from noise on their own respective level, in their own respective terms; contextually relevant, locally pertinent, and globally applicable. Capra's presentation of physicist and cyberneticist Heinz von Foerster's work is an apropos application to students as self-organizing systems, the "real" process of learning and ontological subjectification.

> He coined the phrase "order from noise" to indicate that a self-organizing
> system does not just "import" order from its environment, but takes in en-
> ergy-rich matter, integrates it into its own structure, and thereby increases
> its internal order. (84)

Important to the notion of self-organization are three sub-characteristics that also reflect the position that I am proposing to look at students as open systems. First, is that a self-organizing system creates new structures and new modes of behavior during the self-organizing process; the key word here is "self," not expert, teacher, or authority figure. I am not calling for a recommitment to the ideals of behaviorist psychology that predicates itself upon the notion that learning is a predictable, controllable and measurable change in behavior—that would be representative of a closed system. Is not an open, self-organizing, and self-making student and curriculum representative of a dynamic and Socratic education? Shouldn't the "self" be allowed to create a new self, to transform one's subjectivity, to change one's behavior, ideals, outlook and cognitive processes as a result of learning in a more "natural" and unstructured manner? Shouldn't students have at least some say in the formulation of their "epistemic culture"? Perhaps an open systems curriculum, designed to address and facilitate open systems organisms (students) could provide such growth and transformation in the epistemological, ontological and even axiological realms for all those immersed in such an endeavor.

The second common characteristic to self-organizing systems is that they all deal with open systems operating far from equilibrium, known in thermodynamic circles as entropy, or disorder. Energy (seen as knowledge and experience in the open pedagogical model) is constantly being shuttled within and through living systems (the student), and it is this energy that is required for self-organization to occur when the system is far from equilibrium. This state of relative disorder represents an entropic condition that all open systems go into, and out of on a continual and reformative basis, each time emerging "distorted," transformed, and reformed. Michel Serres differentiates critical, "real" learning from information reception by describing the learning process as being adrift in the turbulent waters, without a foot grounded, uncomfortable, painful, and unsure (1997, 5). Shouldn't students always be operating far from equilibrium? Is Serres' metaphor for learning not an effective representation of disequilibria? Nonlinear connectedness is the third characteristic common to all self-organizing models, a concept covered earlier in this piece as one of the central criteria for systems thinking, and so it need not be reiterated again. Thus, it can be said that self-organizing systems, like students and curricula (both living organisms), are characterized by "the spontaneous emergence of new structures and new forms of behavior in open systems far from equilibrium, characterized by internal feedback loops" (Capra, 85).

Similar to, but perhaps a bit more complex than the self-organizing principle discussed is Maturana's "autopoiesis" concept that stipulates "self-making" as a distinctive organizational property of all living systems (Maturana & Varela, 1997, 43). More specifically, Maturana in his quest to better understand human cognition proposed that the organization of living systems is the set of relations among its components that characterize the system. Capra builds on this theory by defining autopoiesis as "a network of production processes," whereby the function of each component is to participate in the production of the transformation of other components in the network (1996, 98). Largely accepted as at least part of the explanation for our cognitive processes and the intricate network of neurons that we develop and re-develop as we learn and experience, the autopoiesis theory can also serve as an incredibly interesting metaphor or model for a postmodern and chaotic curriculum, as well as students. As it already explains cognition, its relevance to the student is somewhat obvious already, but in curricular terms it begs for a more consilient and Serresian approach to pedagogy and learning whereby transdisciplinary approaches to learning and problem solving work autopoietically to build, support, refute and reformulate each part of the overall curriculum.

The last concept imported into the discussion of open systems is that of dissipative structures first put forth by Nobel chemist Ilya Prigogine in the 1960s (1984). In open systems, Prigogine demonstrated that as the system moves farther away from equilibrium, it reaches a critical point of instability, which to Prigogine represented a spectacular example of spontaneous self-organization. In other words, Prigogine's concept of dissipative structures showed that in open systems, dissipation actually becomes a source of order. According to Prigogine, dissipative structures not only maintain themselves in a stable state far from equilibrium, but may even evolve into new forms, new systems, and in the case of the student as a dissipative structure, into a new subjectivity (1984). Quite simply, when the flow of matter and energy (experience and knowledge) through them increases, the student may go through new instabilities and transform themselves into new structures of increased complexity. Perhaps most importantly, Prigogine's theory showed that while dissipative structures receive energy externally for the most part, the instabilities and jumps to new forms of organization that occur during the instable moments of ordering and reordering are the result of fluctuations amplified by the built in network feedback loops. In the case of students, these feedback loops may be seen as processes like reflective thought, metacognition, exposure to multiple perspectives and realities, and in the engagement of critical dialogue and discourse that can all occur in an open curriculum. In an open curriculum, tempered and softly modulated disorder and disequilibria will actually permit the open systems student to achieve more order for him or herself through autopoietic manifestations of the conscious and subconscious self. Again, Serres' notion that "turbulence" is required to authentically learn or to invent anything, represents a harmonic concept with Prigogine's more physically scientific principle; and so, it provides a very powerful metaphor for a postmodern pedagogical paradigm that treats both the student and the curriculum as dynamic, self-organizing, and reformulating open structures.

In *A Post-Modern Perspective on Curriculum*, William Doll's criticism of knowledge production and education echoes that of many before him, as he constructs a multi-pronged argument for a *megapara-digm change* in the development, philosophy and implementation of curriculum.

> A curriculum that is creative and transformative must combine the scientific with the aesthetic; eclecticism is one feature that makes post-modernism such an exciting movement. (1993, 6)

Within the introductory sections of this noteworthy text, Doll presents his case that the current segregation of knowledge within our culture is a direct by-product of *modernism*, and that a better future can only be reached through a defragmented and unified approach to knowledge inclusive of science, philosophy and art. Although a unifying approach to knowledge may appear to simply be, dare I say it, a *meta narrative* in drag to staunch postmodernists, Doll argues that it is the modernist *adaptations* of Newton's empiricism and Descartes' rationalism that are responsible for this fragmented paradigm of knowledge that defines educational curricula today. As such, Doll posits that a "postmodern perspective" is required to reverse, or at least to neutralize, this modernist deification of science and knowledge that governs much of contemporary culture today.

> One of the educational challenges in the postmodern mode is to design a curriculum that both accommodates and stretches: a curriculum that (combining terms and concepts from both Kuhn and Piaget) has the essential tension between disequilibrium and equilibrium so that a new, more comprehensive and transformative re-equilibration emerges. (1993, 10)

In coalescing E. O. Wilson's theoretical notion of Consilience, the postmodern curriculum arguments put forth by William Doll, and Serres' poststructural philosophy on knowledge and invention into a primary constitutive concept, I am effectively arguing here for a *postmodern consilient curriculum*—one that relates, makes compatible, and interconnects the various, multivocal and chaotic facets of our human existence into complex and unique ontological and epistemological subjectivities; one that centers the action of reasoned philosophizing at the center, not at the marginalized, non-performative periphery. But because of the significant meta narrative limitations in Consilience as Wilson theoretically articulates the term, and so in order to circumvent confusion between Consilience and my more postmodern version, I prefer to use *POST* as the central conceptual paradigm for rehabilitating Dysacademia. In short, I am interested in investigating and articulating a reconceptualization of a University curriculum that is interactively grounded in issues of *knowing* and *knowledge*; one that's less focused on the *doing* and more attentive to *being*. I want to more critically analyze higher education curriculum from a perspective that investigates *what kinds* of knowledge and skill are needed to thrive in, and contribute to our postmodern/posthuman society. My specific intention here is to contribute to the reconceptualization movement by articulating a curricular paradigm that is actually *not* a paradigm, but rather a fragile and open conceptual framework that allows the principle actors in the educational process—the students and the teachers—the mobility, location and impetus to pursue the true meaning of education, that being the ability, energy and desire to wander into open, unknown spaces. A postmodern consilient curriculum would be a curriculum that reflects the theoretical underpinnings of William Doll, in that it would "jump together."

> Life, indeed our working reality itself, is made up of interconnected experiences. Obvious as this statement is, developmentally simple in its approach, it has not played an essential role in curriculum development. (68)

In using a postmodern approach to articulate a relations based *POST* education analogous to Serres' "fragile synthesis," it should be lucid that I am not advocating for the development of, or reliance upon, one comprehensive meta narrative that directs and controls our knowing and understanding, as Lyotard roundly and resolutely critiques modernism of doing. Rather, I am merely looking at a *POST* education as the concept of "association," that being an architectonic process whereby human subjects use ideas, relations, perceptions, associations, and contiguity to represent one way of ordering the chaos (Deleuze & Guattari, 1994, 201). Again, the rhizome model put forth by Deleuze and Guattari expresses my sentiments well.

> In contrast to centered systems with hierarchical modes of communication and preestablished paths, the rhizome is an acentered, nonhierarchical, non-signifying system without a General and without an organizing memory or central automaton, defined solely by a circulation of states. (1997, 21)

Concepts and knowledge construction are innate, local and contextual subjective mechanisms that can be used to create some semblance of order for the subjective self, to grasp contextual and personal chaotic subjectivity; not some *a priori*, censored authoritative semiotic chain of essential factoids. As such, open and rhizomatic modes of inquiry and knowing ought provide the central platform from which we construct and compare our own, self-invented knowledge. In order to address the many social, cultural and political ills that mark our particular epoch, *POST* education needs to be concurrently implemented alongside the professional preparation that now dominates Dysacademia.

Thus located, contemporary academics and others concerned with the plight of the University should be motivated and encouraged to explore the conscious and social constructions of knowledge in a more comprehensive, critical, and gaping manner that accounts for many postmodern and poststructural claims; not to authoritatively explain it ("it" being true knowledge), nor to differentiate between truth/fiction, to play into the modern objective/subjective binary, or to establish a new hierarchical, sedentary and closed language game that presumes hierarchical legitimacy. I don't want to *decelerate* the exciting and open chaos of knowledge into modern, linear and simple categories. Rather, I argue for an active and open *acceleration* and enhanced awareness of intellectual and ontological fractal geometry. In Serresian parlance, I am seeking a paradigm of prepositions that allow mobility and fluidity (between, for, with, to, and), and not one of verbs that imply, insinuate, or demonstrate permanence, rigidity, or linearity (connect, fix, construct, create). Nor am I positing that there exists one true positivist source of knowledge that provides the ultimate blueprint to the universe and its many metaphysical, surreal and multiplistic components. Rather, I argue, as Serres does, that educated citizens and educators in particular, should through active participation in a *POST* based educational experience, strive to gain a certain level of understanding and discovery of how other sources of knowledge effect, influence and interplay with other more familiar sources of knowledge; how the student and the curriculum are deeply connected in one large open, postmodern system.

In order for a *POST* curriculum & pedagogy to be realized, one kind of inquiry would not be able to dominate others as the "way" to knowledge, and thus, the structure of research and curricula would need to be resituated in order to maximize the multiplicity of small narratives. For Michel Serres, classic epistemology in the "modern" sense is thus unattractive, unoriginal, and lazy because it merely reproduces and repackages old ideas and information with "ultra technical vocabulary that breeds fear and exclusion" (Serres & Latour, 1995, 24); and thus, an "authentic epistemology is the art of inventing, the springboard for passing from the old to the new." To Michel Foucault, this represents the essential purpose and critical foundation of philosophy, that being "precisely the challenging of all phenomena of domination at whatever level or under whatever form they present themselves—political, economic, sexual, institutional and so on" (Bernauer & Rasmussen, 1988, 20). It is here that Lyotard's theoretical position seems to comply with the poststructural approach I am proposing (*POST*), but with one caveat—Lyotard seems to contradict his post disciplinary views in other sections of *The Postmodern Condition*. Specifically, Lyotard seems to reject any interdisciplinary organization of knowledge (see Wilson's Consilience), as it implies to him a "common measure" or the development of new language games, which of course reifies narratives and eventually, meta narratives (Lyotard, 50). In "defining" a poststructural structure as "an ordered multiplicity of ordered multiplicities" (1995a, 106), Serres' poetic thoughts can be seen then to effectively soften Lyotard's extreme, and perhaps somewhat nihilistic poststructural concern with a more modest appreciation for the power and epistemological infinity of "multiplicities" and fragile syntheses of thought.

The work of transformation is that of the multiple. (1995a, 101)

It is not an everyday occurrence when there is a potential meeting between refined branches of knowledge, overt phenomena, and everyday language. We need to conceive the multiple as such...we need it in the social sciences and the humanities. (1995a, 103)

Higher education should rightfully provide the same critical and philosophical foundation for all of its subjects; the ability to challenge, to deconstruct, to operationalize, and to appreciate multiple problematic perspectives should be endowed in all college and university graduates, regardless of their chosen field of study, or subsequent professional line of work. As Derrida suggests, this is the responsibility of the University. But perhaps more importantly, a *POST* curriculum and pedagogy would reflect the ethics of Michel Serres, in that it would be lived in the spaces, in between known and unknown, between this and that, between self and other; allowed to wander in the open, unknown spaces without an explicit pressure to reach any specific, predetermined and solid place. Becoming *POST* consilient in our knowledge, understanding and experiences also has the potential for many different levels of application and meaning, depending upon the discipline and setting of specific individuals.

For example, as a university educator and allied health education program director, I must consider and effectively incorporate a diverse multitude of knowledge, perspectives, and experiences relative to pedagogy, curriculum, and educational administration that have profound and dynamic interconnections to my everyday practice as teacher, mentor, parent and citizen. Granted this can be a time consuming, romanticized and daunting transformative process, but one that perhaps all educators and students wishing to be truly educated ought be willing and anxious to embrace. To be sure, this enterprise includes the need for the professorate to address the various concerns presented by Bok regarding university pedagogy (or lack thereof) in his critique of higher education; and it should go without saying that the implications for such a proposal extend far beyond the walls of the academy, and into the halls and walls of our primary and secondary schools, as well as our homes. And as my utterance concerns a problem as complex and gargantuan as Dysacademia, I am fully aware that certain practical, economic, political and sociocultural barriers exist that hinder the potential realization of such a pedagogy, but one must start somewhere; and so in the parlance of Pinar et al., the current discourse is "intended as much to provoke questions as it is to answer questions" (1995, 56).

Wandering Towards a Poststructural Episteme

Joe Kincheloe's work (1993, 1995) reflects a notion similar to Consilience in describing his perception of the *contextualization movement*. It may even seem ironic perhaps, that Edward Wilson could actually be viewed as a soldier of the *contextualization movement* with his modern-day introduction of Consilience. As I understand it, the contextualization scholars are proponents of an ideology that promotes the integration of concepts, and ideas of knowledge against a larger framework. Kincheloe has advocated for an inclusion and coherence of such issues as personal and social history, cultural diversity, and philosophical agendas into school curriculums and in an effort to reverse the modernist trend towards the decontextualization and fragmentation of skills and knowledge in our schools. This fragmentation, Kincheloe feels, separates our schools from the world in which we actually live and work (1995, 347). Inclusion, coherence, separation, and fragmentation—words and concepts that ring similar to myriad scholars from many disciplines investigating the postmodern nature of knowledge and understanding.

In *Schools Where Ronnie and Brandon Would Have Excelled*, Kincheloe writes about modern teachers and the isolation that they have from one another, from their students, and from the outside world of business and politics (Kincheloe, 1995). His frustration with the fragmentation of teachers' experiences, resources, and educational outlooks parallels the discontent expressed by Wilson in *Consilience*. In the latter text, Wilson describes how postmodern academic scientists have become fragmented from their colleagues, and has in effect, become stranded on their own *philistine* research islands. Stranded, they have become cut off from the consilient purpose of science—to unify the knowledge and make sense of the world. Kincheloe expresses similar concern over the failure of our current educational paradigm to recognize the academic, sociopolitical and cognitive capacities that our model students and citizens must possess if they are going to make a real-world difference (Kincheloe, 1995, 349). In support of his argument, he introduces the following challenge (from Grubb, 1991, as cited in Kincheloe).

> Such a recognition can serve to construct a revolutionary consciousness, a way of seeing that will not allow the world to remain the same. (349)

Finding and developing teachers with special insights who are interested in, capable of, and motivated to integrate a consilient, reconceptualized curriculum is what is needed if we are to begin to truly reform our educational system, and thus the Dysacademia that now infects it. Kincheloe goes on to argue that a sense of "dualism" (not to be confused with the now much maligned theory of Dualism presented by Descartes) is also required in today's teaching workforce; whereby teachers not only know "what," but also know "how." In Kincheloe's consilient curriculum, teachers must be able to "...separate theory from practice, thinking from doing, and learning principles from devising applications if they are to be capable of transferring knowledge and skills to the working world" (1995, 356). In William Doll's terms, teachers in such a critical, integrative curriculum must be able to "jump together" knowledge in a connected, coherent way; and to reconnect her/himself to all facets of the educational experience, a point similarly echoed by Kincheloe.

> Integration, no matter what form it takes, should strengthen the teaching of all subjects. When adeptly executed, integration should make history, literature, and the social sciences come alive for previously unmotivated students. (359)

Kincheloe provides a very effective example of this "model" by highlighting the need for vocational students in agriculture and farming to also be well versed and experienced in the environmental sciences. Consilient in the sense that students may gain valuable insight into the connections between farming and pollution; skilled and conversant in the politics of environmental damage; aware of how big business keeps the government from interfering with their insensitive ecological practices. In turn, this requires that future farmers acquire a deep and genuine understanding of how big business works, from Wall Street economics, to the development and perpetuation of corporate culture, to the dynamics of the political lobbying machine in our nation's capital. In integrated *POST* curricula such as this, the key dynamic at work according to Kincheloe is that both the teacher and student are "learning how to learn."

Perhaps the strength of Kincheloe's postmodern consilient philosophy is probably best supported through his *Critical constructivist* concept of education. He aptly defines Critical Constructivism as a form of *world making*, whereby constructivist teachers teach for understanding and application. Included in this critical postmodern curriculum of integration are the central role of student experiences, and their original and personal constructions of the subject matter(s). Here, Kincheloe goes on to criticize the schools of the post-enlightenment era for emphasizing the learning of that which had already been defined as knowledge, rather than emphasizing the actual production of knowledge (1995, 356). A curriculum of true integration attempts to focus its attention on the cognitive processes of the learner. Recall for a moment Wilson's argument for Consilience, and our subsequent over-reliance on the biological sciences to reveal how the mind works in order to answer many of the questions and issues of the modern world. This would mean that consilient intellectuals and postmodern constructivists would thus have to acquire a coherent knowledge in psychology, sociology, biology, anthropology, as well as the humanities and the arts.

A Bell Ringing in the Empty Sky, by David Jardine (1992) also presents several arguments and ideas that reflect a notion of a consilient curriculum. In this very personal and self-reflective essay, Jardine uses the metaphor of a ringing bell that represents the center of all things. As a representation of the coherence and interconnectedness of all things, Jardine also argues that all things are ordered around the ringing bell, that they are linked together in one way or another. Wilson would certainly agree with this precept, but would add that all things are connected through the natural sciences. Jardine's *Empty Sky*, indicating that a lack of interconnectedness is present and thus not allowing the bell's ringing to be heard, represents the discontent found in the works of Serres, Kincheloe, and others with the current state of affairs amongst the post-Enlightenment thinkers, scholars, scientists, and teachers. Jardine's highly effective metaphor depicting our species existing in an empty sky symbolizes the relative lack of understanding of the interdependency and complexity of the world amongst many of those in power in the current educational and social systems. Wilson presents a parallel argument in his quest for Consilience amongst the scientists and policy makers of the world, and presents many specific examples to support his argument including one for education. Jardine argues that our over-reliance on fragmented knowledge and our dependence upon knowledge produced by isolated empiricism has caused our lives to become episodic, and not semantic (1992, 266). If we continue trotting along in such an isolated and fragmented manner, Dysacademia left untreated may prevent us from ever hearing the bell ringing in the empty sky.

To fuel his arguments for the ringing bell to be heard by all, Jardine presents a quote from Hahn that also parallels the Wilson's convictions—"The universe is a dynamic fabric of interdependent events in which none is the fundamental entity" (as cited in Jardine, 1992, 272). Jardine is not advocating, however, that we become totally self-absorbed in seeing ourselves as the center of the universe, or that we employ a "violent colonization" of all things. Merely, he is making the point that we all need to recognize the indebtedness to the existence of all things in one's self. In effect, we need to come to the understanding that all things are not here for us as individuals, but that we are part of all things—in a way connected and dependent, but not self-existent. With more brevity, we need to become more postmodernly consilient by embracing a *POST* way of seeing, thinking and inventing.

Diversified, eclectic, personal, non-restrictive, interconnected and coherent—terms that have been used, discussed, advocated, and implemented by curriculum theory scholars and intellectuals. Perhaps

POST can now be added to this list, and thus incorporated into the current discourse of reconceptualization in the curricular field. Perhaps *POST* can coherently represent all of these words, and initiate a new or modified line of reasoning in the debate on educational reform. As I have attempted to demonstrate in the preceding sections, myriad postmodern reconceptualization scholars such as William Pinar (psychoanalysis theory), Joe Kincheloe (Marxist theory), & David Jardine (phenomenology), each seem to have individually captured the spirit of the *POST* conception I have articulated in their writings and expressions on curriculum theory in unique and expressive ways. Together, the narratives put forth by reconceptualized curriculum theorists present specific challenges to all teachers, administrators and students in a sincere attempt to focus on "the learning of learning" (What is learning? How does one learn? When is learning done?), on the individual self, on developing a true awareness of the inherent and coherent nature of knowledge, on the self-actualization process, and on the discovery and refinement of new *truths* and new, contextual and locally subjective knowledge. Wilson openly admonishes the scientific community concerning the pitfalls of anti-consilient rhetoric and knowledge development, while alternatively advocating for an environment whereby one hand genuinely understands what the other hand is doing. Curricular theorists seem to be arguing for the same type of educational reform—one that intertwines the many diverse faces of the individuals involved, one that addresses the many complex domains of society, human culture and the modern world; and one that regresses from the current empirical model that weighs objectives and performance on a predictable scale of educational competency. A *consilient curriculum* might just be the one, but maybe with a more postmodern twist.

Summarily, my critique is specifically aimed at higher education in the United States, and as such, it is my specific position that university education today no longer serves as the critical springboard to diverse and meaningful intellectual transformation and exploration as it once did when liberal arts and comprehensive pedagogy were more *en vogue*. It can perhaps be surmised that our current educational condition can be traced, but certainly not limited, to at least three co-evolutionary, multifactorial, interrelated and mitigating factors that have metastasized over the last 40 - 50 years in our society. Amongst the principal genealogical and archeological perpetrators contributing to our quasi-necrotic educational condition are, 1) an over-reliance on the processes and mechanisms of objective science (reductionism) and the subsequent development of "quasi-objective" behaviorist psychology (cognitive psychology & learning theories) & Tylerian curricular principles, 2) the neoliberal, performative, and industrio-capitalistic emphases placed on the larger Western educational mission of universities and colleges, particularly in the United States; today they can be distinguished by the myriad specialized academic majors that financially support their respective operation, existence and educational "mission" and the obvious corporative transformation occurring on many campuses across the nation, and 3) the pronounced Foucaultian-Lyotardian-Deleuzian relationship between power, knowledge and control as evidenced by the interrelated concepts of political technology of the body and language games; especially as they pertain to the professional and academic disciplines and their pedagogical utilities. Due to the overwhelming volume of scholarship addressing the pedagogical implications associated with the post-Sputnik social and cultural influences on the development and reliance upon the scientific management and social efficiency paradigms for education, most notably presented and contested in Pinar, Reynolds, Slattery and Taubman's synoptic, yet comprehensive *Understanding Curriculum* (1995, 95), the current focus will extend primarily to the discourses surrounding the latter two interconnected and intricate factors.

Because higher education now seems to rely largely upon a quasi-scientific, compartmentalized disciplinary and foundational model (behaviorist psychology, curriculum guidelines, accreditations standards & objectives) to essentialize knowledge, truth and reality, it is my observation that the contemporary customer of the educational factory that is "higher education" is being denied her/his epistemological and axiological rights, human potential, and ultimately, a free, critical and personal existence. As such, it can quite easily be argued that many of today's college graduates merely symbolize a departmentalized, specialized and highly technocratic "product" that has been sold a bill of goods, an object that has been subsequently duped into believing that they have paid for, and received in full the tools and knowledge necessary to create a substantive and critical ontological and epistemological foundation—a foundation that has traditionally been intended to provide the means necessary to transform each participant into active and productive citizens in a democratic, postmodern society.

On the flip side, there also exists an inordinately high number of students entering the college and university ranks with deep-seated industrial and capitalistic notions of what a college degree signifies, what its utility is, and what the end goal should be of graduating from college—a good paying job. Yes, most colleges still have core requirements steeped in the traditional liberal arts curriculum; yes, many colleges are experimenting with various pedagogical manifestations of interdisciplinary curricula in an attempt to hold on to the liberal arts and humanities; and, yes critical, transformative institutions of higher education do still exist in this country and they are doing their part to turn out critical and reflexive citizens for our democratic society. But the fundamental problem to be addressed here lies in the bare fact that these positive and exemplary instances seem to be in the ever increasing minority, and the majority is now made up of general education institutions, online universities, and money making "degree stampers" who increasingly appear to resemble businesses more so than they do inventors of subjectivity, transformation and intellectual complexity.

If this is indeed the case, that the socio-cultural role of the academy has unashamedly shifted towards neoliberal principles of market value, commodification and technocratic expertise and away from intellectual diversification and maturity, then the majority of young citizens entering our complex, post-human/modern/disciplinary /colonial/911/structural world as professional policy makers, politicians, business leaders, educators, and eventually parents, are lacking a certain critical mass required to confront our immediate and long-term posthuman conditions that are staring the collective "us" right in the face. Something needs to change before this negentropic, but closed system (negentropy in a closed system is dangerous due to the structural constraints that define and objectify the system, in contrast to an open system) self-implodes upon itself and obliterates our civilization, our humanity, and our ecosphere.

It is my concern that far too many contemporary college and university graduates are relatively ill-prepared to carry out the meaningful deconstruction and problem solving skills needed for confronting the myriad critical social, scientific, and political issues that define and characterize our (post) human condition in inventive and creative manners. With reference to Lyotard's' dualistic model for higher education, I am deeply concerned that today's academy may not be producing an adequate amount of the second type citizen he cites—the educated elite capable of maintaining the "internal cohesion" of our society. Rather, it has been my collective experiences as a constituent of higher education that has lead me to the impression that too many general university students today enroll for specific job training skills and knowledge, and the associated lure of economic and social security that higher education promises.

In fact, a recent study conducted by *The Chronicle of Higher Education* supports Wiener's "social status," and Giroux's *neoliberalist* influence claims by demonstrating that 92% of the public it surveyed sees higher education's most important role today as "preparing undergraduates for a career" (Selingo, 2003, A10). Additionally, the Chronicle's fairly inclusive study shows that 90% of all respondents consider higher education to be principally responsible for "providing education for adults to qualify for better jobs." Ironically, respondents also urged universities to focus less on research and economic development, and to focus more on general education, teacher education, leadership and responsibility. How universities should reconcile the public's perceived need to *decrease* initiatives designed to spur local and regional economic growth, educate students *more* for the economic work place, *and* to focus *more* on civic, social and personal responsibilities and general intellectual growth at the same time, is a very interesting and complex social impression that begs further research and analysis.

As a result of our current and long-standing Dysacademic condition, far too many students today are not intellectually capable of inventing the knowledge necessary to deal with the issues that we, as a historical society/culture, have left for them to confront; they either don't have, or aren't allowed the opportunity to live, work and exist from within, or without a Thoureauvian consciousness. Global capitalization and the associated diminishing natural resources and increasing pollution/contamination of our ecosphere; post-Cold War and pre-postmodern war plutonium propagation; the human genome project, cloning and stem cell research; the ecological, social, economic and health complications associated with worldwide rain forest deforestation; and the scientific and technological invasion upon all forms of culture, including the impending development of artificial intelligence and autopoietic robots, are just of the few extremely complex and pressing issues facing our current and future generations.

Another relevant example (in addition to the post 9/11 example) involves the many complex and interconnected issues pertaining to global economic expansion, ecological sustainability, and our [post] human futures. Many students and young adults (and citizens for that matter) erroneously assume that recycling their bottles and newspapers is "all that is needed" to counter the Western world's hyper-consumptive appetite. As such, those who actually do recycle their waste containers are inclined to think that they are doing "their part" to solve this complex and multifaceted problem. Inextricably bound as cogs in the apparatus of consumption and its associated free market policies, much of today's citizenry (including those with higher education degrees) are unqualified to critically deconstruct their respective roles, impact and eventual effects in/on our current neoliberal society dominated by consumption, production, and the mythical American right to material acquisition. Bigger. Better. More. As long as I can afford it…it's my American right!

To further illustrate the need for, and relevance of a more *POST* based model for curriculum and education, consider the following example: most of the issues facing our society and civic leaders today contain important scientific and technological components. Everything from healthcare, to environment and ecology, endemic poverty, and of course, education represent complex, multifarious, and systemically related problems that require more than quick fix, linear solutions based on modern empirical thinking. In his latest book, *The Future of Life*, Wilson laments the prospects for mankind, earth, and our sustainable future by pointing out that we would theoretically require 4 more planet Earths to survive if every country were to reach the current level of consumerism found in America (2002, 46). When compared to the potential implications and complications associated with genetic cloning, stem-cell research, pharmaceutical memory pills, and information technology, these former issues seem somewhat less significant, however they are ALL inherently and problematically connected. Yet, many of our elected and hired professionals who are charged with acting upon these problems are ill equipped to integrate the necessary knowledge from the natural sciences with that of the social sciences and humanities. How can we expect such *(dys)educated* people to develop reasonable and effective strategies for resolving ethnic conflict, arms escalation, global warming, overpopulation, abortion, or rain forest and natural resource depletion? As Wilson suggests in *Consilience*, "...only fluency across the boundaries will provide a clear view of the world as it really is, not as seen through the lens of ideologies and religious dogmas or commanded by myopic response to immediate need" (1998, 13).

As a practicing health care provider, empowered with the care of physically active populations and with the teaching and mentoring of future health care providers, I must also consider how different technical and scientific knowledge developments potentially effect and interplay with current knowledge within my specific disciplinary field. *POST* understanding in this sense includes a masterful understanding of the relevant applications and limitations of empirical and theoretical scientific knowledge produced in the related disciplines, understanding the applicable limits of knowledge generated via the scientific method in sterile laboratory environments, and most importantly, knowing when to use certain techniques and knowledge and how to implement them according to contextual and pragmatic factors relative to individual patients. Thus, in order to provide sound, quality health care services to those under my care, and to provide a dynamic, evolving and "interdisciplinary" education to my students, I must stay abreast of the latest developments in orthopedics, physical rehabilitation, sports psychology, nutrition, exercise physiology, and wellness.

To some, it is painfully obvious that these domains all represent content—skills and knowledge of a "technical nature" required for professional competence and eventual career advancement. True, but what may not be obvious to many is that I must also include in my curriculum other, less tangible skills and knowledge related to ethics, values, professionalism, multiculturalism, and the socioeconomic elements of healthcare, pain, and wellness in order for my students to be more "global" and critical practitioners. Also lacking in this admission is "how" I teach these various domains—my pedagogy if you will. As a member of the academy, I'm also responsible for "higher educating" my students beyond the standards and guidelines constricted upon me by my profession, my discipline and my accrediting body. How I do that comes down to pedagogy, philosophy and in my case by following a *POST* based pedagogy and curricular perspective. As such, I argue that it is equally, if not more so, critical for academicians in all fields to appreciate and make earnest efforts to do the same with their students, their curricula, and their pedagogy. Just consider for a moment what *POST* educated graduates in information technology, education, political science and business, just to name a few might "look" like should they be allowed and encouraged to be dissipative and inventive open system creatures.

As I become more cognizant of, and immersed with, the various sources of knowledge associated with curriculum, teaching, & learning, and how they are each themselves interconnected to the larger web that is society—culture, politics, art, pop culture, history, science, phenomenology, hermeneutics, etc., the more consilient I will become in my pedagogy—the more capable I will be of understanding and connecting some of the dots between knowledge fields. In contrast, the more I remain in my closed and disciplined spaces relative to my professional field, the more I will close down spaces and stunt growth in my students. Because I have worked hard within my discipline to bring various forms of related knowing in my field together both practically and didactically, I feel that I am also in the process of becoming a more *POST* health care provider in that I am more fully aware of the non-linear, fractal and open nature of the human body, wellness and pathology. Discussing, participating in, or attempting to develop resolutions to these contemporary problems, as well as various others, requires both breadth and depth of knowledge; it requires a transdisciplinary and transideological approach that embraces multiples, heterogeneity, complexity and invention. It requires a critical *POST* approach that promotes and encourages the development of what Michel Serres calls "the 3rd person," of multiple 3rd spaces, and one that subsequently relies upon a 3rd pedagogy and curriculum. In this light then, many contemporary college graduates may be ill prepared to demarcate and clarify the various knowledge claims that philosophy, science and art (on a more global level, inclusive of the humanities, music, etc.) construct of our world, and thus are not inclined to think openly, critically and reflexively about issues requiring a certain "chaoplexic" approach (Arnott, 1999, 49). By "chaoplexic," Arnott is integrating the properties and principles of chaos and complexity theories into a postmodern appreciation for the notion that as things appear to get more chaotic, they actually show deeper signs of complexity and organization—students, professionals, human subjects.

If, as noted and self-professed *amodern* philosopher Michel Serres says, "the goal of instruction is invention" (Serres & Latour, 1995, 133), and if the "goal of teaching is to have teaching to cease" (22), then pedagogy today may be exposed as being more "necrotic" (dead, as in lacking nutrition and energy) than alive; or at least "quasi-necrotic." Simply put, in these current times of classroom discipline, rabid standardization, measurable outcomes and teacher accountability that so typify our 21st-century educational paradigm at all levels, the typical American student has very little opportunity or initiative to invent his/her own knowledge, and thus, very little ability to teach the self. As the "founder" of cybernetics, Norbert Wiener, points out, this is not a new or novel argument.

> Our elementary and secondary schools are more interested in formal class-room discipline than in the intellectual discipline of learning something thoroughly, and a great deal of the serious preparation for a scientific or a literary course is relegated to some sort of graduate school or other. (1954, 132)

For Wiener, education in the 1950s was already being viewed as a closed and myopic system, one wherein young minds were no longer implored to think, to invent, or to experience knowledge for themselves; young actors were "taught" how to act rather than being allowed to express their art forms from within, and young writers were schooled in "how" to write from expert sources, rather than being allowed to invent their own form of communicative art. In short time, highly specialized and advanced degrees, especially the PhD, were the standard bearers of knowledge and communication needed to impart learning and skill onto the masses. To Wiener, "forms" of knowledge and occupational skill now superseded critical and intellectual mass as part of a fast moving trend towards an "ever-increasing thinness of educational content"; while the artistic desire to invent was rapidly being structured around particular methods and forms, and thus, subsequently extinguished in all but the most extraordinary of students (1954, 133). In harmony with Serres' and Wiener's critical calls for invention to serve as the primary focus of education, Katherine Hayles suggests that the creative writer is perhaps the best example of a free-floating and chaotic inventor, capable of connecting various epistemic cultures. Working from the "third territory" then, somewhere between order and disorder, is what allows the creative writer to communicate beyond one particular field of study, and thus better capture and articulate the "aura of cultural meanings that surround chaos" (1990, 19).

And so, if individual subjects are not provided a clean canvas, a blank parchment, or an open space with which to invent one's own objective worldview, or one's own self-constructed and reflexive language game, it can be surmised that he/she will more than likely not be able to transform in unknown, open manners, he/she won't be able to cultivate a unique and plastic ontology, nor a critical and multivocal epistemology. Forced to exist with current and historical language games, to acquire a worldview from within an already vulcanized, fragmented and specialized disciplinary field, inevitably and dangerously denies the subject the opportunity to genuinely channel their respective experiences and worldly interpretations into a meaningful and organic subjectivity. Of what aesthetic quality and intellectual depth would Henry David Thoreau's literary work have if he did not have the natural respite that Walden Pond provided? What would have become of Albert Einstein's scientific endeavors if not for his genuine appreciation for poetry, music and the arts and his firm conviction in the value of a well-rounded and balanced education?

Walden Pond provided Thoreau with the opportunity to explore nature in its natural splendor, the opportunity to invent his own biological worldview, and thus a contrast of sorts that allowed him to compare his socially constructed world with his natural ontological and epistemological perspectives; an experience that perhaps allowed him to more critically reflect on the rapidly evolving industrial society and urban life from a different, somewhat self-invented perspective. This contrast of views and experiences provided both Thoreau & Einstein with unique epistemic privileges that infiltrated their literary and narrative works on many levels—a type of dispensation that can be seen as being more consilient than linear, more comprehensive and multiple than singular, more liberated and less restrictive, more inventive and less transparent. In referring to interpretation and aesthetic value as they relate to education, perhaps it would not be a large stretch to surmise that both Thoreau and Einstein would agree with Norbert Wiener's eloquent sentiment on the subject of nature and knowledge when he said that, "no school has a monopoly on beauty" (1954, 134).

From this perspective then, I wish to advance a "curriculum reconceptualized" by integrating what I see as complementary concepts from various scientific frames of thought to the larger framework of pedagogy, curriculum and the student in a postmodern manner. It is my position that much, if not all of the central constructs that characterize *open systems theory* (OST), cybernetics and information theory, and chaos and complexity theories can with a little theoretical creativity, be applied to a postmodern curriculum, and in so doing, create an educational paradigm that maximizes mobility, growth, wandering and eventually negentropy (or, complex order); what I have termed *POST*. In constructing this paradigm, I have intended to introduce and arrange the contributing parameters for my theoretical conception of the 3rd *Person*, and the 3rd *Curriculum*—the focus of my final chapter. It is hoped that the critical development and appreciation of a 3rd *Person* & 3rd *Curriculum* for the postmodern University, as I am attempting to articulate, will be one that extrapolates specific conceptual elements from various theories related to open systems, chaos, information, multiplicities, and rhizomes; and subsequently connects and relates these complimentary concepts as constituent structures of an alternative postmodern curricular discourse that provides openings, possibilities, and recursions. And in an attempt to adhere to the poststructural notion that "theory is not prescriptive," it's merely "idiosyncratic," the discourse I have constructed is offered "up front" with the full awareness that it's effectiveness (real or potential) can only be embodied by a discourse structured by invention, hope, prospects and multiplicity (Pinar et al, 1995, 56).

In short, all students, regardless of their chosen and intended academic/pre-professional field of study, should be invited into the murky, nebulous, and rhizomatic world of postmodern open systems thinking; all students should become 3rd persons at some point in time, and likewise, all members of the professorate should continually and consistently be/come 3rd teachers. Postmodern students suffering from the modern viruses that induce dysgnosia, dyslogia, and dyserethesia as sequelae of their disciplined and controlled dyskinesia, and thus seeking rehabilitation or medication ought to learn to relish in the disorder and turbulence of open spaces (milieu). Members of the professorate can only counteract the "death of the professor" by becoming and remaining the 3rd instructor by entering into, moving amongst, and remaining in multiple 3rd spaces. Students and teachers alike must be allowed to seek gradual and fragile order not through modern disciplinarity and control, but rather through chaos and dissipation. Dysacademics ought be shown, and allowed to enter the passageway to what Serres refers to impassionedly as the "third place" (1997, 8). In order to treat, and prevent Dysacademic dyskinesia from inflicting the self, teachers must teach and allow students "to dance"; for the teacher has failed if the student hasn't learned how to dance among the domains of knowing and being (1995, 45). In expressing his strong dislike for *research* (why re-search, when one can search?), Serres articulates his fervent belief that, "to discover seems the only act of intelligence...ideas that circulate are usually astonishingly old, thus, he who seeks newness remains alone" (Serres & Latour, 1995, 145). Surely then, one cannot discover for oneself, if one allows oneself to be a docile participant in our current disciplined, controlled, and neoliberal-industrial curriculum.

> Thus the issue returns with insistence: how do we change mentalities, how do we reinvent social practices that would give back to humanity—if it ever had it—a sense of responsibility, not only for its own survival, but equally for the future of all life on the planet, for animal and vegetable species, likewise for incorporeal species such as music, the arts, cinema, the relation with time, love and compassion for others, the feeling of fusion at the heart of cosmos? (Guattari, 1995, 120)

Rather, it should be clear at this point that schooling at any level should be based on Serres' contention that invention is education's central purpose, not reproduction and meaningless debate. Furthermore, pedagogy must be connected to the larger socio-cultural mission of education, regardless of what the chosen discipline is/will be. Peter Berger, renowned sociology scholar, coined this *sociological consciousness* and wrote that the critical development of such rigorous intellectual skills would allow the knower to deconstruct, or "see through" the various social structures that form opinions and myth, privilege power and authority, bias certain forms of knowing and knowledge, and situate our social roles and identities (1965). According to the multiple studies cited by Derek Bok in his stinging critique of higher education in America, this is not happening on a large scale. In order to do this—to invent the critical knowledge needed to reach sociological consciousness—students must be allowed to traverse into, between and amongst what Serres calls the "third place" (Serres, 1997, 43). That is, all parties in the pedagogy relation, both student and teacher, must be *allowed to* endure the pain, the discomfort, the uncertainty, and most importantly a certain, undetermined "boundarylessness of self" that accompanies a critical ontological evolution into the third place). For this to happen, teachers, intellectuals, and administrators must reach out and interact with students as subjects viably interconnected with the purposes of education and democracy, rather than merely treating students as objects knotted within an overly determined, objective and fixed educational process. Teachers must of course adhere to academic and professional standards that subsume both the discipline's knowledge base with the teachers' professional experiences; I am not calling for pedagogical anarchy, or professional nihilism in any manner. Standardization of knowledge, of method, of delivery and of thought is unethical, unprofessional, and counter productive to the larger mission of the University, writ large. And above all, university educators of all disciplines must be allowed and encouraged to teach students how "to be" citizens with varied professional lives and purposes, not just merely how "to do" their chosen profession. Young professionals must be critically and ontologically connected to the larger problems of society, and to what is required to live "in" a democracy, not just live "off" of a democracy by coming face to face with their own, disciplined intellectual and cultural myopia. In describing the social forces that now bind the various "intellectual" and "cultural" fields into one homogenous and legitimate competition, Pierre Bourdieu classifies the insular and juvenile condition of what he calls "independent intellectuals."

Everything leads one to suppose that the constitution of a relatively autonomous intellectual field is the condition for the appearance of the in-

dependent intellectual, who does not recognize nor wish to recognize any
obligations other than the intrinsic demands of his creative project. (1969, 91)

It has been the intent of the current chapter to present the various
characteristics, criteria, and phenomena associated with open systems
and chaos, and to communicate them as small elements of a compelling and practical model for a postmodern open systems education,
and for students to be understood, viewed, and handled as living,
undetermined and open systems with equal complexity, depth, and
breadth. All regarded and understood as a paradigm of hope operating underneath a veil of postmodern sensibility; a curriculum that
empowers and enables students to see through the transparent guise
of a preconceived modern utopia, full of happiness and peace for all;
one that affectively harmonizes with Marla Morris' *dystopic* concerns
for a curriculum she sees as "more adequate to the task of becoming
an educated person" (2001, 199). Situated as such, it is my intention to
present a model of pedagogy (inclusive of the curriculum and the
student) that can reasonably and theoretically be seen as a self-
organizing, entropic, fractal, chaotic, dissipative, and autopoietic subjectivity for students entering into the curriculum by appreciating the
power and vitality of Michel Serres' articulation of the 3rd, or middle
place. From here, I wish to add a more postmodern intellect to these
concepts by elaborating more upon the pedagogical and cultural
thoughts of Michel Serres, Gilles Deleuze, Felix Guattari, and others
in an attempt to articulate an alternative, sub-discourse pedagogical
paradigm that I will call the *3rd Curriculum*. As students progress
through a curriculum reconceptualized as such, they don't proceed in
a linear and scientific fashion of objectivity and controlled order;
rather, they transform from entropy (disorder) towards negentropic
(order) and complex forms, but in a more fractal, rhizomatic and
postmodern manner that is not predicted, controlled, or manipulated
by objective ideals, essential knowledge, or modern absolutes.

CHAPTER SEVEN

Inventing Multiple 3rd Persons & 3rd Spaces

I see that clear knowledge contains a blindness almost as far-reaching as the dark knowledge contained in ignorance is. Sometimes one can only under- stand if one liquidates one's knowledge in the loyal narrative of circum- stance. The solutions do not always reside in the place where one looks for them. One must always pay, that is, accept that one must pay off this change of place with some kind of blindness, in order to see better.

--Michel Serres (1997, 66)

Do the patterns of thought and language transmitted by the school, e.g., those which treatises of rhetoric used to call figures of speech and figures of thought, actually fulfill, at any rate among members of the educated classes, the function of the unconscious patterns which govern the thinking and the productions of people belonging to traditional societies, or do they operate only at the most superficial level of consciousness?

--Pierre Bourdieu (1967, 339)

Problematizing the Order of the University

In examining various contemporary curricular discourses across the domains of higher education, it should by now be fairly apparent that a dramatic change has indeed occurred. In short, our Dysacademic in- stitutions of higher learning seem to be increasingly characterized by fewer open and turbulent passages for personal and subjective inven- tions. As a direct result of this institutional metamorphosis, there now appears to be very little opportunity for University students, our fu- ture civic, political, social, scientific leaders to patch up their highly *comminuted curricula* (comminuted as in what a shotgun wound would do to a bone) through invention, subjective scaffolding, and original iteration (Abbott, 2001; Bertalanffy, 1969; Doll, 1993; Martusewicz, 2001; Serres, 1982, 1997, 1995a, & 1995b; Trifonas, 2000; Wilson, 1998). Subtle, but telling support for this somber unease can be seen in the results of a recent study on the reading proficiency of recent college graduates, conducted by the National Center for Education Statistics (as cited by Romano, December 26, 2005). The study cites that, although more and more Americans are now graduating from college, far fewer are graduating, specialized degrees in hand with the skills needed to comprehend routine data or basic instructions, compare competing viewpoints, or read prose in order to understand information expressed via symbolism, metaphors, or analogies. According to the National Center for Education Statistics' findings, only 31% of college graduates were classified as being capable of reading a complex book and extrapolating from it (compared to 40% in 1992), and only 41% of the graduates students tested in 2003 could be classified as "proficient" in prose (down 10% points since 1992). Translation, we are producing more college graduates with highly specialized degrees that "may" indeed contribute to our socio-economic wellness one future day, but they are largely and increasingly less adept at demonstrating skills, awareness, or knowledge outside of their disciplined education.

Viewed differently, there seems to be a subtle but translucent return in the Academy to what Foucault painstakingly described in *The Order of Things*; that being the Lamarckian and Linnaean foundations of rational, objective and controlled order in the various and separated disciplines that defined Classical thinking up to the 18th century (Foucault, 1970). An order that, translucent as it may be, is also sadly connected to the hegemonic power and authority associated with economically based, disciplinary competition. In effect, it can be argued then that education writ large has effectively become a "closed system," one now reflecting the various and sundry values associated with neoliberal, capitalistic, and social efficiency agendas and initiatives that further remove the institution of education from its larger historical, personal and social mission(s). In his call for a new ethico-aesthetic paradigm of thought for psychoanalysis, Felix Guattari connects the institutional and social fragmentation (that I have previously described and subsequently applied to the Academy), to a like process seen in the subjective, living and plastic self—a concept I wish to explore further in the remaining section of this text.

> The devaluation of the meaning of life provokes the fragmentation of the self-image: its representations become confused and contradictory. (1995, 12)

Derrida's Institutional *Dysphilosophy*

Much heralded and influential French philosopher Jacques Derrida is well known for his early and significant work in the area of deconstruction, particularly as it pertains to language, text, and communication. Along the way, Derrida has applied his profound and original thinking in myriad writings and presentations on such varied cultural and social issues as forgiveness, violence, love, being, technology, art, the Internet, ethics, and of course, philosophy (1988; 2000; 2002; 2004). Although not typically viewed as an "ethical" philosopher in the classical sense, Derrida's deconstructive philosophy is deeply concerned with the ethical responsibility we hold in recognizing the difference(s) of the other. Viewed as such, Derrida's various works commonly articulate a philosophy that is deeply axiomatic in both nature and intent, in that the various systems of norms, values and regulating principles that define and contain our culture can all be deconstructed and re-invented with critical reflection, contextual situatedness, and objective modesty (2002, 5). In 1991, Derrida demonstrated his ethical perspective in a lecture given at the first International Conference for Humanistic Discourses entitled "Du droit a la philosphie d'un point de vue cosmopolitique," and hosted by UNESCO (United Nations Educational, Scientific, and Cultural Organization) (first published in 1997; Trifonas, 2002, ix). Translated as "The Right to Philosophy from the Cosmopolitical Point of View," Derrida effectively "reveals how deconstruction can help an institution to reconfigure itself for the better by causing those who are part of it, are it, to question the grounding of the concepts they hold most dear as the keys to the perfectibility of human being" (Trifonas, 2002, x). At this point, it should be fairly evident that a certain deconstructive philosophy ("disguised" as theory) has been the central mechanism used herein to establish the *need* for a "reconfiguration" of the academy by presenting Dysacademia, and its many sub-maladies to the reader.

Naturally then, it is philosophy that begs itself to also be part of the "reconfiguration" needed in order to reconstruct, refigure, and re-invent the Academy for those with vested interests and critical concerns. Indeed, Derrida opens his exposition not by defining or justifying philosophy, but rather by asking the critical and more urgent question, "where ought it take place?" (2002, 2). Because of the institutional relations among universities and the institutions of culture, and the inherent interdisciplinary relation between philosophy and the other disciplines, the answer is actually quite simple for Derrida. Philosophy ought take place in institutions of research and education.

These institutions are already philosophemes...such institutions imply the sharing of a culture and a philosophical language...they are committed to make possible, first and foremost by means of education, the access to this language and culture...commit themselves, in principle, philosophically, to recognize and put into operation in an effective way something like philosophy and a certain philosophy of rights and law, the rights of man, universal history, etc. The signature of these charters is a philosophical act that makes a commitment to philosophy in a way that is philosophical. (2002, 3)

Derrida briefly deconstructs the Dysacademic status of philosophy in the modern University by lamenting its "disciplinary" and "aperformative" existence in modern institutions (2002, 9). He reiterates and updates this concern in other spaces as well, including his essays on the "Eyes of the University: Right to Philosophy 2," whereby he describes and laments how the State has shaped various discourses, rhetoric, and methods in the name of knowledge according to the rhythm of techno-science, while in the process marginalizing those knowledge domains with little, or no "performative value" to the state (2004, 78). Fragmented and excluded from other modes of inquiry by departmental hierarchies, essentialized as chiefly Eurocentric and canonical in character, and dubbed "aperformative" because of its non-impact on neoliberal policies and initiatives ("philosophy is everywhere suffering"), philosophical thinking (situated as a process of reasoned thinking described earlier, and thus rooted in the traditional "liberal arts") in today's academic institutions can be seen then to represent a "value neutral" endeavor. From Derrida's perspective then, value neutral equates to value negative; thus presenting a significant dilemma for those constituents who recognize as he does, that the entire University "is" essentially philosophical, and thus there is no reason to define, or constrain philosophy to one, essentialized and fragmented academic department.

Herein lies Derrida's fundamental and polyfactorial concern over the access to, and the existence of philosophy in contemporary institutions that are after all, philosophical ("love of knowledge"); and thus its critical relevance to the discourse concerning Dysacademia. Philosophy for Derrida has become *Dysacademicized* by the modern University, or better yet, perhaps it may now be thought of as *dysphilosophy*. In effect, modern philosophy is most often manifested by Eurocentric & Western works that operate to essentialize our epistemological, ontological and axiological perspectives and views; and so, it has been effectively dubbed as "the" philosophy of value in our current learning system. In other words, education is now treated like an industry responsible for the production of "knowledge as a valuable commodity," a sharp contrast to the mission put forth by the University of Frankfurt years ago (Derrida, 2004, 85). Sadly but assuredly, today's performative university is now analogous, or reflective even of our larger society, and is now just "one of the parts of the social system" it represents, rather than the organic initiator of new ideas, solutions, and discourses that it once represented. Second, modern philosophy has for the most part, dissipated from the contemporary academy curricula because of its limited powers to improve the performative quality of the University, or the local, regional and national economies. After all, what can one do with a philosophy degree in the 21ˢᵗ-century techno-science world? Of what economical value would subjects (object) liberated with arts be to a hyper capitalistic society? Lastly, Derrida is deeply concerned that when modern institutional philosophy "is" included/required in the curriculum, it is typically and problematically partitioned and fragmented into separate academic departments, and not interspersed "across the curriculum." The disciplinary fragmentation of philosophy effectively eliminates and marginalizes most of its potential for informing the other disciplines, and so its inherent value and utility is minimized even further.

> Thinking is always also compelled by institutional norms and forms, and displaces them. And sometimes it's within an institution, within the limits of an institution, that a philosophical or a thinking event may occur, then displacing the structure of the institution. (2004, 39)

Deconstructing for the Dilation of Space(s)

Having addressed the "where" for philosophy, our institutions, Derrida thus moves on to articulate the "why" and "what" of his thesis in the latter sections of his original lecture. Of critical importance for understanding Derrida's point(s) here is the realization that 1) not just "any" brand or type of philosophy deserves to hold the space, or produce the metalanguage for our many educational and cultural institutions, and 2) that the structure of the institution in which philosophy is housed must be displaced, or deconstructed if we hope to ever "do" anything with our thinking. In keeping with his poststructural legacy, Derrida briefly outlines and critiques the Eurocentric discourse surrounding the historical legacy of philosophy and its Greco-Roman roots, in order to "go beyond the tiresome, worn-out, and wearisome opposition between Eurocentrism and anti-Eurocentrism." Clearly positioned then, Derrida communicates a *different* sort of philosophy that is "no longer determined by a program, an originary language or tongue whose memory it would suffice to recover so as to discover its origin" (2002, 10). So as to avoid history, hegemony, and authority, Derrida articulates a "cosmopolitical" philosophy characterized by reflection, displacement and deconstruction of existing hegemonies, and one that provides the subject access to the philosophical events, signs, languages, and meta narratives that define, legitimate, and constrain our existence and our knowing. In short, a cosmopolitical philosophy is inherently poststructural in that it can be practiced in myriad ways, take multiple paths, and produce polyvocal languages with the intention of liberating the self from the dogmatism and authority that dominant current and historical languages produce/induce; in the current usage, it can be used then to "displace the University."

> It is a matter of putting into operation each time in an original way and in a nonfinite multiplicity of idioms, producing philosophical events that are neither particularistic and untranslatable nor transparently abstract and univocal in the element of an abstract universality. (12)

Contrasting such a cosmopolitical philosophy of openness, subjectivity and multiplicity, is a philosophical discourse based on a sole language (discipline, control, and performativity) that imposes itself upon the subject without any possible discussion—Dysacademia. For Derrida, the right to a cosmopolitical philosophy is not "just" about philosophy itself, nor the obvious applications to our complex technoscience world, but also about a certain "politics of thought," and a "democracy to come" that possesses the faculty to lead to a "rediscovery of an irreducible autonomy in science, law, religion, and democracy " (13). A worldwide philosophy is needed for all walks of life, all professionals, all who call themselves educated; a worldwide political philosophy that helps us understand what's happening through a deconstructive analysis capable of revealing the open systems nature of things and events; a worldwide philosophy that aids us in deconstructing the various social, cultural, scientific, and political myths that govern and distort our subjectivities and world views. A philosophy that helps more than 31% of college graduates read a complex book and be able to extrapolate from it, and subsequently contextualize and apply this type of thinking towards all sorts of "real world" problems in the professional, scientific, political, and economical realms of being. After all, as Derrida says, "every kind of thinking, of thought, is philosophical" (2002, 22), and "sometimes it's within an institution…that a philosophical or a thinking event may occur." A *cosmopolitical* philosophy, as Derrida suggests, is needed to deconstruct the system of Dysacademia and to displace the current [hyper]structure of the University; to open up the epistemological and ontological spaces for subjective growth and understanding (*POST* thinking), and for the transformation and development of 3rd person(s) and 3rd space(s). For Derrida, the responsibility of the university and of those associated with it are thus centered at the heart of the discourse (2004, 83), and his views on invention are clear, and interestingly very compatible with those of his contemporaries, e.g., Michel Serres. For both of these highly influential thinkers, there exist no essential, singular or natural events; deconstruction & displacement opens and dilates passages for philosophical and poetic re-invention; turbulence is required for invention; and the disciplined reproduce the discipline(s) with cultural reproduction and closed, modern thinking.

A Serresian Curriculum:
3rd Person(s) & 3rd Space(s)

In using a multitude of profound metaphors to express his "amodern" views of the larger, more philosophical undertaking for pedagogy in *Troubadour of Knowledge*, Michel Serres poetically articulates his visions of the purposes, processes and pains of true learning, while concurrently highlighting the pedagogical constraints that disciplinary boundaries impress upon one's epistemological and ontological development. To communicate this, Serres situates the learner in the midst of a turbulent river crossing (Serres).

> In crossing the river, in delivering itself completely naked to belonging to the opposite shore, it has just learned a third thing. The other side, new customs, a new language, certainly. But above all, it has just discovered learning in the blank middle that has no direction from which to find all directions. At the apex of the cranium, in a vortex, twists the cowlick's tuft, a place/milieu were all directions come together. Universal means what is unique yet versed in all directions. From then on, the solitary soul, wandering without belonging, can receive and integrate everything: all directions are equal. (1997, 7)

Knowledge for Serres then, is elliptical; it becomes decentered just like the world eventually does to each separate individual. Thus, the *third place* can only be borne if one enters the turbulence, the disorder, and the chaos that ironically and inevitably produces the order that the learner seeks (1997, 9). This third place requires the experience of experience, of exposure, of transformation, and even death; death in this case signifying the purging of old knowledge, old ideas, and misplaced opinions, and being replaced by new, invented ideas. It is here, in the 3rd place that Serres sees the educated soul residing, dilated only by experience and by learning. And, as many poststructural theorists often remind us, there are indeed many, multiple 3rd spaces *ad infinitum*, from wich to enter, exit and reside in; hence, the recognition of 3rd place(s) and space(s) (Deleuze, 1995; Deleuze & Guattari, 1987; Serres, 1995a). Characteristic of all such descriptions, the 3rd place(s) requires motility, hypermobility, plasticity, and even buoyancy; it is where both modes of knowledge (verification and inventiveness) can be addressed, and where each individual can form a *syrrhese*, or a mobile confluence of fluxes on his/her own topographical terms (Serres, 1995a, 126). It is the 3rd space(s) then that welcomes, comforts, and produces even, the 3rd person. Via a cosmopolitical philosophy capable of deconstructing and displacing the system, the 3rd person removes him/herself from the argumentative and perpetual binaries of conventional dialogue (from taking *one* side, or the other), and rather, invents her/his own version of events, dialogue, and concepts. Rather than taking part in one side of an existing argument, the 3rd person creates new tangent(s), new interpretation(s), and new possibility(s); multiple multiplicities, in fact. Wisdom or the intelligent use of knowledge, requires us then to invent a *3rd curriculum* and so to embrace and utilize a *3rd pedagogy*. A curriculum or pedagogy built upon the 3rd person, the 3rd space(s), and the 3rd conversation(s) is one that may prove to be more generally characterized by the instructed third (le Tiers-Instruit), or more simply, as a *Troubadour of Knowledge* (Serres, 1997, 184).

To Serres, knowledge is typically constructed in our Cartesian and Newtonian world around 2 dichotomized and comminuted poles (right/wrong, truth/fiction, good/bad, winner/loser, light/dark, etc.); and sadly, the 1st or 2nd instructed (her symbolized by the dysacademic) tend not to linger at the center of the two poles, in the turbulent, fluxed, hyperreality of the knowns and unknowns that reside in the middle (Serres, 1997, 161). Our *educated dislike* of the 3rd place (which incidentally, can often be confused as an *a priori* element of "human nature") is largely founded upon our learned avoidance of the pain, the disorder, the anxiety, and the discomfort that is associated with insubstantial concepts, things that reside in the middle and in between, things that wander and live in the third place; things that can't be tracked, predicted, measured or standardized. In research parlance, things deemed *subjective* are not given the same weight or consideration as "official knowledge" (largely because of their perceived neoliberal *nonsignificance*), and thus can be seen to represent what Guattari has called the "conservative reterritorializations of subjectivity" (1995, 3).

Modern, Dysacademic and dysphilosophic based learning has qualified its subjects to favor linear and objective certainty, and simplicity; and thus to seek order for the duration of all learning experiences (negentropy). It has contributed (if not outright caused) to the shocking findings of the National Center for Education Statistics regarding college graduate literacy ("dysliteracy"). Again, Guattari's concerns regarding the fate of subjectivity in our culture is significant, and although not included explicitly in this passage, its relevance and applicability to the discourse of education should be apparent.

> As things stand, sociology, economic science, political science and legal studies appear poorly equipped to account for the mixture of archaic attachments to cultural traditions that nonetheless aspire to the technological and scientific modernity characterizing the contemporary subjective cocktail. (1995, 4)

Paradoxically, looking at things through a poststructural lens that re-situates and contextualizes the observer, much of the living natural world can be seen to tenuously reside in the 3rd place; and so we must enter the 3rd place(s) if we ever hope to see, touch, hear, or taste it (the natural and social world) with our full sensory apparatus. Pedagogically and socially, absolute knowledge, technical expertise, and ultimately power and concrete order reside at/in these poles, away from the disordered center that provides much of the security and ease associated with modern (disciplined) thinking and being.

Thus, these *ordered poles* are far more comfortable, predictable and reliable for the subject who resides at the margins. In contrast, wandering into the center of the 3rd place(s) is like drifting into the middle of a turbulent river, wading without any sure footing, without the safety and assuredness of firm terra cotta, distant from the safety of the banks (Serres, 1997, 5). *Loitering* in the center is like entering into the nebulous and sticky cauldron of dissipative structures, where there are no absolutes, no determined directions in which to turn for safety, for assuredness, for light, or for immediate and concrete order. Swimming in the dissipative center allows the self to freely roam the waterways between the archipelagos, temporarily and transiently struggling to float, suspended in undetermined uncertainty (disorder) until the support of land can be discovered, somewhere, somehow, ideally different for all (subjective entropy). Here, in the middle spaces between the poles of light (knowledge) and dark (non-knowledge), there is no protection from the dark, from the heat of entropy, from the unknown and the chaotic, or from the murky and strident waters that cloud our vision, our hearing, and our senses. Here, in the 3rd place(s), one sees that knowledge is *not* represented exclusively by light, and concurrently that dark doesn't represent the *absence* of knowledge; dichotomies are broken, binaries split into multiples, and realities shattered into chaotic localities and contextualities.

For Derrida, this is represented by the "novel problematic," or something "other"; a process where language opens the passageways necessary for the inventive thought and insight needed to counteract the hegemonic rhetoric associated with the performative University (2004, 98). In effect then, it is within and amongst the 3rd spaces that the disciplines, and the disciplined are made to be irregular, abnormal, and "dys" 'ed; thus, they are re/de situated as *dysciplines*, and eventually, the *dysciplined*. In, within, and amongst the 3rd space(s), it is accepted and expected that the 3rd person be represented by an autopoietic subjectivity that is "in fact plural and polyphonic" (Guattari, 1995, 1).

Getting Into 3rd Spaces: Problematizing Subjectivity

In problematizing and resituating the notion of subjectivity that our modern epoch now essentially realizes and accepts as "objectivity," Felix Guattari believes it obligatory to *include* the various semiotic productions that mass media, informatics, telematics and robotics have constructed when thinking of our collective, and individual psychological subjectivities (1995, 4). Specifically, Guattari maintains that the various technological machines of information and communication our society has produced "operate at the heart of human subjectivity, not only within its memory and intelligence, but within its sensibility, affects and unconscious fantasms." Recognizing these technological connections to our subjective selves then, requires us to redefine the heterogeneous nature of the production of subjectivity on three interconnected, and discursive levels.

> Thus one finds in it: 1. Signifying semiological components which appear in the family, education, the environment, religion, art, sport...2. Elements constructed by the media industry, the cinema, etc., 3. A-signifying semiological dimensions that trigger informational sign machines, and that function in parallel or independently of the fact that they produce and convey significations and denotations, and thus escape from strictly linguistic axiomatics. (1995, 4)

As it pertains to Dysacademia's affect(s) upon the subjective formation of 3rd space(s) and 3rd persons, Guattari's redefinition works on all 3 levels to resituate the constituencies of the Academy's organic subjects (both the professorate and the student body).

First, knowledge, truth, value, meaning, democracy, and all other discursive elements, concepts, and notions that are historically and actively constructed, disciplined, controlled, and reinforced under the "guise" of education, must be realized for what they really are— signifying semiological components. Secondly, other semiological constructions from the media and popular culture outlets must also be recognized and realized for what they are and for their interconnected meaning to each subjective "lived curriculum"—important and very real rudiments of one's formulated and reflexive subjectivity. Lastly, the poststructural dimensions found in the a-signifying semiological systems that define much of our educational machine have been fully elaborated upon in the many works of Jacques Derrida, including *The Right to Philosophy* (both parts 1 and 2).

For Guattari though, a subsequently recognized "provisional subjectivity" based on this poststructural insight would be thus defined as "the ensemble of conditions which render possible the emergence of individual and/or collective instances as self-referential existential territories, adjacent, or in a delimiting relation, to an alterity that is itself subjective" (1995, 9). Situated as such, in its entire multiple and heterogeneic robustness, Guattari envisions and calls for an "immense complexification of subjectivity," replete with "harmonies, polyphonies, counterpoints, rhythms, and existential orchestrations, until now unheard and unknown," or to be more succinct, a "schizo unconscious" characterized by flux, autopoiesis, and ethico-poetic subjectivity. It is specifically here that Guattari's Derridean associations and affinities, and thus their relevance to the current discourse surrounding disciplinarity and control emerge, as his suggested "method" for complexifying subjectivity is founded upon 1) imperceptible bifurcations capable of overthrowing the framework of dominant redundancies (i.e., the classical order), and 2) the shifting of subjectivation, courtesy of the a-signifying existential functions typical of poststructural deconstruction (20). Thus, the first (and only?) step towards creating, maintaining, and re-inventing 3ʳᵈ space(s) and 3ʳᵈ persons in the pedagogical realm involves the active and open deconstruction of the classical order found in the inorganic University, and the perpetual shifting and movement of the multiple individual subjectivities that comprise the organic components of the University.

In combining the profound and deeply entrenched existence of Dysacademia with the seemingly difficult poststructural challenge to de- and re-construct individual subjectivities and the institutions which give life to them, those interested in just such an undertaking may be inclined to wonder "how," or "where" to begin just such an undertaking. In fact, the cynical postmodern theorist, or even the well-meaning modernist, may wonder aloud if the potential for such a transformation really exists with the current state of affairs being as bleak as I have portrayed (are they?). If there is potential to engage in such a reconstructive, yet open discourse (and I believe there is), what form will/does it take? Additionally, just how does one begin to develop and partake in the necessary actions needed to underscore the discourse, in order to actualize the discourse's reconstructive intentions for inducing change? In keeping with the theoretical threads presented herein then, it should be readily apparent that the "how" must be *through*, or *with* some strain of philosophical thinking. And, as it has been previously presented, Derrida has offered a suggestion that addresses both questions, as well as what he feels is "the" responsibility of the University; 1) it ought to take place in our philosophemes, or our philosophical institutions, and that 2) it ought to take the form of a cosmopolitical philosophy, rather than the tired Eurocentric/anti-Eurocentric discourses that perpetuate our malaise (2002).

All is not that simple and clean for critical theorists, however, as a serious dislike of "centers" and fixed positions (which ironically & typically serves as the foci of the deconstructive discourses) can also work to paradoxically construct potential barriers for the reconstructive effort(s); a censorship of sorts is created that selects and excludes. Simply put, once the deconstruction of a discourse or system is under-

taken, postmodern and poststructural theorists are notionally reluctant to replace it with "another" center in lieu of the deconstructed
one; even when an alternative "is" desired, and arguably needed. But,
if there is ever to be "some thing" that can tenuously and temporarily
dwell in the "center" of the discourse (even Derrida modestly admits
that "there is always censorship") ; something with the potential to
reconstruct "other," something "new" and undetermined; without
permanently and hegemonically *taking* the open space, resolutely, authoritatively, and statically; perhaps poststructural and/or cosmopolitical philosophy represents that "some thing." For Deleuze and
Guattari that "some thing" can be appreciated with rhizomes, multiple lines of flight, and schizoanalysis; for Derrida, with the right to a
reason based, "cosmopolitical philosophy," for Serres with turbulent
passageways that ontologically and epistemologically illuminate multiple 3rd spaces; and for Felix Guattari, that "some thing" exists in the
form of "Chaosmosis" (1995); all of which can be seen as poststructural extensions of the *POST* discourse submitted in the previous
chapter, and succeeding sections of this text.

Towards a Chaosmotic Subjectification of Space & Self

In theoretically attempting to reconcile chaos and complexity into
a workable and meaningful discourse capable of supporting and ex-
plicating the formation of multiple and diverse autopoietic subjectivities, Guattari has metamorphosed chaos and osmosis into
"Chaosmosis" in an attempt to describe the homogenesis of ontological referents.

> A world is only constituted on the condition of being inhabited by an um-
> bilical point—deconstructive, detotalisating and deterritorialising—from
> which a subjective positionality embodies itself. The effects of such a nucleus
> of chaosmosis is to make the ensemble of differential terms the object of a
> generalized connectivity, an indifferent mutability, a systematic dequalifica-
> tion… This oscillation at infinite speed between a state of chaotic "grasping"
> and the deployment of complexions anchored within worldly coordinates
> takes place before space and time, before the processes of spatialisation and
> temporalisation. (1995, 80)

More specifically, chaosmosis means that any attempt to construct an
ontological heterogenesis requires a continual and reflexive reconstruction of the operational narratives that govern and shape our social realities; or, a "relative chaotisation in the confrontation with
heterogeneous states of complexity." In an eerily similar sentiment,
Hosek & Freeman (2001) articulate this self-formation process as "osmetic ontogenesis," a neurodynamical process whereby conceptuali-
zations of the postmodern self converge and resonate with the various
mechanisms we possess for sensation, perception, representation, and

meaning (510). Or to put it in another, a chaosmotic reconstruction of that knowledge is required in order to function beyond the signifying properties of information and communication is possible because the communication and information that we process in the formation of our individual epistemologies and ontologies is structured by language. To draw an analogy, Guattari likens this schizoanalytic construction of the self to the free and open construction of jazz music. Jazz music can be comprehended as chaosmosis because of its spontaneous ability to self-generate without a set script (autopoietic), its reliance on multiple and disparate parts to form a whole (heterogeneous), and because of its inherently and individually determined aesthetic quality (93). If the chaosmotically self-constructed self is viewed as a jazz song then, "being crystallizes through an infinity of enunciative assemblages associating actualized, discursive components with non-discursive, virtual components," and "it is out of this chaos that complex compositions...constitute themselves" (58).

Interestingly, the game of soccer (football) provides another apropos and philosophically connected metaphor for the open, undetermined and aesthetic qualities and potential for chaosmosis. To those who know the game, soccer is a game of limited structure, open spaces, and reactionary movements, the nuances of which take years of exposure to master for most participants. Aside from the physical-technical mastery required, those who play and coach it at a high level possess a profound understanding of closed and open spaces; offensively they know how to open space(s), defensively they know how to limit and close space(s), and the flow of the game is comprised of a continual and undetermined series of opening and closing of undetermined space(s). In the intriguing documentary film entitled simply "Derrida" (2002), Jacques Derrida himself briefly expresses his love and past experiences with soccer, while the application of his work to soccer is readily apparent to those who know both provinces well. Similarly, Michel Serres creatively uses myriad soccer and rugby (and dance) exemplars as metaphors for the "anti-structural" and chaotic nature of true learning and education, and the various relations based syntheses that are capable of being formed. For example, he incorporates the open, undetermined, responsive and agile movements/reactions/actions required by the goalie in order to respond to the play at hand, and the dissipative flow of the game (1997, 9).

In translation then, the self and the knowledge that can be seen to inform and shape individual subjectivity, is constructed through the chaotic contribution and quasi-random assemblage of various, disparate, and undetermined notes; much in the same way that a jazz song materializes from the open spaces that silence occupies, or in the way that all soccer players on a field are related to each other based solely on the position of the ball, and their adjacency to others. Impromptu jazz jams and sophisticated soccer games alike materialize out of chaotic and dissipative relations; they are not prescripted, rigidly conducted, or a priori determined by any omniscient being or force. In short, both the jazz song and the soccer game are invented each and every time they are played. Sometimes, the constructed song (part of the self) is aesthetically pleasing from the initial moments; other times it requires reworking, reconstruction, and new information in order for it to "stick." Sometimes, the constructed song needs a new melody, a new beat, or the addition of a new instrument or player; or perhaps, just new audiences in order for it to become part of the subjective self. Over time, some songs are kept, some are deleted, but most of them are reworked, reconstituted and resynthesized with parts of other songs, other notes and other rhythms to continually construct and crystallize new ones. The same goes for any particular soccer game. In this sense, the entropy associated with chaos gradually and perpetually becomes negentropic by bleeding, blending and reformulating (osmosis) with other existing and incoming nodules of thought and experience. For Guattari, the inventive powers of art, like those expanded upon with jazz music, offer the potential for "mutant coordinates to extremes: it engenders unprecedented, unforeseen and unthinkable qualities of being," that if encouraged and promoted, offer a new ethico-aesthetic paradigm for the construction of subjectivities (1995, 106). Yes…art.

For Guattari, as for Maxine Greene (2000), the inventive and creative powers of the arts possess the capacity to resist and counter established boundaries, to highlight and re-evaluate the creative dimensions that traverse all domains of thought and praxis, and to invent heterogeneous views, perspectives and ethical positions. Largely removed and marginalized from today's contemporary curriculum, and perhaps even in the large scope of our culture, an aesthetics based paradigm positioned from within the arts' creative powers has ethico-political implications because, "to speak of creation is to speak of the responsibility of the creative instance with regard to the thing created, inflection of the state of things, bifurcation beyond pre-established schemas" (Guattari, 107). For Maxine Greene, democracy needs the arts because the cultivation of imagination is important to the making of a democratic community that respects, embraces and encourages multiple perspectives, ethics, and subjectivities.

> One of the primary ways of activating the imaginative capacity is through encounters with the performing arts, the visual arts and the art of literature…Such encounters make possible an education of feeling; an education in critical awareness, in noticing what there is to be noticed…The arts hold no guarantee as to true knowledge or understanding, nor should they replace other subject matters. They should become central to the curricula and include exhibitions and deliver performance, thus adding to the modalities by means of which students make sense of their worlds. With aesthetic ex-

periences a possibility in school, education will be less likely merely to transmit dominant traditions. (2000, 277)

More specifically, because the ethical purpose(s) of creative invention ought to rightfully focus on the subjective invention of the self in ways capable of freeing the self from established political and social boundaries of being, and for the creation of truly free, critical and subjective communities (democracies), art represents a double process learning machine that possesses autopoietic-creative and ethical-ontological dimensions. In other words, osmetic ontogenesis demonstrates how bio-epistemologically unique subjects shift over time in intra-action with the world; or more simply, it refers to the ways in which the body/brain (self) is constructed in, and through the world. In this light then, chaosmosis and osmetic ontogenesis can both be seen as Foucaultian and Serresian mechanisms capable of allowing subjects to subjectively invent and transcend the self through reflection, deconstruction and reiteration (Guattari, 1995).

> The chaotic nothing spins and unwinds complexity, puts it in relation with itself and with what is other to it, with what alters it. This actualization of difference carries out an aggregative selection onto which limits, constants and states of things can graft themselves. Already we are no longer at the speeds of infinite dissolution…In symbiosis with infinite complexions, finite compositions insert themselves within extrinsic coordinates, enunciative assemblages fit together in relations of alterity. Linearity, the matrix of all ordination, is already slowing down, an existential stickiness. (114)

Inventing Other Educational Space(s)

As for a specific *stratagem* for developing a 3ʳᵈ curriculum capable of opening 3ʳᵈ space(s) and allowing the open, subjective, chaosmotic, and philosophical formation of the 3ʳᵈ person, I again turn to the poststructural thinking of various contemporary scholars for guidance and insight. Rebecca Martusewicz (2001) recognizes the Serresian need for a more uplifting and explorative notion of pedagogy, one that sharply diverges from the fairly cynical view of the "educated condition" currently predominating our standardized, objectified and accountable time period.

> To think about education…is to be interested in the transformation of 'the way things are' into more just and healthy relations, structures, and ways of thinking and being. (8)

Michel Serres, whom Martusewicz leans upon heavily in articulating her poststructural pedagogy and ethical position, creatively intertwines various concepts from science and history, literary imagery and metaphors, and poetic narratives to judiciously communicate his position concerning the modern fragmentation and partitioning of knowledge in modern times.

> The passage is rare and narrow…From the sciences of man to the exact sciences, or inversely, the path does not cross a homogeneous and empty space. Usually the passage is closed, either by land masses or by ice floes, or perhaps by the fact that one becomes lost. And if the passage is open, it follows a path that is difficult to gauge. (1995a, xi)

> For Serres, as well as for other French postmodern thinkers like Deleuze, Guattari and Foucault, the natural sciences, literature, mathematics, philosophy, mythology, and the human sciences have largely been separate "islands" of thought that when effectively linked, inform us of the political and cultural landscape that is human life. Serres trusts that education ought to allow the individual to "see on a large-scale, to be in possession of a multiple and sometimes connected intellection." (1995a, xiii)

But what consistently seems to qualify the diverse works of Michel Serres, Gilles Deleuze and Felix Guattari are critical, poststructural attempts to find epistemological passages, rhizomes, lines of flight and chaotic nodules, or what Katherine Hayles calls "archipelagos of chaos," between the complicated branches of knowledge while simultaneously identifying and overcoming the hegemonic obstructions and assumptions that prevent traveling in such passages. In echoing the sentiments put forth by Martha Nussbaum's call for the cultivation of humanity (1998), Serres extends this discourse further into the axiological realm by arguing that morality, or in his terms a "science of humanity" is only achievable through a complementary marriage between the natural and social sciences and the humanities (Serres & Latour).

> The future will force experts to come quickly to the humanities and to humanity, there to seek a science that is humane. (1995, 179)

For Derrida, this means that there is a minimal responsibility for all those vested in teaching at the University wishing to emancipate subjectivities into more free, critical beings that can, in turn, enhance and give back to society in other, non-performative manners. Derrida contends that individuals enmeshed in the responsibility of higher education must admit and confront the power of the" institution as a text" concept, and the political implications that accompany such a performative concept (2004, 102). More specifically, the institution as text model signifies that, like all technical systems the University is complicit in "parasating and simulacra" because of its role in the production and publication of state censored, and performative based knowledge. Rather than inventing knowledge itself then for the creative and emancipative powers of thought and being, the University is more concerned with the publication of knowledge that appeases and validates the various politico-juridical forces that control and fund the institution. Central to the institution as text concept today is the ever increasing power that external agencies, institutions and forces have had upon the faculties of the University, most notably external accrediting agencies and their hyper-technocratic and performative based standards and guidelines. The hegemonic control that state governments, accrediting and professional agencies now have upon the faculties and their institutions extends into every fabric of the University identity and utility (Derrida).

> We posit or acknowledge that an institution concept is at play, a type of contract signed, an image of the ideal seminar constructed, a 'socius' implied, repeated or displaced, invented, transformed, threatened, or destroyed…it is also and already the structure of our interpretation. We must all first interpret 'what' the University is and thus what our responsibility is (or should be). (2004, 102)

In athletic training (my home discipline), as in other allied health care fields like medicine and physical therapy, this is indeed a complicated task for the faculty members that teach and direct highly organized and advanced technical fields of study that also require program accreditation in order to be in existence. In addition to the myriad and ever changing bioscientific skills and knowledge proficiencies required to work in a certain healthcare scope of practice, all health care givers must also understand the open and chaotic nature of all science (including medical science), the contextual and local nature of each patient presentation, the socio-cultural perspectives, anxieties, fears and biases that caregiver and patient bring to the relationship, and the various economic and emotional baggage that each patient possesses. Pedagogically, this amounts to the development of advanced skill-sets and level of consciousness that allows practitioners to go beyond the mechanical and modernistic delivery of health care services, and into the various socio-cultural, political, economical and historical domains of human interaction and service. In short, all caregivers must never forget that helping people is the primary objective of all care decisions and plans of action, and as such, that health care is a very complex and interconnected venture for even the most seasoned caregiver. Additionally, all allied health care educators must also actively embrace their higher responsibility to the University, that being to the development and proliferation of Derridean reason. The same could, and should be said of University faculty members empowered to educate the teachers, lawyers, engineers, politicians, and business people of tomorrow.

Plastic, mobile, perpetual and chaotic—Serres refers to these channels of exploration and invention metaphorically as the "*Northwest Passage*"; an opening that must be traversed with great pain, but also one that gives birth to unpredictable, unexpected and spiritual transformations of the self (Serres, 1997, 47). To Serres, it is during the turbulent travels through the symbolic *Northwest Passage* that the journeyman/woman will come to see, feel and interpret the myriad vortexes that exist between the various branches of knowledge. Traversing the *Northwest Passage* then, will subsequently provide the much needed opportunities for inventing knowledge at the various crossovers that one experiences. Similarly, Deleuze and Guattari inscribe "lines of flight," "schizoid flow drawings," and multiple "folds" as their preferred manner to describe a more open and gradually negentropic process of inquiry, while introducing "essentially inexact yet completely rigorous notions" into the discourse of knowledge and objectivity in *A Thousand Plateaus*.

> Here once more, it's to do with the way someone's own work can lead to unexpected convergences, and new implications, new directions, in other people's work. And no special status should be assigned to any particular field, whether philosophy, science, art or literature. (1997, 30)

And, as Serres states, "even if specialties are divided, the inventive remains undivided" (1997, 55). To Serres, a chaotic and convergent curriculum constitutes the *third conversation*, one that allows time and locality to make networks fluctuate, to be unstable, and to bifurcate; one that forms a mobile confluence of fluid and turbulent fluxes (Serres & Latour, 1995, 114). The challenges to do this, to recognize the inherent and natural connectedness and interstices of different knowledges, should not be an intimidating and negative experience but rather, one that enlivens and challenges the conscious spirit within all of us (Serres & Latour).

> Indeed, one of the exciting problems of our era consists of rediscovering the chaotic nature of knowledge. (127)

Clearly, elements of recursiveness, unpredictability, dissipation, self-organization, and interconnectedness resonate loudly throughout the various writings of Derrida, Serres, Deleuze and Guattari, and thus so too should the inherent connectedness and association of their philosophy of prepositions, chaos, multiplicity, and inventiveness reverberate with many of the central tenets associated with open systems theory, chaos and cybernetics. From here then, an attempt can be made to combine the central notions of chaos, open systems, & cybernetics with the poststructural thinking of Serres, etc. into a pedagogical sub-discourse that might prove capable of rivaling, and/or resisting the dominant one now in place. Whereas the dominant modes of mechanistic and scientifically based processes that drive the American educational paradigm seem intent on reducing all complexity and chaos to a rational, stable, predictable and linear structured order, it is the manner in which order seems to perpetually and almost magically come about from the "immanent threat" that chaos intonates that makes this sub-discourse seem so radical and theoretically unlikely. In its simplest terms, an open & chaotic 3ʳᵈ curriculum regards and situates students as individual and open systems, as organic entities that are actually capable of creating order (*negentropy*) out of what appears to be complete disorder (chaos/entropy). Above all, a *3ʳᵈ Curriculum* will be based on a Derridean/Kantian reasoning that empowers the possessor of such mass and ability to see, to feel and be in context with his/her constructed reality, and lived "text". In essence, students will progress through a 3ʳᵈ curriculum as learner directed self-dissipating systems. A *3ʳᵈ Curriculum* is a transient, tenuous, plastic and mobile order that traverses many fractal landscapes of knowledge, is presented and experienced in full (three) dimension, and is capable of creating many vortexes (syntheses); some aesthetic, some phenomenological, some experiential, some objective, some real, some mythical; all fragile, and all personally subjective. Although pedagogical issues for Deleuze and Guattari may not appear as readily noticeable as they are in Serres' works, they are very clear in denouncing the typical didacticism so prominent today as the imposition of hegemonic doctrines on innocent and made-docile bodies in later works (1994, 3).

In contradistinction to the typical, modern curriculum characterized by a controlling, power laden, and self-limiting pedagogy, Deleuze and Guattari offer a model of *apprenticeship pedagogy* that provides a "taste" of knowledge and skill without hindering the creative possibilities, a process that if approached with an open and reiterative mindset, would allow for dissipation, for autopoiesis, and for self-organization of the student (1994, 3). In *What Is Philosophy?* Gilles Deleuze and Felix Guattari introduce their notion of three *Chaoids*, a trinity of thought encompassing and intertwining art, science and philosophy into a demarcated, but non-hierarchized understanding of thought (1994, 197). It is this dynamic and infinite play between chaos and order, local and global that makes Deleuze and Guattari appreciate the open, fractal and contextual nature of knowledge, of the power of invention, and of the potential schizoanalytic topography of "reality." All three of these factors, argue Deleuze and Guattari, complement one another, are connected with a type of ontological and epistemological chaos, and are dissipative in that they continually reformulate into something new as they come into contact with other heterogeneous elements; and as such, together represent "thought as heterogenesis" (1994, 199).

Additionally, Deleuze & Guattari's chaoplexic concept reinforces their philosophical belief in an anti-essentialist process based approach to the development of concepts, rather than the typically modern, classical scientific approach to essentializing what things "*are*."

Rather, Deleuze is more interested in "the circumstances in which things happen: in what situations, where and when does a particular thing happen, how does it happen, and so on" (1995, 25). The focus for Deleuze and Guattari is thus placed on the vortexes, the fragile synthesis—how are/were they developed, and most importantly, what do they *mean* for the subjective mind. Deleuze was also fond of the concept of chaos, or as he liked to refer to it "the virtual," and how it was a common element of science, art *and* philosophy (1994); while Guattari metamorphed the term into what he called "chaosophy" in his final book *Chaosmosis* (1995). Careful not to confuse the philosophical notion of chaos as a transcendent phenomenon (as transcending the real), Deleuze and Guattari perceive chaos as a positive kind of pool of resources that is capable of producing new ideas, new ways of thinking—a source of creativity and inventiveness. In their last book together, *What Is Philosophy?* the long time co-authors give several "operational definitions" of chaos worth including in the current dialogue because of the innate relation to the views of Serres, and to those put forth by systems and chaos theorists alike.

> Chaos is defined not so much by its disorder as by the infinite speed with which every form taking shape in it vanishes. It is a void that is not a nothingness but a virtual, containing all possible particles and drawing out all possible forms, which spring up only to disappear immediately, without consistency or reference, without consequence. (1994, 118)

> Chaos is characterized less by the absence of determinations than by the infinite speed with which they take shape and vanish. This is not a movement from one determination to another but, on the contrary, the impossibility of a connection between them, since one does not appear without the other having already disappeared, and one appears as disappearance when the other disappears as outline. Chaos is not an inert or stationary state, nor is it a chance mixture. Chaos makes chaotic and undoes every consistency in the infinite. (1994, 42)

Opening(s) for Undetermined Space(s)

In *Understanding Curriculum*, an entire chapter is devoted to curriculum as poststructuralist, deconstructed and postmodern text whereby the authors attempt to provide an explorative, yet nonessential background of these complex and interrelated theories (Pinar, Reynolds, Slattery & Taubman).

> At its most general level, Poststructuralism, deconstruction, and postmodernism share a rejection of structuralism, humanism, and modernism, a repudiation of the ways various academic disciplines have "traditionally" presented their versions of reality. (1995, 452)

As it regards poststructuralism in general, it is important to realize that it denies all claims to meta narratives, foundational, essential, universal, or homogenous truths; but rather pays more critical attention to the symbolism, status and power that fundamentally reside in language, desire, and representation (Pinar et al, 1995, 452). Furthermore, poststructural theorists see nearly everything that is not fundamentally "natural" (like water, air and matter) as text and/or discourse that is fundamentally bounded by language games, socially constructed paradigms (of thought and practice), and elements of assumed "normativity"; while concurrently attacking structuralism's linguistic idealism, ahistoricism and relative misunderstanding of language's inherent power to substitute for the lack of a true, objective reality. In short, theorists beginning with Michel Foucault and Jacques Derrida, most notably, have effectively asked if the underlying structures of "things" constitute any sort of fixed, ahistorical, and *a priori* objective reality or meaning; while simultaneously charging that the structuralist approach to deconstruction fails to take into account the historical, social and political constructions that drive and constitute contemporary language systems. In this light then, PS theorists argue that concepts, systems, and structures become socially constructed signifiers of "things," while simultaneously deriving their largely unexplored meaning(s) and symbolism from "man made" signifiers.

As such, everything is a text, and all texts and discourses that can easily be seen as representing objective "reality" by modernist thinkers, can thus be deconstructed by the theorists into their constitutive, mythical and reiterative parts as part and parcel of a cosmopolitical philosophy. Deconstructive practices and readings in this frame of mind then can be subsequently traced to their historical, social, cultural and political elements to reveal reiterations, commonalities, and discrepancies that challenge linear and modernist authority. Because he firmly believes that "ultratechnical vocabulary" breeds fear and exclusion, poststructural author Michel Serres detests the "ultra technical vocabulary" that is produced by groups, cliques, and so-called "experts" (1995, 24); and it is for this reason that Serres (wanting to avoid authentic structuralism) was forced to find a "new language" for his inventive thought—each time he produced a new piece of work. For Serres, both the causes and the fixes of modernity's rigid epistemological and ontological barriers that constrain thought, creativity, and invention, while also strangulating identity and subjectivity can be traced to the academy, writ large (as cited in Serres & Latour, 1995).

> The obstacles come from divisions, both ancient and very recent, improved by academia. The passage is natural, and the obstacle is artificial. (1995, 74)

Michel Foucault is often credited with "coining" the term "discourse," meant to signify a discursive practice which itself forms the objects of which it speaks (Pinar et al., 1995, 462). Perhaps Michel Serres' version is more capable of illuminating the nature of what Foucault meant by the notion of discourse.

> An idea opposed by another idea is always the same idea, albeit affected by the (-) sign. The more you oppose one another, the more you remain in the same framework of thought. New ideas come from the desert, from hermits, from solitary beings. (1995, 81)

Quite simply, Serres, Foucault and myriad other prognosticators contend in varied, yet analogous ways that in order to engage in a discursive encounter with someone, or with some text, one has to know the boundaries, the histories and the ramifications of thought that structure the concept. From the particular signifiers used to articulate the signified, to the various parameters that have been historically formulated in order to define and essentialize the concept's objectivity, a deconstructive thinker must look from within, and from without in order to deconstruct the structure, language, rules, and signs that construct the image, identity, truth, or conception under investigation. In other words, it is impossible to authentically and neutrally see, or speak from "outside" a discursive concept; even though one may be attempting to deconstruct and rearticulate the concept with an honest scholarly intent, or what is more readily known as a "neutral" approach to inquiry.

For example, it is impossible for any of us to have a "non-discourse" dialogue about the white and black races because the antecedent concepts of "black" and "white" have already been socially constructed and embedded in our mind's experience; qualified by language, signifiers, and experiences now inherent in our internal system of understanding and articulation. Likewise, we as University educators need to situate and appreciate the discourse that is the institution, and thus too the "responsibility" that we have as active, living members within the institution as text. As vital cogs in the text, we must face our responsibilities seriously, and in order to do, we must begin by deconstructing the various texts that define and shape our lives—our curricula, our pedagogy, our utility, and most importantly, our responsibility. We can't possibly remove ourselves from the discourse that exists, and so we cannot authentically work from any sort of neutral subjectivity.

Thus said, authority, objectivity and rationality can be effectively destabilized and deconstructed into multiple subjectivities, localities, and contextualities that are capable of illuminating what Derrida calls the "reiterability" and "différance" of the various signs, marks, signs, texts, and modes of thought that characterized our postmodern epoch

(2000, 7). *Intelligence* is an excellent example of how discourse operates in our consciousness and vernacular—the "concept" of intelligence has been created by a discourse that has been fed by various scientific and authoritative narratives, not by truly objective and essential knowledge, and thus it is the discourse itself that creates and recreates the "reality" of what it means to be (or not to be) intelligent. Educational "outcomes" and "excellence" are other bothersome and problematical signs and signifiers that must be addressed first from the inside before they can be given any rational meaning. For a poststructural thinker then, knowledge does not represent reality—discourse constructs reality, and power is thus represented by the ability to define, unify or totalize phenomena into a discourse (Pinar et al., 1995, 462). The same can be said of any discourse, including the current one surrounding the effective utility and identity of higher education in the United States—Dysacademia.

In the introduction to the "anthology like" *Cultural Studies* text, an attempt is made by its authors to articulate the tenuous project of the cultural studies field by describing it as, among other things, "antidisciplinary" (Nelson, Treichler & Grossberg, 1992, 2). Specifically, the authors make no haste in pointing out that by critiquing the various domains, methods and intellectual legacies of the traditional disciplines, the field of cultural studies is itself "reluctant" to become a "real" discipline. When one stops to consider just how difficult it is to define culture itself, it becomes easier to see just how difficult it might be to define cultural studies; and therein lies the essential challenge facing cultural studies scholars. It is precisely this critical, transdisciplinary, and postmodern identity that gives cultural studies its mobility, creativity, and reiterative power of invention that allows its workers to "draw from whatever fields necessary to produce the knowledge required for a particular project." Careful to avoid a destructive turn towards "intellectual nihilism," cultural studies scholars are clear in announcing that their field(s) of study is/are not merely "anything." Rather, it is critical for the neophyte and inquisitive outsider to realize that multiple, open avenues for inquiry are available to the cultural studies scholar and that various modes of inquiry in cultural studies usually involve the attempt to draw relations between cultural concepts and phenomena with power, critical theory and historical forces (Nelson, Treichler & Grossberg, 1992, 3). As noted cultural theorist Stuart Hall writes, "Cultural studies is not one thing, it has never been one thing" (as cited in Nelson, Treichler & Grossberg, 1992, 3), rather, it is a diverse enterprise that encompasses different paradigms of thought and knowledge in specific localities, it addresses any and all questions of cultural significance. In the process, the critical study of culture poses new questions and traces multiple roots of thought, all the while aligning itself with different institutions and locations.

That being said, perhaps the best "definition" to work from may be that cultural studies is "an interdisciplinary, transdisciplinary, and sometimes counter-disciplinary field that operates in the tension between its tendencies to embrace both a broad, anthropological and a more narrowly humanistic conception of culture" (Nelson, Treichler & Grossberg, 1992, 4). Thus, cultural studies does not equate "high culture" exclusively with culture, is not just another intellectually snobby name for "popular culture," and is committed to studying the entire range of a culture's arts, beliefs, institutions, and communicative practices (including popular culture) in an earnest attempt to actively deconstruct what John Fiske labels as "the social order that constrains and oppresses the people," while offering action based, politically engaging sub-discourses and counter-narratives that "offers them resources to fight against those constraints" (cited in Nelson, Treichler & Grossberg, 1992, 5). In this sense then, cultural studies is not just another popular, yet passive and "value-less" academic phase, but rather, a politically engaged interference mechanism that possesses the potential to produces sub, or counter-discourses to contextual hegemonies and political technologies of oppression and subjectification. On this important point, Nelson, Treichler & Grossberg are worth quoting at length.

> Cultural studies thus believes that its practice does matter, that its own intellectual work is supposed to—can—make a difference. But its interventions are not guaranteed, they are not meant to stand forever. The difference it seeks to make is necessarily relevant only for particular circumstances; when cultural studies work continues to be useful over time, it is often because it has been rearticulated to new conditions. Cultural studies is never merely a theoretical practice, even when that practice incorporates notions of politics, power, and context into its analysis. (1992, 6)

In reconciling the field(s) of cultural studies with a postmodern sensibility of reiteration, openness, contextuality and locality, then cultural studies must be mindful of its capacity and responsibility to articulate insights about "the constitutive and political nature of representation itself, about its complexities, about the effects of language, about textuality as a site of life and death" (Nelson, Treichler & Grossberg, 1992, 7). In effect then, cultural studies scholars must be equally aggressive in deconstructing cultural phenomena and concepts, as they are reconstructive in creating new avenues, strategies, and voices for counter action, correction and ultimately social change. Cultural studies theorists can not simply "lay down like lambs" after they have deconstructed the political, economic, cultural, racial and social manifestations and subaltern dynamics at work in the global AIDS epidemic, or likewise for the myriad of complex social and humanistic issues associated with deforestation, technology, science and innumerable other dilemmas facing our cultural epoch.

Emphasizing real world problems, possible solutions and the inherent contingencies involved in deconstructive theorizing is central to contemporary cultural studies, and to the "theory of articulation" that cultural studies workers intend to formulate (Nelson, Treichler & Grossberg, 1992, 8). The ultimate goal then of cultural studies work is to carry out "conjectural analysis" or analysis that is "embedded, descriptive, and historically and contextually specific...to address the changing alliances within contemporary political movements and to sort out contingent intersections of social movements from long term 'organic' change." To carry out conjectural analyses, cultural studies theorists use any and all relevant cultural texts, or artifacts such as film, books, art, etc. to draw connections, show relations, describe discourses, and highlight society's myriad power structures that define, control and maintain the various Foucaultian "political technologies of the body," or "biopower," and their resultant and perpetual stranglehold on individual identity, subjectivity, and other elements of postmodern discourse.

As I alluded to earlier, cultural studies is not just another name for popular culture, in fact the scope and breadth of cultural studies work is considered to be much broader and inclusive, more reflexive and reiterative, and most importantly, much more political (Nelson, Treichler & Grossberg, 1992, 11). Cultural studies is, however, more deeply concerned with what is considered "popular" in other more critical ways, such as 1) interrogating the mutual determination of popular belief with other discursive formations (as can be seen between popular belief and science), and 2) the everyday terrain of people, and with all the ways that cultural practices speak to, of, and for their lives (language, hierarchies, power, categorization, homogenization, marginilization, etc.). As an example of what "is" and what "is not" considered to be cultural studies as it may be applied to curriculum discourses, consider the current challenges to the traditional literary canon and its relation to pedagogy and curriculum. Merely "redrawing" or "eliminating" the traditional line between high culture and low culture, or between "official knowledge" and "unofficial knowledge," in and of itself does not constitute cultural studies according to Nelson, Treichler & Grossberg (1992, 12). If, and only if, the analysis or argument interrogates the "cultural practices" within both the academy and private worlds that create, sustain, or suppress contestations over inclusion and exclusion can the work be considered "true" to the cultural studies field.

In other words, merely making an intelligent and coherent argument that the Western canon of knowledge should be "opened up" and diversified to include works from other repressed and marginalized voices does not fit the bill for true cultural studies work; the analysis must also articulate how textbook companies exert their considerable power over the curriculum, and how current policy makers with vested political and economic interests work to uphold this hegemonic infrastructure. Of course, cultural studies as a field is not that simple—those who *are* cultural theorists don't get to whimsically decide "who is" and "who is not" a cultural studies scholar, or "what is" and "what is not" cultural studies work. Rather, cultural studies requires of its workers to identify the operation of specific practices and what they accomplish as potential texts, while at the same time they must constantly interrogate their own connections to contemporary relations of power in order to prevent itself from becoming irretrievably woven into its own discursive web. Nelson, Treichler & Grossberg summarize the various and complex responsibilities, challenges, and legacies facing the cultural studies field.

> Continually engaging with the political, economic, erotic, social, and ideological, cultural studies entails the study of all the relations between all the elements in a whole way of life. This is at once an impossible project and the necessary context of any objects or traditions rescued...from the enormous condescension of posterity. (1992, 14)

For Derrida, the two-part process and responsibility afforded to cultural studies and poststructural theorists constitutes the intentional and effaceable value of "deconstruction," that being the primary challenge to deconstruct a particular phenomenon, discourse or text, followed closely by the more challenging task of subsequently offering up some type of performative possibility for change (2000, 21). Deconstruction for Derrida then, "does not consist in moving from one concept to another, but in reversing and displacing a conceptual order as well as the nonconceptual order in which it is articulated," and further it is thus intended to offer "the chance and the force, the power of *communication.*" Why this long expose' on poststructural theory and cultural studies? What's the relevance to the current discourse surrounding Dysacademia? Because I believe that Derrida is correct in his assertion that "there is always censorship anyways," some type of censorship must be uttered following a lengthy deconstruction if I hope to have done anything "constructive." I believe that poststructural cultural studies has the potential power to be the thread that can connect and illuminate the various disciplines, allow the various disciplined technocrats adequate, 3rd space to expand their pedagogy and knowledge production, AND adequately address the responsibility of the University as the principle of reason. Thus appreciated, it is the responsibility and challenge for me in this current discourse, to offer some type of performative possibility for change and transformation in Dysacademia.

For most, watching disparate films like *Bowling for Columbine* (2003) forces the viewer to use a certain cosmopolitical philosophy in order to enter the 3rd place, to embrace the 3rd person, and to have the

3rd conversation. As a text that resides in, and arises out of, the 3rd place, Michael Moore's critical and thought provoking film directly challenges and disorders our notions of a media generated reality, and thus our conceptual ideas concerning how justice, crime, politics, education and social responsibility operate in our nation are fundamentally and critically challenged. In deconstructing the discourse surrounding the tragic events of Columbine High School, America's gun culture, and today's youth, Moore proceeds to ask difficult questions in *Columbine.* In doing so, Moore presents a noteworthy amount of relevant cultural comparison and deconstructive analysis of the competing themes and arguments concerning the central issues of the film. In viewing the film in its entirety, the viewer gradually becomes aware that Moore is not necessarily intending to find answers to the problems he addresses; but rather, he seeks to pose the thorny questions relating to children and gun murders that make most of us "uncomfortable" being in the center of such a discourse. Articulately dispelled by Moore are the various mythical "causes" of our "kid gun" problems: the presumed overabundance of violent movies and videogames in our culture, the satanic musical and lyrical influences by cult rockers like Marilyn Manson, and the relative number of guns present in our nation's households. Despite one's impressions, biases, or political dislike of Michael Moore and his work, *Bowling for Columbine* forces the viewer to critically confront the bothersome sociocultural and economic factors that give rise to behaviors whereby American kids and teenagers find refuge in violent homicidal action as outlets for their fears, problems, and various sociocultural dilemmas.

For Serres, experiencing 3rd texts such as *Columbine* embodies or represents the true meaning and purpose of education—to enter a *third world*, to have the *third conversation*, to become the *third person.* For chaos theorists, this open space between order and disorder, between entropy and negentropy, represents the "third territory" (Hayles, 1990, 18), while Foucault refers to this concept as a "double space" when speaking of the complex coherences between interior and exterior forces and events in living subjects (1970, 274). To engage in, and to live in a world of relations, of prepositions, *between, in, amongst, with, and.* A third self that dwells at the center, in the murky, turbulent waters of uncertainty and "non direction"; dissipating, allowing energy and matter to flow through the self, in due course finding order amongst disequilibria; self-making, organizing the self and the consciousness; inventing knowledge, finding one's own way towards the safety of the banks, all the while chaosmotically drifting in a tense, but anxious and stimulated state, somewhere between known and unknown, between comfort and anxiety, between truth and myth, between hot and cold. Embracing the self *and* the process as an open, autopoietic system, a multi-dimensional network constructed and reconstructed by innate feedback loops; not by closed, linear, static, and dead-end essentials. Foucault elaborates on this post Classical sort of epistemology as it relates to living organisms in a sentiment that is remarkably "open systems" influenced.

> The living being must therefore no longer be understood merely as a certain combination of particles bearing definite characters; it provides the outline of an organic structure, which maintains uninterrupted relations with exterior elements that it utilizes in order to maintain or develop its own structure. (1970, 273)

Thriving in 3rd spaces requires the 3rd person to be situated, not seated, moving, not static; amongst the paradoxical and elliptical uncertainty between light and dark, in the shadows; welcoming the dark, the unknown, *nonknowledge* even. The 3rd person is allowed to embrace and even seek out the "unknown unknown," they are amused by the possibility of possibilities; they regale in the "multiplicity of multiples" (Serres, 1995b, 106). As such, knowledge, learning, experience, transformation, pain, and uncertainty are compulsory to illuminate this dark, shadowy, fragile, circumstantial and complex place. The 3rd person—the educated, enlightened individual—is plastic, vibrant, hypermobile, chaotic and perpetual; "it never stops being exposed. It evolves and travels." It is hypermobile; it is autopoietic; it is dissipative. It/they cannot be evaluated or measured with standardized tests; it cannot be subject to an Academic Bill of Rights that censors and silences controversial or "meaningless" discourse.

For the 3rd person, "the known is constructed in the same way that the knower is instructed" by inclusion and exclusion; "it finds the sciences and the humanities as it moves towards the discovery of a Northwest Passage, where one is born in both senses" (Serres, 1997, 52). The 3rd person refuses to see a hemiplegic dichotomy between the left brain and the right brain; rather, they work together hermetically to create consciousness only by meeting in the middle; they fully realize that right-handed people are no different from left-handed people, but rather that they are really the same—they both use both hands, they both have the "other" in them. For Serres, Hermes represents the messenger that communicates between the various branches of knowledge, amongst, in, to and from this and that. Hermes connects things; delivers the messages, both implicit and explicit in all types of knowledge. In this fashion then, the 3rd person ought to be cultured in a postmodern, hermetic manner of philosophical sensibility that promotes the formulation of an inventive, plastic, and individualistic external reality, outside any first or second person subject. A 3rd curriculum that constantly moves from the local to the global and back, forwards and back, sideways, obliquely, all the while taking full advantage to travel in and amongst Serres' "reversible, folded time"

(Serres & Latour, 1995, 71). A reversible time and a like-consciousness avoids being comminuted by appreciating the reversible nature of time that occurs with real learning and exploration, and by valuing the inherent connectedness of all forms of knowing.

For Deleuze, Serres' 3rd space can be seen as apt descriptors of Hume's "theory of association" whereby the human subject is perpetually formed through association with ideas, thoughts, and perceptions in a chaotic, open and transformative manner that helps establish some degree of personal, subjective order (Deleuze & Guattari, 1994, 201). It is through a continual and chaotic use of philosophy, art *and* science, that the subject learns differing ways to order the chaos that is the natural and phenomenological world, or in Serres' parlance the 3rd place. Once capable and comfortable residing in the middle 3rd, the educated 3rd is capable of recognizing the vortexes, the middle and "natural" double spaces which exist between the sciences and the humanities, where the global (science) touches the local (culture). Thus experienced, the instructed 3rd is capable of inventing one's own language and one's own phenomenological worldview, which are both required for and produced by the wandering that is so vital to a critical ontology. Thus lived, the 3rd person will also invent one's own culture.

The educated 3rd is capable of deconstructing and resisting the frenzy of what I am inventively calling *"mediality"* (*a.k.a.,* media generated version of reality), and our political spin machines, as does Michael Moore in *Bowling for Columbine*. The 3rd citizen can thus work to temper and extinguish the culture of fear that predominates our societies' anxiety and misgivings over "others," over the reported intents and motivations of our worlds' "evildoers," and can be more at peace with both the unknown, and challenging the "known." As Serres puts it, "to discover seems the only act of intelligence...ideas that circulate are usually astonishingly old, thus, he who seeks newness remains alone" (Serres & Latour, 1995, 145). And, because of the inextricable link between culture and education that Pierre Bourdieu points out, the educated 3rd, or the "self-taught man" will be "distinguished straightaway from a school-trained man" (1969, 347). As such, the self taught 3rd person will possess the courage required for, and will be capable of withstanding the pain associated with the infirmity of the new, the invented, and the dark shadows.

In harmony with Serres' critical call for invention to serve as the primary focus of education, Katherine Hayles suggests that the creative writer is perhaps the best example of a free-floating and chaotic inventor, capable of connecting various epistemic cultures (1990, 19). Working from the "third territory" then, somewhere between order and disorder, between form and flow, between fact and fiction, between dark and light, is what allows Hayles' creative writer to communicate beyond one particular field of study, and thus better capture and articulate the "aura of cultural meanings that surround chaos." Upon reflecting on Michael Moore's *Columbine*, it can be argued that his text is not only a direct critique of America's social and political systems, but also of the American educational system for denying the 3rd space(s) and the open development of the subjectivity of the 3rd person. Interestingly, it is also apparent that Moore himself has been immersed in, and enjoys residing in the 3rd space—he savors the middle, the opportunity to invent, to question, to challenge everything and anything. In the end, it appears as though it is the freedom of this 3rd space that stimulates and nourishes his artistic and critical texts. Michael Moore—a self educated, dystopic 3rd person, inventor of 3rd texts and conversations, and dilator of multiple and dystopic 3rd space(s).

In light of Serres' pedagogical contentions and the sociocultural commentary presented in texts such as *Columbine*, it is my contention that schooling, at any level ought to be based on Serres' argument that *invention* is education's central purpose, not ontological censorship or meaningless epistemological reproduction. Furthermore, it should be apparent after watching *Columbine* that education writ large must be connected to the larger socio-cultural mission of our society and democracy, regardless of the perceived economic implications of various curricular models, the en vogue scientific trends that spark our consumptive and restorative appetites, or the respective and future professional aspirations of the students. Renowned sociologist Peter Berger coined the ontological attribute that Moore is attempting to construct, *sociological consciousness,* and wrote that the critical development of such rigorous intellectual skills would allow the knower to deconstruct, or "see through" the various social structures that form opinions and myth, privilege, power and authority, bias certain forms of knowing and knowledge, and situate our social roles and identities (1965). From this perspective then, *Columbine's* investigation into youth violence and culture, media frenzies and their role in our "culture of fear", and its historical and contemporary critique of our country's foreign and fiscal policies can be seen as a potentially liberating and enlightening pedagogical text for sparking the growth of a *sociological consciousness*. As such, myriad pop culture texts like *Bowling for Columbine, The Matrix, Minority Report, Vanilla Sky,* and myriad others too numerous to mention, may indeed prove suitable for inclusion into a cosmopolitically based 3rd *curriculum* because of their potential for deconstructing and displacing the various systems that constrain and define our cultural epoch.

In order to do this—to invent the critical knowledge needed to reach sociological consciousness—students must be allowed to traverse into, between and amongst the pedagogical *third place(s)* (Serres, 1997, 43). They must be taught how reason, how to think, how to invent, and thus, how to deconstruct a text. That is, administrators, teachers and students, alike must be *allowed to* endure the pain, the discomfort, the uncertainty, and most importantly the "boundary-lessness of self" that accompanies critical ontological evolution into the 3ʳᵈ place(s). For this to happen, all pedagogues must address their University and intellectual responsibilities and reach out, interact with, and liberate students as subjects viably interconnected with the purposes of education and democracy, rather than merely treating students as objects knotted within an overly determined, objective and fixed educational process. They must be allowed to watch, to interpret, to experience, and most importantly to discuss critical texts such as *Bowling for Columbine*. Michael Moore effectively entered the 3ʳᵈ space, and thus generated a 3ʳᵈ conversation with *Columbine*—he has provided a very difficult, sober and yet sometimes humorous "passageway" that offers teachers and students a promising potential to enter, to confront, to struggle and argue, to challenge, and hopefully, to transform. Teachers and social leaders must do *more* of what Marilyn Manson suggests in *Columbine* when asked what he would say to the students of Columbine HS; that is they must do more listening [of students], and less speaking [to students]. Above all, educators of all disciplines must be allowed and encouraged to teach students how "to be" citizens with varied professional lives and purposes, not just merely how "to do" their chosen profession, including at the postsecondary level. All of our citizens must be critically and onto-logically connected to the larger problems of democratic and pro-foundly political society, and to what is required to live "in" a democracy, not just live "off" of a democracy. As evidenced by the closing interview in *Columbine*, our culture could certainly be improved with fewer subjects like Charlton Hestons, and perhaps more Michael Moores...less 1st persons and more 3ʳᵈ persons. Come to think of it, we just might also be better off with more Marilyn Man-sons who know the power of listening to children and young adults as they elucidate their experienced and invented worldviews.

A 3ʳᵈ curriculum centralizes the myriad issues presented by Moore in *Columbine* as equally relevant, critical, and primary nuclei of all, and any educational discourse or inquiry, regardless of chosen academic major or field of study. Sadly though, the modern educational process is fundamentally in many ways, antithetical to the pedagogical concerns of Derrida, Deleuze, & Guattari, and to what Serres sees as the essential goal of instruction, that being "invention" (Serres & Latour, 1995, 133). Modern dysciplined curricula, by and large don't allow for the students to enter into turbulent and undetermined spaces void of linearity, to experience disequilibria, or to have the freedom to self-invent their own subjective views, or a deeply seated phenomenological and subjectively reflexive understanding of events, concepts, and metaphysical phenomena. In fact, it may even be rightfully argued that modern curricula actually work to prevent turbulences, uncertainty and discomfort for all of its participants (by rely-ing on standardized tests, rigid lesson plans, and accreditation guide-lines as the primary pillars of their operational identity). Certainly then, *Bowling for Columbine* can be seen as an excellent and important schizoanalytic text that challenges our conception of reality as it per-tains to violence, fear, race, power, politics, and education. It certainly was for my 12-year-old son and me on the day we entered into these particular unknown 3rd space(s) presented by Moore's deconstructive text. Excluding socially conscious texts such as *Columbine* which have the potential to deconstruct the various hegemonies constructed by our different political and media institutions, can thus be seen as "preventing turbulence" in our schools.

Seen in this light then, the current discourse concerning a Ser-resian 3rd curriculum incorporates very specific ethical considerations as they pertain to ontological and epistemological freedom, the sub-jective and critical generation or invention of knowledge, self-transformation and subjectification, postmodern notions of identity and truth; and their subsequent interconnectedness to pedagogy, and our socio-global existence. Likewise, a Deleuzian and Guattarian em-phasis on the "process" of education, self-transformation, critical in-quiry and discourse may better enhance and develop the aesthetic and affective convictions required to authentically value these critical and qualitative self-organizing and self-generating domains of knowledge. Personally, an *amodern* and poststructural perspective, similar to that put forth by Serres, Martusewicz, Deleuze & Guattari, have better enabled me to look at all forms of education as open, complex, multifarious, and chaotic processes that possesses the poten-tial for, and even demands a more critical, meaningful and transfor-mative curriculum. In my view, a 3rd curriculum is also pragmatic and realistically attainable, but only if our central operating paradigms and collective social values can be simultaneously transformed from the ever increasing neoliberal and industrial tendencies that now characterize our cultural epoch.

And so, if individual subjects are not provided "some" clean can-vas, "some" blank parchment, or "some" open space for which to in-vent one's own objective worldview, or one's own self-constructed and reflexive language game, it can be surmised that he/she will more than likely not be able to transform in unknown, open manners; he/she won't be able to cultivate a unique and plastic ontology, nor a critical and multivocal epistemology. Forced to exist with current and historical language games, to acquire a worldview from within an al-ready vulcanized, fragmented and specialized disciplinary field, in-evitably and dangerously denies the subject the opportunity to genuinely channel their respective experiences and worldly interpre-tations into a meaningful and organic subjectivity. She/he will remain dysciplined. This is indeed a dangerous road to travel—for all of humanity.

Walden Pond provided Thoreau with the opportunity to explore nature in its *natural* splendor, the opportunity to invent his own biological worldview, and thus to compare *nature* to *the natural*. With repeated exposure to these types of open and reflective spaces, Thoreau was allowed to create an epistemic culture characterized by an ontological and epistemological reformation and self construction that allowed him to more critically reflect on a rapidly evolving and socially constructed industrial society. This contrast of views and experiences provided Thoreau with a unique epistemic privilege that infiltrated his literary and narrative works on many levels—a type of dispensation that can be seen as being more consilient than linear, more comprehensive and multiple than singular, more liberated and less restrictive, more inventive and less thin. On one particular day in the fall of 2003, I watched *Bowling for Columbine* with my oldest son (then, 12 years old); we wandered out into our own ontological and epistemological Walden Pond, we swam into and across the turbulent waters of this particular 3ʳᵈ space that Michael Moore dilated, we reveled in, and grew out of a 3ʳᵈ conversation together, we moved individually towards becoming our own 3ʳᵈ person, and we imbibed in our own subjective 3ʳᵈ curriculum. And on different, heterogeneous and subjective levels we consumed a 3ʳᵈ text…a text that contrasted our previously existing worldviews…a text that will ruminate, reiterate, and recapitulate all that we see, hear, and say in the future…all that is different…like a rhizome. I…he…we invented something that day…something that now exists between us…within us…amongst us…in the 3ʳᵈ space(s) between his subjectivity, and mine.

Concluding Remarks

The concept of universitas is more than the philosophical concept of a re-search and teaching institution, it is the concept of philosophy itself, and...the principle of reason as institution.

--(Derrida, 20004, 105)

The paradox of this university topology is that the faculty bearing within it-self the theoretical concept of the totality of the university space should be assigned to a particular residence and should be subject, in the same space, to the political authority of other faculties and of the government they rep-resent. By rights, this is conceivable and rational only to the degree that the government should be inspired by reason.

--(Derrida, 2004, 106)

Although I have intended to situate my analysis and subsequent commentary in order to avoid making an essentialist and nihilistic claim regarding the contemporary University condition, I comply with the various deconstructive analyses put forth by myriad scholars that *gone* are the days when university education critically served as the springboard for diverse and meaningful intellectual transforma-tion and exploration. In contrast, it can be viewed that *here* are the days whereby academic majors have been explicitly and deftly de-signed to produce technical experts capable of adequately contribut-ing to the economic and technological growth "needed" for our society's democratic, social and industrial "progress." Obviously, such a radical transformation cannot occur quickly or simply, and so there are various cultural factors, events, and dynamics that are in-herent of the analysis of this particular aspect of our culture. With our society facing an increasing bevy of complex and potentially fatalistic problems with which to deal with or else risk our own annihilation, we cannot afford to continue "producing" what Aronowitz calls "techno-idiots" from our institutions of higher education (2000, 172). Although today's graduates may indeed be in possession of impressive and complex levels of industrio-economic based skill and insight, far too many of them possess relatively little insight into the complex ways of the natural and man-made worlds that are needed to be considered "intelligent" outside their chosen field of study or work. Indeed, these concerns have been somewhat supported, if not validated by recent emperical studies analyzing the "literacy" skills of today's college graduates, and by the ironic commentaries made by business executives in venting their frustration with the need to "re-train" new, college educated employees.

If one stops to consider higher education's "other" traditional utility, that being the development of the individual, subjective self and the associated responsibility to society that the higher educated possess, an ethical imperative can also be perceived within the discourse I have attempted to articulate. Ontologically, today's vocationalized university and its rigid and balkanized curricula designed largely to contribute to our economic well-being, can also be seen as one that subversively prevents the free and open subjectification of individual students. In short, it is readily apparent today that most parents and students today seek out a college degree in order to better their chances of economic success, or cultural and material survival. In fact, a recent survey of public opinion on higher education conducted by the *Chronicle of Higher Education* found that vocational and professional preparation was indeed the most important role for colleges and universities today with 71% of respondents rating this role as "very important" (2003, A11). In contrast, only 35% and 31% of the respondents felt that "providing useful information to the public on issues effecting their daily lives," and "promoting international understanding," were very important, respectively. In today's "student as customer," teacher as "worker" culture, the corporate university is more than happy to oblige the student seeking a technocratic and neoliberalist based "higher education." Most often lost in this "professionalization of the curriculum" is general education as universities move to meet the demands of their customers, and the increasing demands of global capitalization. Sadly, students seeking the cultural capital, job training and "excellence" commonly associated with holding a college degree don't usually recognize, embrace, or take advantage of the "other," more enlightening and liberating experiences such as "the world," and the utility and meaning of "their daily lives" that true "higher education" has historically offered for most of its constituencies.

In light of the current state of the *Dyscademy,* higher education and its end product—the "educated citizen," it is my belief that modern society has an intense need for an educational experience that strongly contrasts with the modernistic behavior modification curriculum; one that typically and problematically produces a dirge of technocratic and professionally competent consumers with limited intellectual depth, diversity and understanding. A cursory glimpse of today's various sociocultural, environmental, economic and political problems should easily expose the pressing necessity for a more postmodern curriculum, one reconceptualized to abolish absolute and hegemonic boundaries and demarcations between the disciplines, one that deconstructs authoritative & closed meta narratives that promise objective truth and natural reality, and one that allows...no one that *requires* invention, dissipation, and gradual, turbulent and negentropic transformations of knowledge and individual subjectivities. Irregardless of academic major and chosen program of study, all college and university students seeking to be higher educated should be exposed, and immersed in such a curriculum so that they enter the "real world" with the scope of consciousness, intellectual depth, and responsibility needed to address the increasing complexity of our current and future sociocultural maladies. Because of the cyclical and reproductive nature of education and social progress (or stagnation?), perhaps teacher education exists as the most critical arena for such an adventurous and rational agenda dedicated to critical ontological, epistemological and axiological change. Imagine what higher education would be like if the University were helping to create 3rd teachers, who in turn helped invent 3rd students in primary and secondary schools, who in turn arrived college and university campuses capable and anxious to continue with their 3rd education at a "higher level."

A poststructural cultural studies based higher education, although admittedly censored as Derrida confesses, has the potential and rationale to address the chaotic nature of knowledge by deconstructing the modernistic boundaries, rules, and hierarchies constructed by the disciplines; whilst allowing students to be courageous apprentices, nomads and seekers of "heretofore uncharted passages" (Martusewicz, 2001, 9). A postmodern 3rd education, one tenuously taking up the tenets of open systems, complexity and chaos theories, one that embodies a schizoanalytic and rhizomatic topography, and one founded upon a certain cosmopolitical philosophy will permit, foster and even encourage the student to chaosmotically "be" an open system; to compete with their own contextual and local forms of self-organization, invention, disequilibria, feedback, dissipation, and of course, their initial and welcomed states of decreasing entropy. In short, it is optimistically proposed that a 3rd education, presented as such will be adroit in producing sociologically conscious and autopoietic subjects, fully capable of "self-making," self-adjusting, self-organizing, and thus of "treating the Dysacademic self." Imagine the possibilities.

• BIBLIOGRAPHY •

Abbott, Andrew. *Chaos of disciplines*. Chicago: The University of Chicago Press, 2001.

Amariglio, Jack, Stephen Resnick, & Richard D. Wolff, R. Division and difference in the "discipline" of economics. In E. Messer-Davidow, D. R. Shumway, & D. J. Sylvan (Eds.), *Knowledges: Historical and critical studies in disciplinarity*. Charlottesville, VA: University of Virginia Press, 1993.

Apple, Michael W. *Education and power* (2nd ed.). New York: Routledge, 1995.

---*Educating the "right" way: Market, standards, God and inequality*. New York: Taylor & Francis, 2001.

Arenson, K. W. Panel explores standard tests for colleges. *The New York Times* (available at http://www.nytimes.com/2006/02/09/education). February 9, 2006. Last accessed February 9, 2006.

Arenson, K., & D. A. Henriques. SAT errors raise new qualms about testing. The New York Times (available at http://www.nytimes.com/2006/03/10/education). March 14, 2006. Last accessed March 14, 2006.

Arnott, S. In the shadow of chaos: Deleuze and Guattari on philosophy, science, and art. *Philosophy today*, 1999.

Aronowitz, Stanley. *The knowledge factory: Dismantling the corporate university and creating true higher learning*. Boston: Beacon Press, 2000.

Berger, Peter. *Invitation to sociology*. Garden City, NY: Doubleday Books, 1963.

Bernauer, J., & D. Rasmussen (Eds.). The ethic of care for the self as a practice of freedom. In *The final Foucault*. Cambridge: The MIT Press, 1988.

Bertalanffy, Ludwig Von. *General system theory: Foundations, development, applications*. New York: George Braziller, 1969.

Best, Steven, & Douglas Kellner. *The postmodern turn*. New York: The Guilford Press, 1997.

---*The postmodern adventure: Science, technology, and cultural studies at the 3rd millennium*. New York: The Guilford Press, 2001.

Blauch, L. E. (Ed.). *Accreditation in higher education*. New York: Greenwood Press, 1959.

Boggs, C. *Intellectuals and the crisis of modernity.* Albany: SUNY Press, 1993.

Bok, D. K. *Universities in the marketplace: The commercialization of higher education.* Princeton, NJ: Princeton University Press, 2003.

Bourdieu, Pierre. Systems of education and systems of thought. *International social science journal,* 1967.

---Intellectual field and creative project. *Social science information,* 1969.

Capra, Fritjof. *The web of life: A new scientific understanding of living systems.* New York: Anchor Books, 1995.

---*The Hidden Connections: Integrating the biological, cognitive, and social dimensions of life into a science of sustainability.* New York: Doubleday, 2002

Carnegie Foundation. *Missions of the college curriculum: A contemporary review with some suggestions.* San Francisco: Jossey-Bass Publishers, 1977.

Carnochan, W. B. *The battleground of the curriculum: Liberal education and American experience.* Stanford, CA: Stanford University Press, 1993.

Cetina, Karin K. *Epistemic cultures: How the sciences make knowledge.* Cambridge, MA: Harvard University Press, 1999.

Chomsky, Noam. *Chomsky on miseducation.* (D. Macedo, Ed.). New York: Rowman & Littlefield Publishers, 2000.

Cohen, S. A question of boundaries: The response of learned societies to interdisciplinary scholarship. *Learned societies and the evolution of the disciplines.* New York, NY: American Council of Learned Societies, 1988.

Colby, A., T. Ehrlich, E. Beaumont, & J. Stephens. *Educating citizens: Preparing America's undergraduates for lives of moral and civic responsibility.* San Francisco: Jossey-Bass, 2003.

Commission on Colleges, Southern Association of Colleges & Schools. *General accreditation in higher education.* Atlanta, GA, 1963.

Commission on Colleges, Southern Association of Colleges & Schools (2003). Compliance certification. Atlanta, GA, 2003.

Council for Higher Education Accreditation. *Fact sheet #1: Profile of accreditation.* Washington, DC. (available at http://www.chea.org), August, 2003. Last accessed January 10, 2004.

Council for Higher Education Accreditation. *Strengthening higher education through strengthening accreditation.* Washington, DC. (available at http://www.chea.org), February, 2003. Last accessed January 10, 2004.

Dandaneau, S. *Taking it big: Developing sociological consciousness in postmodern times.* SAGE Publications, 2001.

Davis, Brent, & Dennis Sumara. Curricular forms: On the assumed shapes of knowing and knowledge. *Journal of curriculum studies,* 2000.

Deleuze, Gilles. *Negotiations.* (M. Joughin, Trans.). New York: Columbia University Press, 1995.

Deleuze, Gilles & Felix Guattari. *A thousand plateaus: Capitalism and schizophrenia* (B. Massumi, Trans.). Minneapolis: University of Minnesota Press, 1987.

---*What is philosophy?* (H. Tomlinson & G. Burchell, Trans.). New York: Columbia University Press, 1994.

Derrida, Jacques. Structure, sign and play in the discourses of the human sciences. In *Writing and difference*. (A. Bass, Trans.). Chicago: University of Chicago Press, 1980.

---*Archive fever: A Freudian Impression*. (E. Prenowitz, Trans.). Chicago: University of Chicago Press, 1998.

---*Limited, inc*. (S. Webster, Trans.). Baltimore, MD: Johns Hopkins University, 1998.

---Where a teaching body begins and how it ends. In Trifonas (Ed.), *Revolutionary pedagogies: Cultural politics, instituting education, and the discourse of theory*. New York: RoutledgeFarmer, 2000.

---The right to philosophy from the cosmopolitical point of view (The example of an international institution). In Trifonas (Trans. & Ed.), *Ethics, institutions, and the right to philosophy*. New York: Rowman & Littlefield, 2002.

---*Eyes of the university: Right to philosophy 2*. (J. Plug, Trans.). W. Hamacher & D. E. Wellberry, Eds. Stanford, CA: Stanford University Press, 2004.

deRussy, C., Langbert, M. & Orenstein, P. *New* York academia vs. the academic bill of rights. *FrontPageMagazine.com* (http://www.studentsforacademicfreedom.org), January 1, 2006. Last accessed January 1, 2006.

Dick, K. (Director) & A. Z. Kofman (Director & Producer). *Derrida* [Motion picture]. United States: Jane Does Films, Inc., 2002.

Doll, William E. *A post-modern perspective on curriculum*. New York: Teachers College Press, Columbia University, 1993.

Einstein, Albert. *Ideas and opinions*. (C. Seelig, Ed.). New York: Three Rivers Press, 1982.

Eliot, T. S. *Notes towards the definition of culture*. London: Faber & Faber, 1962.

Etzkowitz, Henry, Peter Healey, & Andrew Webster. *Capitalizing: New intersections of industry and academia*. Albany, NY: State University of New York Press, 1998.

Etzkowitz, Henry, & Andrew Webster. Entrepreneurial science: The second academic revolution. In H. Etzkowitz, P. Healy, & A. Webster (Eds.), *Capitalizing: New intersections of industry and academia*. Albany, NY: State University of New York Press, 1998.

Ford, M. *Beyond the modern university: Toward a constructive postmodern university*. Westport, CT: Praeger, 2002.

Foucault, Michel. *The order of things: An archaeology of the human sciences*. New York: Vintage Books. (Original work published 1966), 1970.

---*Discipline and punish*. New York: Vintage Books. (Original work published 1975), 1977.

---*Michel Foucault: Politics, philosophy, culture*. In L. D. Kritzman (Ed.). New York: Routledge, Chapman & Hall, 1980a.

---*Power/Knowledge: Selected interviews and other writings 1972-1977*. (C. Gordon, Ed.). New York: Harper & Row, 1980b.

---*Language, counter-memory, practice: Selected essays and interviews*. (D. F. Brouchard, Ed.). Ithaca, NY: Cornell University Press, 1990.

Fuller, Steven. Disciplinary boundaries and the rhetoric of the social sciences. In E. Messer-Davidow, D. R. Shumway, & D. J. Sylvan (Eds.), *Knowledges: Historical and critical studies in disciplinarity*. Charlottesville, VA: University of Virginia Press, 1993.

Galison, Peter. *Image & logic: A material culture of microphysics*. Chicago: University of Chicago Press, 1997.

Giroux, Henry A. *Corporate culture and the attack on higher education and public schooling*. Bloomington, IN: Phi Delta Kappa Educational Foundation, 1999.

---*The abandoned generation: Democracy beyond the culture of fear*. New York: Palgrave Macmillan, 2003.

Gould, E. *The university in a corporate culture*. New Haven, CT: Yale University Press, 2003.

Greene, Maxine. Imagining futures: The Public school and possibility. *Journal of curriculum studies, 32(2)*, 2000.

Guattari, Felix. *Chaosmosis: An ethico-aesthetic paradigm*. (P. Bains & J. Pefanis, Trans.). Bloomington, IN: Indiana University Press, 1995.

Halnon, K. B. (In) Academic McCarthyism in Pennsylvania. *FrontPageMagazine.com* (http://www.studentsforacademicfreedom.org), January 16, 2006. Last accessed, February 25, 2006.

Hayles, Katherine N. *Chaos bound: Orderly disorder in contemporary literature and science*. Ithaca, NY: Cornell University Press, 1990.

---*How we became posthuman: Virtual bodies in cybernetics, literature, and informatics*. Chicago: University of Chicago Press, 1999.

Horowitz, D. *The problem with America's colleges and the solution. FrontPageMagazine.com* (http://www.studentsforacademicfreedom.org), September 3, 2002. Last accessed February, 25, 2006.

Horowitz, D. Why an academic bill of rights is necessary: Testimony before the education committee of the Ohio senate. *Frontpagemagazine.com* (http://www.studentsforacademicfreedom.org), March 15, 2005. Last accessed February, 25, 2006.

Horowitz, D. *Hating whitey and other progressive causes*. Spence Publishing Company, 2000.

Hoskin, Keith W. Education and the genesis of disciplinarity: The unexpected reversal. In E. Messer-Davidow, D. R. Shumway, & D. J. Sylvan (Eds.), *Knowledges: Historical and critical studies in disciplinarity*. Charlottesville, VA: University of Virginia Press, 1993.

Hoskin, Keith W., & Richard H. Macve. Accounting as discipline: The overlooked supplement. In E. Messer-Davidow, D. R. Shumway, & D. J. Sylvan (Eds.), *Knowledges: Historical and critical studies in disciplinarity*. Charlottesville, VA: University of Virginia Press, 1993.

Jardine, David. A bell ringing in an empty sky. In W. Pinar (Ed.) (1999), *Contemporary curriculum discourses: Twenty years of JCT*. New York: Peter Lang, 1992.

Katz, S. N. The pathbreaking, fractionalized uncertain world of knowledge. *Chronicle of Higher Education* (http://www.wws.princeton.edu/snkatz/papers/CHE), September 20, 2002. Last accessed April 1, 2005.

Keller, Evelyn F. Fractured images of science, language, and power: A postmodern optic or just bad eyesight? In E. Messer-Davidow, D. R. Shumway, & D. J. Sylvan (Eds.), *Knowledges: Historical and critical studies in disciplinarity*. Charlottesville, VA: University of Virginia Press, 1993.

Kincheloe, Joe. *Toward a critical politics of teacher thinking: Mapping the postmodern.* Westport, CT: Bergin & Garvey, 1993.

---Schools where Ronnie and Brandon would have excelled: A curriculum theory of academic and vocational integration. In W. Pinar (Ed.) (1999), *Contemporary curriculum discourses: Twenty years of JCT.* New York: Peter Lang, 1995.

Kingston, Jack. Press release on National Public Radio. Savannah, GA, October 22, 2003.

Kirp, D. L. Degrees of influence: How the marketing mindset overtook higher education. *Boston Globe.* (available at http://www.boston.com/news/globe/ideas/article), November 16, 2003. Last accessed February 16, 2003.

Klein, Julie & T. Blurring, cracking, and crossing: Permeation and the fracturing of disciplines. In E. Messer-Davidow, D. R. Shumway, & D. J. Sylvan (Eds.), *Knowledges: Historical and critical studies in disciplinarity.* Charlottesville, VA: University of Virginia Press, 1993.

Kozol, J. *Savage inequalities: Children in America's schools.* New York: Harper Collins Publishers, 1992.

Laszlo, Ervin. *The systems view of the world: A holistic vision for our time.* Cresskill, NJ: Hampton Press, 1996.

Lattuca, L. R. *Creating interdisciplinarity: Interdisciplinary research and teaching among college and university faculty.* Nashville, TN: Vanderbilt University Press, 2001.

Lenoir, Timothy. The discipline of nature and the nature of disciplines. In E. Messer-Davidow, D. R. Shumway, & D. J. Sylvan (Eds.), *Knowledges: Historical and critical studies in disciplinarity.* Charlottesville, VA: University of Virginia Press, 1993.

Levin, R. C. *The work of the university.* New Haven, CT: Yale University Press, 2003.

Liston, Delores D. *Joy as a metaphor for convergence:* A phenomenological and aesthetic investigation of social and educational change. New York: Hampton Press, 2001.

Lyotard, Jean Francois. *The postmodern condition: A report on knowledge* (G. Bennington & B. Massumi, Trans.). Minneapolis: University of Minnesota Press, 1984.

---*Just gaming* (B. Massumi & W. Godzich, Trans.). Minneapolis: University of Minnesota Press, 1990.

---Foreword: Spaceship. In M. Peters (Ed.), *Education and the postmodern condition.* Westport, CT: Bergin & Garvey, 1997.

Margolis, E. (Ed.). *The hidden curriculum in higher education.* New York: Routledge, 2001.

Marshall, J. Dan, James T. Sears & William H. Schubert. *Turning points in curriculum: A contemporary American memoir.* Upper Saddle River, NJ: Merrill, 2000.

Martusewicz, Rebecca A. *Seeking passage: Post-structuralism, pedagogy, ethics.* New York: Teachers College Press, Columbia University, 2001.

Maturana, Humberto R., & Francis J. Varela. *The tree of knowledge: The biological roots of human understanding.* Boston: Shambhala, 1997.

Merriam-Webster Dictionary. Springfield, MA: Merriam-Webster Inc, 1997.

Messer-Davidow, Ellen, David R. Shumway, & David J. Sylvan, (Eds.). *Knowledges: Historical and critical studies in disciplinarity.* Charlottesville, VA: University of Virginia Press, 1993.

Michael, J. *Anxious intellects: Academic professionals, public intellectuals, and enlightenment values.* Durham, NC: Duke University Press, 2000.

Miller, B. F. & C. B. Keane. *Encyclopedia and dictionary of medicine, nursing, and allied health*. (3rd ed.). Philadelphia: W. B. Saunders Company, 1983.

Miller, G. E. *The meaning of general education*. New York: Teachers College Press, Columbia University, 1988.

Miller, J. H. *Speech acts in literature*. Stanford, CA: Stanford University Press, 2001.

Moore, M. (Writer/Director). *Bowling for Columbine* [Motion picture]. United States: MGM Studios, 2003.

Morris, Marla. *Curriculum and the Holocaust: Competing sites of memory and representation*. New York: Lawrence Erlbaum & Associates, 2001.

---Curriculum, cellos, and dreams: On a winter's night a teacher travels. *Journal of curriculum theorizing, 20(1)*, 2004.

Musil, C. M. Educating for citizenship. *PeerReview*. Spring, 2003.

National Commission on Accrediting. *The role and function of the national commission on accrediting*. Washington, DC, 1966.

Nelson, C., A. Treichler, & L. Grossberg. Cultural studies: An introduction. *Cultural Studies*. New York: Routledge, 1992.

Nussbaum, Martha C. *Cultivating humanity*. Cambridge, MA: Harvard University Press, 1988.

Nuyen, A. T. Lyotard and Rorty on the role of the professor. In M. Peters (Ed.) *Education and the postmodern condition*. Westport, CT: Bergin & Garvey, 1997

O'Neill, J. *The poverty of postmodernism*. London: Routledge, 1995.

Peters, Michael. Legitimation problems: Knowledge and education in the postmodern condition. In M. Peters (Ed.) *Education and the postmodern condition*. Westport, CT: Bergin & Garvey, 1997.

---Derrida, pedagogy, and the calculation of the subject. In Trifonas (Ed.), *Pedagogies of difference: Rethinking education for social change*. New York: RoutledgeFalmer, 2003.

Pickering, Andrew. Anti-discipline or narratives of illusion. In E. Messer-Davidow, D. R. Shumway, & D. J. Sylvan (Eds.), *Knowledges: Historical and critical studies in disciplinarity*. Charlottesville, VA: University of Virginia Press, 1993.

Pinar, William F., William M. Reynolds, Patrick Slattery, & Peter M. Taubman. *Understanding curriculum: An introduction to the study of historical and contemporary curriculum discourses*. New York: Peter Lang, 1995.

Prigogine, Ilya, & Isabelle Stengers. *Order out of chaos: Man's new dialogue with nature*. New York: Bantam, 1984.

Readings, Bill. *The university in ruins*. Cambridge, MA: Harvard University Press, 1996.

Reynolds, William M. In *Curriculum: A river runs through it*. New York: Peter Lang, 2003.

Reynolds, William M., & Julie A. Webber (Eds.). *Expanding curriculum theory: Dis/positions and lines of flight*. Mahaw, NJ: Lawrence Erlbaum Associates, 2004.

Romano, Lois. *Literacy of college graduates found in decline*. The Ithaca Journal, December 26, 2005.

Rosenthal, S. A Marxist critique of E. O. Wilson's Consilience: The unity of knowledge. Paper presented at the 1998 Southern Sociological Society Meeting. (http:/www./tomweston.net/rosent). 1998. Accessed February 15, 2004.

Rudolph, F. *Curriculum: A history of the American undergraduate course of study since 1636*. San Francisco: Jossey-Bass, 1977.

Saporta, M. Georgia Tech strips DuPree name from school. *Atlanta Journal-Constitution*, March 6, 2004.

Schwartz, Jeffrey M. & Sharon Begley. *The mind and the brain: Neuroplasticity and the power of mental force*. New York: HarperCollins Publishers Inc., 2002.

Selden, W. K. *Accreditation: A struggle over standards in higher education*. Published by the National Commission on Accrediting. New York: Harper & Brothers, 1960.

Selingo, J. What Americans think about higher education. *The chronicle of higher education*, May 2, 2003.

Serres, Michel. *Hermes: Literature, science, philosophy* (J. V. Harari & D. F. Bell, Eds.). Baltimore: Johns Hopkins University Press, 1982.

---*Genesis*. (G. James & J. Nielson, Trans.). Ann Arbor: University of Michigan Press, 1995.

---*The natural contract*. (E. MacArthur & W. Paulson, Trans.). Ann Arbor: University of Michigan Press, 1995.

---*The troubadour of knowledge* (S. F. Glaser & W. Paulson, Trans.). Ann Arbor: University of Michigan Press, 1997.

Serres, Michel & Bruno Latour. *Conversations on science, culture and time* (R. Lapidus, Trans.). Ann Arbor: University of Michigan Press, 1995.

Sherman, Scott. David Horowitz's long march. *The Nation* (available at http://www.thenation.com), July 3, 2000. Last accessed February 25, 2006.

Short, Edmund C. *Forms of curriculum inquiry*. New York: State University of New York Press, 1991.

Snow, C. *The two cultures: And a second look*. Cambridge, England: Cambridge University Press, 1964.

Southern Association for Accreditation in Colleges & Schools. *General accreditation in higher education*. 1963.

Taylor, Michael C. Unplanned obsolescence and the new network culture. *The Chronicle Review*, December 14, 2001.

Tierney, W. G. *Curricular landscapes, democratic vistas: Transformative leadership in higher education*. New York: Praeger, 1989.

Trifonas, Peter. Technologies of reason: Toward a regrounding of academic responsibility. In Trifonas (Ed.), *Revolutionary pedagogies: Cultural politics, instituting education, and the discourse of theory*. New York: RoutledgeFarmer, 2000.

---Preface. In Trifonas (Trans. & Ed.), *Ethics, institutions, and the right to philosophy*. New York: Rowman & Littlefield, 2002.

---Toward a deconstructive pedagogy of diffe'rance. In Trifonas (Ed.). *Pedagogies of difference: Rethinking education for social change*. New York: RoutledgeFarmer, 2003.

---Postmodernism, poststructuralism, and difference. *Journal of curriculum theorizing, 20(1)*, 2004.

Tyler, Ralph W. *Basic principles of curriculum & instruction*. Chicago: University of Chicago Press, 1949.

United States Department of Education. (Press release). Secretary Spellings announces new commission on the future of higher education. (available at http://www.ed.gov/news/pressreleases/2005/09/09192005), September 9, 2005. Last accessed March 9, 2006.

Webber, Julie A. *Failure to hold*. New York: Rowman & Littlefield Publishers, 2003.

Wiener, Norbert. *The human use of human beings: Cybernetics and society*. New York: Da Capo Press, Inc, 1954.

Wilson, Edward O. *Consilience: The unity of knowledge*. New York: Alfred A. Knopf, 1998.

---*The future of life*. New York: Alfred A. Knopf, 2002.

T

Questions about the Purpose(s) of Colleges and Universities

Norm Denzin,

Joe L. Kincheloe,

Shirley R. Steinberg

General Editors

What are the purposes of higher education? When undergraduates "declare their majors," they agree to enter into a world defined by the parameters of a particular academic discourse—a discipline. But who decides those parameters? How do they come about? What are the discussions and proposed outcomes of disciplined inquiry? What should an undergraduate know to be considered educated in a discipline? How does the disciplinary knowledge base inform its pedagogy? Why are there different disciplines? When has a discipline "run its course"? Where do new disciplines come from? Where do old ones go? How does a discipline produce its knowledge? What are the meanings and purposes of disciplinary research and teaching? What are the key questions of disciplined inquiry? What questions are taboo within a discipline? What can the disciplines learn from one another? What might they not want to learn and why?

Once we begin asking these kinds of questions, positionality becomes a key issue. One reason why there aren't many books on the meaning and purpose of higher education is that once such questions are opened for discussion, one's subjectivity becomes an issue with respect to the presumed objective stances of Western higher education. Academics don't have positions because positions are "biased," "subjective," "slanted," and therefore somehow invalid. So the first thing to do is to provide a sense—however broad and general—of what kinds of positionalities will inform the books and chapters on the above questions. Certainly the questions themselves, and any others we might ask, are already suggesting a particular "bent," but as the series takes shape, the authors we engage will no doubt have positions on these questions.

From the stance of interdisciplinary, multidisciplinary, or transdisciplinary practitioners, will the chapters and books we solicit solidify disciplinary discourses, or liquefy them? Depending on who is asked, interdisciplinary inquiry is either a polite collaboration among scholars firmly situated in their own particular discourses, or it is a blurring of the restrictive parameters that define the very notion of disciplinary discourse. So will the series have a stance on the meaning and purpose of interdisciplinary inquiry and teaching? This can possibly be finessed by attracting thinkers from disciplines that are already multidisciplinary, for example, the various kinds of "studies" programs (women's, Islamic, American, cultural, etc.), or the hybrid disciplines like ethnomusicology (musicology, folklore, anthropology). But by including people from these fields (areas? disciplines?) in our series, we are already taking a stand on disciplined inquiry. A question on the comprehensive exam for the Columbia University Ethnomusicology Program was to defend ethnomusicology as a "field" or a "discipline." One's answer determined one's future, at least to the extent that the gatekeepers had a say in such matters. So, in the end, what we are proposing will no doubt involve political struggles.

For additional information about this series or for the submission of manuscripts, please contact Joe L. Kincheloe, joe.kincheloe@mcgill.ca. To order other books in this series, please contact our Customer Service Department at: (800) 770-LANG (within the U.S.), (212) 647-7706 (outside the U.S.), (212) 647-7707 FAX, or browse online by series at: www.peterlang.com.